A COMPANION TO
WILLIAM CARLOS WILLIAMS'S
PATERSON

A
COMPANION
TO
WILLIAM CARLOS WILLIAMS'S
Paterson

BENJAMIN SANKEY

UNIVERSITY OF CALIFORNIA PRESS
BERKELEY · LOS ANGELES · LONDON
1971

University of California Press
Berkeley and Los Angeles, California
University of California Press, Ltd.
London, England
Copyright © 1971 by The Regents of the University of California
Previously unpublished or uncollected material,
including letters, by William Carlos Williams,
copyright © 1971 by Florence H. Williams.
ISBN: 0–520–01742–0
Library of Congress Catalog Card Number: 72–121193
Designed by W. H. Snyder
Printed in the United States of America

PREFACE

This book is an interpretation of *Paterson*, and also an attempt
to supply in a convenient form some of the information that
readers of the poem will find useful.

My interpretation is based on a good many readings of *Paterson* and on a survey of what Williams himself had to say about
the poem from time to time. Sometimes Williams's own interpretive comments seem to go beyond anything for which there is a
warrant in the text. But even so, the comments have their interest,
and I have attempted to reproduce a good many of them, without,
however, meaning to imply that Williams's statements are always definitive statements about what the poem "means."

I have consulted the notes, drafts, and other manuscript material in the collections of Yale University and the State University of New York at Buffalo. And I have attempted to supply
information about some of the works consulted by Williams,
specifically those he used as "sources" for some of the prose
passages.

I have learned a number of important things about Williams's
poetry from my friend Alan Stephens, who also read the manuscript of this study at an early stage. George Zabriskie of Washington, D.C., gave valuable information and advice, and I have
relied heavily on his essay, "The Geography of 'Paterson.'" I am
also grateful for information supplied by Mrs. Else B. Lorch and
others at New Directions, and by Professor Ralph Nash, Professor John C. Thirlwall, and Mrs. Linda Welshimer Wagner.
Members of the library staff at the University of California,
Santa Barbara, have been very helpful; and so have librarians at
Emory University, the Library of Congress, the Paterson Free
Public Library, the State University of New York at Buffalo,
and Yale University. I should also like to thank Miss Karen
Malone, who typed the manuscript, Mark Ferrer, who helped
select and prepare the illustrations, and James McCord, who

helped with the research. Mrs. Teresa Joseph of the University of California Press made a number of excellent suggestions.

The reader will probably want to use this "companion" with a copy of the poem open before him. Page numbers refer to the fifth printing of *Paterson*, New Directions Paperbook (New York, 1969), and are cited without the designation "p." or "page." This text was printed from new offset plates in June 1969, and its pagination differs from that of earlier printings. The fifth printing has 246 pages; earlier printings had 284 pages.

Several corrections were made in the text of the fourth printing of *Paterson* (1968), of which two are worth noting. Earlier printings gave the date of Sam Patch's death as 1826; this was corrected to 1829 (27 of the fourth printing, 17 of the fifth printing). "Ibibio," the name of an African tribe, had been misspelled "Ibidio" in earlier printings (171 of the fourth printing, 143 of the fifth printing). A passage from Williams's *Autobiography* (pp. 390–392) is printed at the beginning of the volume in the fourth and subsequent printings of *Paterson*.

Publication data on Williams's works are found in the first section of the bibliography at the end of this volume. Williams's notes and other manuscript material from the State University of New York at Buffalo and Yale University are identified in the text as "Buffalo MS" or "Yale MS." Essays and books to which frequent reference is made are identified as follows:

Barber and Howe.	John W. Barber and Henry Howe. *Historical Collections of the State of New Jersey*. Newark, 1853.
Cambon.	Glauco Cambon. *The Inclusive Flame: Studies in American Poetry*. Bloomington, 1963.
Davenport.	Guy Davenport. "The Nuclear Venus: Dr. Williams' Attack on Usura," *Perspective*, VI (Autumn 1953), 183–190.
Longwell.	Charles P. Longwell. *Historic Totowa Falls and Vicinity*. [Paterson], 1942.
Martz.	Louis L. Martz. *The Poem of the Mind*. New York, 1966.

Nash.	Ralph Nash. "The Use of Prose in 'Paterson,'" *Perspective*, VI (Autumn 1953), 191–199.
Nelson.	William Nelson. *History of the City of Paterson and the County of Passaic, New Jersey*. Paterson, 1901.
Nelson and Shriner.	William Nelson and Charles A. Shriner. *History of Paterson and its Environs: The Silk City*. 3 vols. New York and Chicago, 1920.
Peterson.	Walter Scott Peterson. *An Approach to Paterson*. New Haven, 1967.
Quinn.	Sister M. Bernetta Quinn. *The Metamorphic Tradition in Modern Poetry*. New Brunswick, 1955.
Seldes.	Gilbert Seldes. *Mainland*. New York, 1936.
Thirlwall.	John C. Thirlwall. "William Carlos Williams' 'Paterson': The Search for the Redeeming Language—A Personal Epic in Five Parts," *New Directions 17* (1961), 252–310.
Van Derhoven.	O. Van Derhoven. *Visitors' Guide to Passaic Falls*. Paterson, 1859.
Wallace.	Emily Mitchell Wallace. *A Bibliography of William Carlos Williams*. Middletown, Conn., 1968.
Zabriskie.	George Zabriskie. "The Geography of 'Paterson,'" *Perspective*, VI (Autumn 1953), 201–216.

An earlier version of my Introduction appeared in *Spectrum*.

Permission has been granted by Florence H. Williams to quote from *The Selected Letters of William Carlos Williams*, copyright 1957 by William Carlos Williams; and by Mrs. Williams and the publishers named below to reprint passages from the writings of William Carlos Williams:

New Directions Publishing Corporation: *Selected Essays of William Carlos Williams*, copyright 1931, 1954 by William Carlos

B. S.

CONTENTS

ix

Introduction

THE PROGRAM

Williams described the overall design of *Paterson* in a note prefacing the first book (in 1946), at which time he intended for the poem to consist of only four books:

Paterson is a long poem in four parts—that a man in himself is a city, beginning, seeking, achieving and concluding his life in ways which the various aspects of a city may embody—if imaginatively conceived—any city, all the details of which may be made to voice his most intimate convictions.

The clause beginning "that a . . ." suggests an argument—at least a partially didactic mode; so does the phrase "his most intimate *convictions*" (which also hints at an "apologia pro vita sua"). Some correspondences are proposed: and so there will be something like an allegory. Also a direction for the poem to take—a narrative, though general and symbolic rather than particular and "realistic." (Beginning, achieving, and so forth.)

A few other features of the poem should be mentioned: a habit of detailed attention to particular occasions; and, in moving from subject to subject, a disregard for conventional transitions—even for the conventions of psychological "association."

Williams elaborated on his plan at various times, for instance, on the occasion of the publication of the third book:

I began thinking of writing a long poem upon the resemblance between the mind of modern man and a city. The thing was to use the multiple facets which a city presented as representative for comparable facets of contemporary thought, thus to be able to objectify the man himself as we know him and love him and hate him. . . . From the beginning I decided there would be four books following the course of the river whose life seemed more and more to resemble my own life as I more and more thought of it:

1

the river above the Falls, the catastrophe of the Falls itself, the river below the Falls, and the entrance at the end into the great sea.[1]

To write a long poem exploring an analogy between a city and a man, illuminating this main analogy by detailed accounts of particular objects and events, juxtaposed unpredictably; to employ a number of organizing principles (including narrative, allegorical description, topical "reflection"), using these principles intermittently and in unexpected combinations; to avoid the staleness of conventional argumentation, but still to "make a point": such hopes and purposes seem to have guided Williams when he worked out the overall design of *Paterson*. The prefatory note, of course, indicates only a plan. No doubt Williams changed his mind about certain things; and no doubt there were some things he was never entirely sure about.

THE POET'S JOB

Williams's subject is the poet's attempt to come to terms with the experience of his own time and place—his "locality," represented in the poem by the industrial city of Paterson, New Jersey. *Paterson* is both a poet's autobiography, schematized and translated into symbolic terms, and a poem about itself (since the "poet" of *Paterson* is a version of Williams himself). It is also a poem about the place in which the poet finds himself, and about his troublesome relations with that place. The place—modern urban civilization in the United States, "synecdochized," so to speak, by Paterson of the depression and war years—has been given its present shape by forces outside the poet's control, and so damaged in the process that it is difficult for him to "love" it as he must do in order to make it his theme.

Yet he can't reject it; he senses, more or less clearly, that only through the mediation of his own place can the earth's elemental powers enter his work. Part of the story of *Paterson*, then, is the poet's struggle with himself to accept the present world. But to accept this world, and to give meaning to it, he must discover a language appropriate to it; and this is the other part of the story.

[1] Quoted by Thirlwall, p. 254.

In a sense, the entire poem concerns what Williams announced as the subject of Book Three: the search for a language by means of which to make vocal the elemental features of the place and the modern "replicas." This language must be one appropriate to American people living now, here, in this place: a language distinct from that brought over by settlers from England, but also "rising above" the stunted languages actually used by the people who live here. The example of Walt Whitman was perhaps never far out of Williams's mind as he was writing *Paterson*; he respected, and attempted to continue, Whitman's search for an "American" language.

These main terms, and the relations among them, appear in the poem metaphorically, and often in a very complicated form. Before introducing the poem's main metaphors, it will be well to outline the attitudes at stake.

First, the poet's "world." Williams had dealt with the significance of American history in a number of prose works of the twenties and thirties, the best known and most influential of which was *In the American Grain*.[2] These writings were polemical accounts of the cultural implications of the way in which this country was settled. They were "polemical" in much the same way that many other historical writings of the postwar period were polemical; like the writings of Waldo Frank, for instance, they sharply criticized the role of the Anglo-Saxon in the New World. Frank wrote in *Our America* that "the European cultures, swept to America and there buried, were half-killed by the mere uprooting. They were never American: they could never live *in* America. . . . But a great and varied cultural world already lay upon America before the coming of the pioneer."[3] *In the American Grain* stressed the destruction of the native cultures and the failure of transplanted European culture to replace them. In the discussion of the American writer's heritage that

[2] *In the American Grain* was published in 1925 by Albert and Charles Boni, and was reisssued in 1939 by New Directions, with an introduction by Horace Gregory (Wallace, A9). I have used the third paperbook printing (1966), and page numbers refer to that printing. The essay "The American Background," first published in 1934 in *America and Alfred Stieglitz*, edited by Waldo Frank *et al.* (New York, 1934), appears in *Selected Essays*, pp. 134–161.

[3] *Our America* (New York, 1919), p. 106.

Williams presents as a dialogue with Valery Larbaud, Williams
went on from the subject of Cotton Mather and Puritanism to
define the present-day American as "an Indian robbed of his
world" (p. 128):

> If the Puritans have damned us with their abstinence, re-
> moval from the world, denial, slowly we are forced within
> ourselves upon an emptiness which cannot be supplied,—
> this IS the soul, according to their tenets. Lost, in this (and
> its environments) as in a forest, I do believe the average
> American to be an Indian, but an Indian robbed of his
> world—unless we call machines a forest in themselves. . . .
>   From lack of touch, lack of belief. Steadily the individ-
> ual loses caste, then the local government loses its author-
> ity; the head is more and more removed. Finally the
> center is reached—totally dehumanized, like a Protestant
> heaven. Everything is Federalized and all laws become
> prohibitive in essence.

As Williams interpreted it, the colonization of the New World
meant the imposition of the settlers' will on the new land, an imposition carried out successfully up to a point, but leaving an
unfortunate heritage. The settlers and pioneers bequeathed what
Williams called an "unrelated" culture: a culture derivative from
Europe and not properly responsive to the new conditions. The
Indian societies had possessed cultures that were "related" to the
local landscape, but the white man with his technological su-
periority had destroyed these cultures without replacing them.
The destruction of the native cultures, and the subsequent degradation of the natural environment, brought gradually into
being the world inhabited by Williams and his contemporaries.
The present-day American was called upon to devise a living culture on this land that his ancestors had taken from the Indians.
   The essential fact of American experience, according to this
account, was the contrast between the promise of the land and its
actual history—an opposition Williams emphasized in an early
draft for an "introduction" to *Paterson*:

> A fragmentary sort of poem in four parts, strung together
> with notes and comments for what may come of it; a de-
> sign to off-set the shortsightedness and indifference of the

present age—a near Paradise what with plenty staring us
in the face on all sides—by defects of a different order.
(Buffalo MS)

(The "defects of a different order" would be those of the poem
itself, including its deliberately fragmentary nature.)

In *Paterson*, then, the poet's "world" has three aspects: the
elemental promise or "primitive destiny" of the place, its history
since the coming of the white man, and the present scene. The
promise and destiny define a latent presence in the modern scene,
available to the poet, but even to him only in brief glimpses, hard
to sustain. The present scene, molded by historical forces (for
instance by Alexander Hamilton's plans for utilizing the power
of the Falls), is characterized by what Williams calls a "stasis"—
a static order protecting the interests of a few while damaging the
environment and "scanting" the lives of the rest. The prevailing
"stasis" explains the actual ugliness confronting the poet.

What confronts the poet is, so to speak, a fallen world, a world
that has been betrayed (Williams suggests that Hamilton was a
kind of Judas). The poet, at great cost to himself, attempts to
"redeem" it by means of language. There seem to be two ways in
which the poet can be thought of as saving or rescuing his people.
One is by giving a permanent record of their lives, as Homer did
for the heroes of the *Iliad*. The other is by providing a living
myth, something to unify and sustain them. Together these two
aims define the scope of the poet's work: "The poem to me (until
I go broke) is an attempt, an experiment, a failing experiment,
toward assertion with broken means but an assertion, always, of
a new and total culture, the lifting of an environment to expression. Thus it is social, the poem is a social instrument—accepted
or not accepted seems to be of no material importance. It em-
braces everything we are."[4]

But the language available to the poet is an Old World language, English, a language that had developed in response to
quite other conditions and experiences: *"They saw birds with
rusty breasts and called them robins. Thus, from the start, an
America of which they could have had no inkling drove the first
settlers upon their past. They retreated for warmth and reassur-*

[4] Letter to Henry Wells, April 12, 1950, *Selected Letters*, p. 286.

ance to something previously familiar. But at a cost. For what they saw were not robins. . . ."[5] The poet is called upon to "invent"—to devise a new poetic language (and a new shape for the line), appropriate to the New World and to the lives actually lived here. He cannot hope to produce a "finished" work, since his job at this stage of things must inevitably be a form of quarrying, of preparing the language for poets to come.

To express this negative view of the present order of things, and this conception of the poet's mission, Williams assigns a metaphorical role to the concepts "marriage" and "divorce." American society is made up of a number of disparate cultural strands, none of them presently thriving, and not yet fused into a single living culture. Our civilization is "divorced" from its setting; and the various cultural elements are isolated ("divorced") from one another. Our cities, imposed upon a landscape from which they draw raw material and power, fail to become a living part of the land; this also is "divorce." The universities are cut off from the actual life of the people, their knowledge only a semblance of knowledge because it can't live without *circulating*. The fact that knowledge does not circulate is both a cause and a consequence of the failure of language: and our language is another instance of the "divorce" (the divorce of official language, or poetic language, from the American experience). The people of America may look into their minds, but when they do, what they see is foreign to them, since there is no language for interpreting it. The poet is asked to do something about the "divorce," to officiate at a metaphorical marriage, reconciling (as Williams puts it) the people and the stones, and bringing together the disparate by means of a principle of unity, the "common language" he hopes to discover or invent. But can he do this? In a good brief summary of Williams's argument, Glauco Cambon calls attention to the sense of urgency: "America as a civilization in the making, then, is the central theme of Wil-

---

[5] "The American Background," *Selected Essays*, p. 134. Benjamin T. Spencer provides a good analysis of Williams's theories about America and the proper language for American experience, distinguishing "three interrelated yet distinct Americas" in Williams's theories, "what may be termed the Platonic, the unconscious, and the cultural" ("Doctor Williams' American Grain," *Tennessee Studies in Literature*, VIII [1963], 1–16).

liams, who, after presenting in his mythological way what he considers the facts of the case in 1925, now asks the urgent question: Is marriage still possible between Americans and America? or, to paraphrase it unmythologically: Granted our pioneer start, is real civilization still attainable. Can we "integrate" with our land? And with ourselves? *Paterson* is this cry of alarm. . . ."[6]

For a time, as Williams tells the story, the poet, offended and baffled by the world in which he finds himself, turns to the past, hoping to find there a "quiet" that he can offer as an alternative to the noise and confusion of his own time. (This search is the subject of Book Three.) But the poet finds that the past was no quieter than his own day. Reading about the early days of his own region, he finds simply a background, a record of the forces that have brought about the present. The past offers no solution to his difficulties, and the poet determines that he must go it alone, using the tools that are ready to hand, though these may be inadequate.

Though the past is not a usable source, the poet does catch a glimpse of a permanent "source" concealed within the violence and multiplicity of the present scene. This is the *elemental*, manifesting itself through the local.

Does the poet in fact succeed at the job he has proposed for himself? That is, does Williams attempt to present him as succeeding? The conclusion of *Paterson* is ambiguous, and presumably deliberately so. Book Four ends with a passage combining the notions of death and birth. Someone dies (a murderer is hanged, and there are other references to death); but there is also a kind of resurrection, as Paterson, pictured as Odysseus, swims to shore and heads inland, accompanied by his dog. There is both a termination (death, the completion of the poem—and its possible failure), and the promise of a beginning (the afterlife of a work of art). Book Five is an afterthought, added perhaps because Williams felt that he had not affirmed sufficiently the symbolic "emergence" at the end of Book Four. The idea of Book Five is that the work of art does enjoy some kind of survival after the death of the man who made it; and this is "the hole in the bag" through which death is eluded.

[6] Cambon, p. 187.

THE CITY OF PATERSON

Williams had come to believe that the poet could best work through his own locality—indeed, that he was under an obligation to do so. The doctrine could claim philosophical support. Not a philosopher himself, nor very philosophically minded, Williams had been much impressed by Dewey's saying that "the locality is the only universal": "We are discovering that the locality is the only universal. Even the suns and stars have their own times as well as their own places. . . . When the discovery sinks a little deeper, the novelist and dramatist will discover the localities of America as they are, and no one will need to worry about the future of American art."[7]

Williams found roughly the same message in the work of contemporary writers: Joyce, for instance, whose method he praised as

a reaffirmation of the forever-sought freedom of truth from usage. It is the modern world emerging among the living ancients by paying attention to the immediacy of its own contact; a classical method.

And in proportion as a man has bestirred himself to become awake to his own locality he will perceive more and more of what it disclosed and find himself in a position to make the necessary translations. The disclosures will then and only then come to him as reality, as joy, as release. For these men communicate with each other and strive to invent new devices. But he who does not know his own world, in whatever confused form it may be, must either stupidly fail to learn from foreign work or stupidly swallow it without knowing how to judge of its essential value.[8]

Though he had visited Europe and had been impressed by what he saw, Williams had chosen to "return" at a time when

[7] Quoted by James Guimond from *The Dial*, LXVIII (June 1920), 687–688; Williams quoted the phrase "the locality is the only universal" in *Contact II* (Jan. 1921), p. 7. See also *Selected Letters*, p. 224. Guimond also notes Williams's debt to Count Hermann Keyserling, who had argued in favor of "increasing provincialism" for America (*The Art of William Carlos Williams* [Chicago, 1968], p. 55 and 55n).

[8] "Comment" (1921), in *Selected Essays*, p. 28.

a good many American writers were choosing Europe; and the act of returning had a moral significance to him—a significance most clearly evident in the conclusion of *A Voyage to Pagany* and in the dialogue with Valery Larbaud reported in *In the American Grain*. The return meant choosing to work against odds, but to remain in Europe (or to become "cosmopolitan," as Pound had done) meant to give up one's only real hope, the local as a source. The plan for *Paterson*, developed gradually over a good many years, was a plan for using and celebrating the local. Williams gave two main reasons for his choice of Paterson. He wanted a large image by which to pull together the things he knew; and he wanted to write about a place and people he knew well:

> The first idea centering upon the poem, *Paterson*, came alive early: to find an image large enough to embody the whole knowable world about me. The longer I lived in my place, among the details of my life, I realized that these isolated observations and experiences needed pulling together to gain "profundity." I already had the river. Flossie is always astonished when she realizes that we live on a river, that we are a river town. New York City was far out of my perspective; I wanted, if I was to write in a larger way than of the birds and flowers, to write about the people close about me: to know in detail, minutely what I was talking about—to the whites of their eyes, to their very smells.[9]

Paterson makes extensive use of local geography and history; and it is apparently pretty accurate. George Zabriskie, whose father spent the first thirty-five years of his life in Paterson, and who himself spent his first twenty years on the upper reaches of the Passaic River, points out that "in its geography and history *Paterson* is as literal as a Baedeker, with the special qualification that Williams does not feel restricted in time."[10]

[9] *Autobiography*, p. 391. This passage is quoted in full by the publishers in the fourth and subsequent printings of *Paterson*. There are other accounts of the origins of the poem: a very interesting one, for instance, in *I Wanted To Write a Poem*, pp. 71–74. See also the account quoted in Thirlwall (pp. 263–264) from a publishers' release. Williams's preparation for *Paterson* is discussed by Gordon K. Grigsby, "The Genesis of *Paterson*," *College English*, XXIII (Jan. 1962), 277–281. See also Martz, pp. 125–146.

[10] Zabriskie, p. 201.

The city's topography supports the poem's basic symbolism: a sleeping male giant resting against a female giant (the mountain). The course of the Passaic River, originating in the mountains, forming the Falls, then moving out to the sea, gives Williams a local embodiment for the "river of life" concept; and the roar of the Falls provides a symbolic challenge to the poet to find a voice for his region. The city's history provides a synecdoche for the history of the United States as Williams saw it—colonization, struggles with the Indians, the exploitation of natural resources, industrialism, and the gradual degradation of the environment. The growth of Paterson tests the program that Williams associates with Alexander Hamilton: to make the new country a commercial and manufacturing nation along European lines by encouraging local industry, repaying the debts incurred during the Revolution, and harnessing the country's natural resources. Hamilton's ambitious plans for the city of Paterson, though never fully implemented, determined the direction it was to take. For Williams the plans ignored the "local genius" and in trying to reproduce European civilization in this country thwarted the promise latent here. Paterson grew into a company town known for its labor troubles; the Passaic River became a "swillhole."

METHOD AND PRINCIPAL SYMBOLS

The method of *Paterson* is allegorical, but there is no straightforward narrative base, and no unambiguous system of allegorical meanings for the literal terms. Like *Endymion, Paterson* belongs to what Sister Bernetta has called the metamorphic tradition.[11] Its symbolic terms merge and overlap, and these mergings and transformations make interpretation difficult at times; but there is a logic governing them, and Williams's conception of his theme required them. Perhaps it is not wise to attempt to fix on a genre for *Paterson*, but a few approximations may help to locate the poem with respect to traditions available to Williams. Most obviously it is a modern "experimental" poem, like

[11] In a review of *Paterson II*, Robert Lowell commented that "the symbols are not allegorical, but loose, intuitive, and Protean" (*Nation*, CLXVI [June 19, 1948], 693).

The Cantos or *The Bridge*, relying on postsymbolist ways of handling metaphor and transition. (And like other experimental poets, Williams owed a good bit to the prose writers, notably Joyce.) It is an "inclusive" poem, containing narrative, lyrical, and even dramatic elements; there are editorial-like passages of reflection; there is news and documentation. But all of these "modern" practices are governed in Williams's case by an over-all procedure derived from two Romantic forms: the allegorical (or symbolic) narrative, as managed by Keats (or Blake), and the selective autobiography of a poet's mind, as carried out by Words-worth in "The Prelude." Which is not to say that Williams was consciously indebted to Keats or Blake or Wordsworth.[12] In a limited sense, of course, *Paterson* is an attempt at a "national" epic—certainly no *Iliad*, nor even an *Aeneid*, but an epic in roughly the sense that *Leaves of Grass* is sometimes called an epic.

The characters of *Paterson* form a miscellaneous group, rang-ing from historical figures and people Williams knew to large allegorical personifications. The key notion is Williams's con-ception of a man like a city and a woman (or many women) like a flower or flowers (7). "Paterson" is the elemental city—the basic landscape on which the present city is built, and the hidden promise that the present industrial city thwarts; his wife is the mountain nearby, whose "head" forms Garret Mountain Park. The male figure of the poem is a man as well as a city; and he is also a mythic giant, whose dreams (like those of Joyce's Finnegan, or those of Havelock the Dane in the patriotic fairy tale) animate

[12] Williams's early poem "The Wanderer: A Rococo Study," *Collected Earlier Poems*, pp. 1–12, was apparently based on an earlier work Williams himself remembered as an imitation of Keats. *Paterson* develops certain themes from "The Wanderer," and even includes a few passages from that poem. Certainly the "metamorphoses" of *Paterson* can be traced back to Williams's early reading of Keats; they may also have been encouraged by surrealist work, including Soupault's *Last Nights of Paris*, which Williams translated. In a review Richard Ellmann called attention to the similarity between Williams's characters and some of Blake's (*Yale Review*, XXXIX [Spring 1950], 544). The general principle could have come to Williams at second or third hand, through Joyce, for instance. As a "form," the writer's autobiography was available to Williams from many sources other than Wordsworth, of course. A good many poems since the Romantic period have been poetic autobiographies of one kind or another.

the people who inhabit the place. The idea of a sleeping giant, animating the people of the area, expresses Williams's notion that a poet must "give life" to his people if they are truly to live. It also describes the relationship between individuals and the permanent elemental forces active, though unrecognized, in their lives. (These forces are the powers of *earth*, acting through the *place*, and through the persistent psychological energies of sexual love and religious awe; Book Two presents poor modern "replicas" of them.)

The figure of Paterson, then, appears both as a particular person—"Dr. P.," a persona for the poet—and as a mythic concept, the sleeping force and genius of Paterson, the spirit and elemental promise of the place, distinct from its modern embodiments, yet nourishing and guiding them. As an individual, Paterson visits patients, receives letters, takes a walk in the Park, and tries to write the poem; as city and giant, his thoughts are "listed in the telephone directory."

The female of the poem, pictured as a mountain ("the Park's her head"), as a flower, and as various specific women, stands for the poet's world. She is his counterpart, his subject matter and the source of his inspiration. As the poet is the formative principle, she is what he *forms*. In one set of meanings, the woman is the American wilderness, mauled and raped by invaders from Europe, as well as the "ravished Park," invaded and abused on Sundays by picnickers from the city.[13] In other terms, she is "reality" (contemporary reality—the back streets) offering herself as wife to the reluctant poet. She is Paterson's "first wife," and appears, for instance, as the oldest wife of the African chief in the *Geographic* photograph (13). She is also "Beautiful thing," a symbolic notion which Williams embodies as a fire attacking the city, and as one or more young Negro women. Even Phyllis, the tough young girl from the back country featured in Book Four, manifests the elemental feminine principle of the poem, serving (as Williams put it) as "a female Paterson."

[13] This is a motif that Williams might have picked up, for instance, from Lewis Mumford, who wrote of the American pioneer in terms of rape: "Instead of seeking Nature in a wise passiveness, as Wordsworth urged, [the pioneer] raped his new mistress in a blind fury of obstreperous passion" (quoted in Seldes, p. 15). The personified wilderness had appeared in *In the American Grain*.

Marriage is the condition of the primal landscape, and it is still the mythic norm. But in fact our own time is characterized by "divorce," as we wait for the poet who can bring things together ("marry" them) by means of language. As the one who "marries," the poet is both a minister performing rites and a bee transferring pollen from one flower to another; he is also, of course, the husband.

Of the other metaphorical figures drawn from the local geography, most important are the Passaic River and its Falls, the waterpower of which had called the city of Paterson into existence. The river suggests the course of life (the "river of life," which ends in a "sea of blood").

The roar made by the Falls as it hit the rocks below is used by Williams to represent the challenge faced by the poet to articulate the meaning of life, and specifically the life of *this* place *now*. The roar is a confusion and noise to be "unravelled"—its multiple strands sorted out, ordered, supplied with a meaning. The roar stands for uninterpreted experience, that of the poet and that of the people of the area (and of the United States). The multiple waters of the Falls stand for the poet's or giant's thoughts, or people, or the multiple racial and linguistic strands found in this country. The roar suggests the gabble of languages and cultures which must be given significance and unity by a poet. Challenged by the roar (as Oedipus was challenged by the Sphinx), Paterson listens intently for the "voice" that will provide his answer to it: the new language, expressive of the place and its people.

Associated with the Falls are several figures from local history, notably Sara Cumming (who fell to her death from above the Falls), the famous daredevil Sam Patch, and a tightrope walker named Harry Leslie. Patch and Leslie are figures for the poet—suggesting the risk and showmanship of the poet's work. To write a poem is to take a chance, as Sam Patch took a chance when he leapt from the Falls. (It may also be to "fail," as Patch failed in his final leap from the Falls of the Genesee River.) The poet, like the leaper or tightrope walker, can be thought of as risking failure (and in a sense death) in full view of the public. If he fails, the reason may be lack of skill: "language failed" Patch in his last jump. Simply to leap, without the necessary skill, is simply to commit suicide; simply to write an ambitious poem, without "invention," is to risk oneself foolishly. Mrs. Cumming, whose death came while visiting the Falls with her husband, a minister, supplies a punning symbol for that kind of death which comes to those who lack a language—plunging into the waters "without minister." (The poet and his language fail to save her from oblivion.)

Other key figures in the poem include a number of dogs, mentioned offhandedly, sometimes simply as counterparts for people. The poet himself, for instance, is described at the outset as "just another dog among a lot of dogs." But the collie bitch who appears in Book Two is a manifestation of the female principle of the poem—a Venus, newly washed, inhabiting a sea chamber (and the strands of her coat, resembling the waters of the Falls, stroked into order by her master). "Musty," the dog who while in heat escapes the careful surveillance of the friend entrusted by her owner, provides a comic symbol for the natural passions, unruly and generative. (And she is also, perhaps, an instance of the "unmastered" feminine principle: subject matter without a poet.) At the end of Book Four, when Paterson emerges from the sea, he is accompanied by his faithful dog (a Chesapeake Bay retriever, as Williams later noted)—a birth of Venus, in which the dog represents beauty, or the poem itself.

THE SHAPE OF THE POEM

As the Author's Note suggests, *Paterson* is in part a "logical" structure laid out in advance, in part an improvisation. The books of the poem have titles, and the arrangement of events is topical, to an extent, while within each book the movement has a kind of chronology. The four books correspond roughly to stages in a man's life, seasons of the year, and so on.

Such schematism gives the poem a clarity of structure, an overall order and direction, but the argument often seems to move along abruptly and without a plan. This also, of course, is part of the plan. Williams means the poem to appear not only as a completed design but as a recorded struggle—his own struggle to write the poem. And he favored a certain obscurity, analogous to what he saw in some modern paintings, as the source of a "necessary impact" on the person looking at a painting or reading the poem:

> It's like some kinds of modern painting. The painter tries to produce a particular emotion in the beholder. To do so he does not necessarily have to paint a photographic representation of his subject. The result is something that isn't popular and it isn't always successful; but that's the way I've always tried to work.
> Obscurity, once it is penetrated, is found to be a relatively simple matter. It's a very necessary impact to the listener and reader when anything new is presented. Once a man has penetrated the obscure jungle, he is likely to come on a plateau where he has a much broader vision than he ever knew in the past.[14]

Unexplained juxtaposition in support of narrative has become a familiar convention by now, and there is perhaps less need to defend it or explain it than when *Paterson* was first appearing. Even then, of course, there was good modern precedent; Glauco Cambon describes the method of *Paterson* as "a montage technique whose direct antecedents are to be found in Pound's *Cantos* and in Dos Passos's *U.S.A.* trilogy."[15]

Among the narrative uses of loose juxtaposition the most familiar is that used by Joyce and others to represent the movement of a character's mind, the so-called "stream of consciousness." A character's mind "wanders," as when Paterson sits in the Library trying to read.

Generally, however, Williams is less concerned with exhibiting the various "associational" moves of a character's mind than he is with establishing connections or analogies. Paterson, whether he stands for the poet himself or for the genius of the place, is actively searching for meaning within the apparent chaos of modern experience. This means that the chaos Williams exhibits at the surface of the poem is a kind of mask, and that the reader is given a job somewhat like that of his character, to locate the principles latent in "things" or in the "facts." In a very early work (*Kora in Hell*, 1920), Williams had argued that the imagination "discovers in things those inimitable particles of dis-

[14] Newspaper interview in 1950, quoted by Thirlwall, p. 289.
[15] Cambon, p. 191.

similarity to all other things which are the peculiar perfections of the thing in question," that the "loose linking" of one thing to another has effects of destructive power, but that by virtue of the imagination's harmonizing power, "on this level of the imagination all things and ages meet in fellowship."[16] In this way the imagination destroys old groupings, gives the particular its due, yet goes on to create a new fellowship among all things. Something of this conception is operative in *Paterson*. The skipping around from one thing to another is an imitation of what the mind does as it acts—not just accidents of association, but active perception. Working at full speed the imagination notices a connection or resemblance and quickly makes its move—can make its move more rapidly and convincingly than one can explain it.

In general, then, the collocations of *Paterson* have two aspects: the deliberately achieved impact, caused in part by a violation of the reader's expectations, by a surprise at finding these things brought together; and a logic, clear to Williams, increasingly clear to the reader—a largely thematic logic, as it turns out.

THE USE OF PROSE

The most striking of Williams's innovations was doubtless the extensive use of prose, not simply in notes at the back of the poem (as in *The Waste Land*), nor blocked out as part of the verse (as in *The Cantos*), but conspicuously inserted into the text and conspicuously unpoetic in shape. Pound's *Cantos* had presumably suggested to Williams what might be done with prose material; he had justified Pound's procedure in an early essay, arguing that it exhibited a special movement of the intelligence: "That is the way Pound's verse impresses me and why he can include pieces of prose and have them still part of a *poem*. It is incorporated in a movement of the intelligence which is special, beyond usual thought and action—.[17] There were other models, including *Aucassin and Nicolette*, which in later years

---

[16] Prologue to *Kora in Hell*, in *Selected Essays*, p. 16; *Imaginations*, pp. 18–19.
[17] "Excerpts from a Critical Sketch," *Selected Essays*, p. 108.

he remembered having read while attending medical school: "Together with Hilda Doolittle ('H.D.') I discovered, in those days, the wonders of *Aucassin and Nicolette*, the prose and the verse alternating."[18]

Interestingly enough, Williams's use of prose in *Paterson* had metrical significance for him. Since one main subject of the poem is the "search for a language," Williams tries in various ways to exhibit the language that already exists—whether in what people say, in what they write in a letter, or in the prose of local newspapers and local antiquities. The prose exhibits what the poet has to work with: ordinary American prose, colloquial or stilted, good or bad, its rhythms and phrasing hinting at the essential idiom for which the poet is searching. "All the prose, including the tail which would have liked to have wagged the dog, has primarily the purpose of giving a metrical meaning to or of emphasizing continuity between all word use."[19] To take one example, the workaday prose of the old account of Mrs. Cumming's death gives Williams something to lean on, to work against: not a model but a point of departure. True enough, it may be a "false language," as he suggests in that case. The true language will be that invented by the poet.

Another reason for the prose has been mentioned in connection with Williams's practice of juxtaposing ostensibly unrelated items. This is the principle of "counterpoint," discussed intelligently by Ralph Nash:

As for the contribution of the prose to the techniques of presentation, the actual speaking of the poem, the inevitable key word is counterpoint. There is the counterpoint affecting pace and tempo—the intrusion of flat prose rhythms, in passages of varying length, the occasional rhythmic and vivid prose, the ironic juxtaposition of lyric affirmations and unpleasant "facts," or the opposite juxtaposition of a grimly urban scene and an excerpt from the days of a more pastoral village life. Closely related is the counterpoint of the materials of the poem: the balancing of the pure with the dirty, the resolution with the confusion, the dream with the fact, the past with

[18] *Autobiography*, p. 52.
[19] *Selected Letters*, p. 263. (The tail wagging the dog refers to Cress's letter at the end of Book Two.)

the present (but cutting both ways, not neglecting the old newspapers, the murders, the suicides, the child aflame in a field trying to crawl home). And over all this—and over the tone of impersonal observation, the outright *examples* of the failure of language, and the many effects I have probably missed—is what we might call the counterpoint of poet and city. Yesterday's weather, last week's meeting, a nineteenth-century artesian well: they crop up out of past and present like the flint ("the flinty pinnacles") out of the ground, insisting on the here and now and then of Paterson as place.[20]

And Nash's summary touches on another principle at work. The outcropping to which he refers is not intended to make the poem more like a work in prose but to give the imagination a different kind of room from what it has in verse where "yesterday's weather" is not mentioned. As Williams comments in Book Three, 99: "The province of the poem is the world./ When the sun rises, it rises in the poem/ and when it sets darkness comes down/ and the poem is dark ." For Williams the proposed continuity was itself a problem. The poem—prose, yesterday's weather and the rest of it—remains an artifact.

THE STYLE

Williams is sometimes thought of as essentially a descriptive writer, and it's true that many of his unquestionably successful works are short poems in which the main work is done by descriptive means. But though his program and the bent of his mind led him again and again to describe particular impressions and events, Williams at the same time experimented pretty elaborately with procedures for indicating the meaning he perceived in, or wished to draw from, what he was describing. The collections of verse, and the short stories—not to mention such works as *Kora in Hell* and *A Novelette and Other Prose, 1921–1931*— can be examined as records of this experimentation. In the short descriptive poems the argument may be implicit in the slant of a few words used in the description, and in the direction of the poem's movement; in such cases the poet's abstention from direct comment may seem to justify the judgment that the poem

[20] Nash, pp. 198–199.

is "nothing but" a description. But even such ostensibly "pure" descriptive poems do more than simply describe. And often, of course, Williams directly states his meaning. Williams was a good observer, and he took pains in arranging words on a page to convey an impression; but he was also a man with opinions, something of a theorist, and not always inclined to omit his theories from his verse. A characteristic feature of Williams's style—just as characteristic, perhaps, as his close attention to detail—is a habit of exploding into semiphilosophical commentary. (Often, however, a move in the direction of general argument will also be a *formal* move, intended mainly to help organize the detail.) This habit, a kind of controlled self-indulgence, carries over into *Paterson*, where one of Williams's problems is to see to it that the reader divines the import of the materials.

There is plenty of good description in *Paterson*, but there is little that is purely descriptive in intent. Just about everything mentioned participates in the poem's symbolic argument, either as an instance or a symbol, referring by the logic of synecdoche or analogy (or by the quasilogic of pun) to one of Williams's major symbolic terms. When he describes the Park and the people in it, he is also describing the American people and the American continent. "Sunday in the Park" implies an elaborate myth about the American past. When he describes the leaps and recoveries of the waters at the Falls, he is also describing the course of a man's thoughts; and so on. As the reader learns to recognize the poem's recurrent metaphors (wind for spirit and inspiration, for instance) he will also begin to notice quick allusions to these key terms in passages that are ostensibly descriptive. (When Williams notes that there is "no wind," he can be taken to mean that inspiration is lacking, say, in the preacher's sermon.) The motto "No ideas but in things" does not mean that there will be no general ideas in the poem, or that the ideas will be "implicit," but only that the ideas at stake will be grounded on things present in actual experience and actually described in the poem. The consequences of this working principle are not the same as those that would follow if Williams were also committed to "realistic" conventions for drawing meaning from the things described. In *Paterson* a description can be entirely "realistic" (an exact presentation of something the poet has seen), and its implications nevertheless managed "nonrealistically" by means of pun or allegory.

Because Williams varies his procedures for deriving meaning from detail, *Paterson* is an unusually *tricky* poem.

The language of *Paterson* can be intricate and discontinuous; it can also be very natural and clear. Generally it is clear and natural except where special exigencies of transition or metaphor tempt Williams to skip over steps in the presentation of an idea, or to move without explanation or apology to a new subject. A certain calculated obscurity is, as we have seen, part of Williams's plan for the poem; it is as if he does not wish the reader to be entirely sure of the meaning of particular passages until he has grasped the overall argument. Where the language is obscure, it will often be because Williams breaks off a sentence or introduces an ambiguous pronoun reference. (Often a change in line form or a shift to prose will signal a change of the foreground subject, though the general line of argument continues despite the shift.) Other obscurities are caused by Williams's handling of metaphor. He is willing to let the meaning of a metaphorical term be influenced by (or depend on) an oblique relation to one of the poem's main symbols; he is also willing to mix his metaphors pretty drastically, and a passage of complicated mixed metaphor with syntactic loose ends can present the reader with some problems. Yet, with all his indulgence in tricks and special usages, Williams remained "a stickler for the normal contour of phrase which is characteristic of the language as we speak it."[21]

The naturalness and clarity of Williams's language can be illustrated by a descriptive passage from Book Two:

> At last he comes to the idlers' favorite
> haunts, the picturesque summit, where
> the blue-stone (rust-red where exposed)
> has been faulted at various levels
>   (ferns rife among the stones)
> into rough terraces and partly closed in
> dens of sweet grass, the ground gently sloping.   (56)

Here the purpose is to describe a scene clearly while at the same time carrying along the symbolic argument, not too obtrusively.

---

[21] *Selected Letters*, p. 317.

WILLIAM CARLOS WILLIAMS
From a painting by Donald Lent. Courtesy of the artist.

THE PASSAIC FALLS
Courtesy of James B. Kenyon.

THE MILLRACE SECTION OF PATERSON AS SEEN
FROM GARRET MOUNTAIN, LOOKING NORTH
Courtesy of James B. Kenyon.

"LOVELY RINGWOOD" (*Paterson*, 12)
Courtesy of the New Jersey Department of Environmental Protection.

CARVED GRASSHOPPER FROM CHAPULTEPEC (*Paterson*, 47)
Instituto Nacional de Antropologia e Historia S.E.P. Photograph by B. A. Stewart.
Copyright National Geographic Society, 1968.

THE UNICORN IN CAPTIVITY. SEVENTH TAPESTRY
IN THE HUNT OF THE UNICORN SERIES AT THE CLOISTERS.
FRENCH OR FLEMISH TAPESTRY, LATE XV CENTURY,
FROM THE CHÂTEAU OF VERTEUIL

Reproduced by courtesy of the Metropolitan Museum of Art, The Cloisters Collection,
Gift of John D. Rockefeller, Jr., 1937.

The language is quiet and precise, but not ostentatious about its precision, ranging from the offhand public phrasing of "the picturesque summit" to a technical formulation ("has been *faulted* at various levels") and to the visual precision of "rust-red where exposed." The reader can picture the terraces caused by the faulting; at the same time, some of the words point to an abstract argument. The *rifeness* of the vegetation, for instance, indicates the unguided profusion of natural growth (an aspect of the "elemental" scene) and also the multiplicity of the poet's material (in contrast with the simplicity and unity of the supporting rock).

The lines have a structure firm enough to give force and movement to the description. The clear shape of the lines on the page makes available the runover principle, which helps to produce the relaxed but quick movement and a certain matter-of-factness of tone.

The versification of *Paterson* is reasonably varied, and it should be pointed out that the verse of *Paterson* dates from various stages of Williams's career. Some of the verse is quite early (specifically, passages from "The Wanderer . . ." used in Book Two with slight revision). Again, the passages of descriptive reminiscences in Book Four, section 3, are earlier than one would think; Williams seems originally to have written them as a beginning for the poem, set them aside, and then returned to them when he had (as he felt) almost completed a later version of it. (Among the latest material in *Paterson* is much of the prose: prose passages often replace verse.)

Like everything else in the poem, the versification is uneven—deliberately so, since the verse includes unfinished fragments intended to be set off against finished passages. (The typescripts show that almost everything was carefully reworked, often typed and revised and retyped many times, and that the placement of words in the line was a prominent consideration as Williams revised.) Still, though the versification is various and to an extent uneven, it should be possible to generalize a bit about the line forms employed. For one thing, the verse is "free," in the obvious sense that it is not governed by any system for counting accents or syllables or feet; there is almost no rhyme (and what little there is aims for special effects). The lines have sufficient structure to support the syntax and to allow for clear variations of movement and emphasis. (The line structure, indeed, seems conceived mainly as a principle to support and play off against the syntax.) The lines are firm enough for the runover principle to function effectively.

There are some little "songs," scattered throughout the poem, with short lines and stanza-like shapes on the page.

In general, I should say, the verse is not nearly so "proselike" as some of the reviewers found it. There is a form—or, rather, a set of related forms—and Williams knew what he was doing with them. Whatever may be said of the overall plan of the poem, the construction of the poem's elements, and particularly the management of the line, was very careful. The success of the versification (and it seems to me largely successful) was a result of Williams's experience and tact, and of extremely attentive revision. Williams also had theories about versification, and it may be useful to conclude this account by quoting from a discussion of these theories as they relate to William's practice. In a review of *Pictures from Brueghel*, Alan Stephens points out that Williams's late notion of a "variable foot" could not quite do what Williams claimed for it. " 'Measure' calls for a unit of measurement, and in our verse you can select your unit from only a few possibilities: you can count beats, or syllables, or feet constructed of definite and recurrent combinations of stressed and unstressed syllables; the identity of the line is a matter of simple arithmetic, and you will search in vain for such a basis in Dr. Williams's line."[22] But Stephens goes on to point out that there is a traditional basis for Williams's line; and this would apply to *Paterson* as well as to the later verse.

I believe that the identity of Dr. Williams's line has no metrical basis, but that nonetheless the line has a definable identity. The general principle is this: a line is a line because, *relative to neighboring lines*, it contains that which makes it in its own right a unit of the attention; and it is as precisely various in its way as are the shadings of accent that play about the abstract norm of the metrical foot, for it too has a norm against which it

[22] Review of *Pictures from Brueghel and Other Poems*, *Poetry*, CI (Feb. 1963), 360–362.

almost constantly varies, allowing for feats of focusing on values that would be otherwise indistinguishable. The norm is the ordinary unit of the attention in language— the formal architecture of the sentence. This principle, it seems to me, also underlies verse with a metrical basis— is indeed the ultimate principle of all verse; if this is so, then audible rhythm, whether produced by a formal metric or by improvisation, is not the supreme fact of the verse line (though it is of course indispensable) and Dr. Williams will have been working in the tradition all along.

Williams in *Paterson* experiments with the mixture, or alternation, of highly sophisticated "literary" procedures and the spontaneous, uncalculated. Certain features of the poem are inconceivable apart from a self-conscious literary tradition going back to Joyce and early Pound (and, through these writers, to the pre-Raphaelites, say, or to Gautier or Flaubert). But other features are inconceivable apart from Williams's temperament— his impatience, his distrust of logic, his quickness to invent procedures, to take chances without much concern about the implications of particular maneuvers. The effect of this hybrid procedure is to keep the reader fascinated and a bit dazed. As he reads *Paterson*, the reader will be condemned to a certain amount of wondering and guessing, sometimes because mechanical clues are missing, sometimes because there seems to be a gap in the design. Sustaining him in his attempt to come to terms with the poem will be an appreciation of how clearly Williams sees particular things and how well he can show the principles active in what he sees. There will be a favorable impression of Williams the man—a gambler sometimes but not an impostor; the writing is honest, in unpredictable ways. These favorable impressions will be accompanied by the refreshment and surprise of reading a long poem in which so many different things can happen. The reader will want to believe that such a skillful and various writer knew pretty clearly what he was doing.

The next few chapters follow the action of the poem.

PATERSON

Book One

THE DELINEAMENTS OF THE GIANTS

PREFACE

On the page facing the beginning of *Paterson: Book I* Williams placed the following passage (after having considered in earlier typescript versions a number of other locations for it):

> :*a local pride; spring, summer, fall and the sea; a confession; a basket; a column; a reply to Greek and Latin with the bare hands; a gathering up; a celebration;*
>
> *in distinctive terms; by multiplication a reduction to one; daring; a fall; the clouds resolved into a sandy sluice; an enforced pause;*
>
> *hard put to it; an identification and a plan for action to supplant a plan for action; a taking up of slack; a dispersal and a metamorphosis.* (2)

That is, the poem at one time or another will be all these things. The method will be schematic, but not all that schematic: spring, summer, fall, and the sea—Williams will suit himself about how to complete a list, and here "fall" is a pun, serving as pivot: it's a season and the Falls of the Passaic River, leading to the sea.

Book One begins with three pages of Preface, stating the subject problematically as a quest for "rigor of beauty."

> "Rigor of beauty is the quest. But how will you find beauty when it is locked in the mind past all remonstrance?" (3)

The question states the central theme of *Paterson*, the poet's attempt to find a language by which to express the beauty that is "locked" in the mind. The next passage provides the beginning of an answer, a way of getting started. The poet will "make a

27

start,/ out of particulars," intending "to make them general,
rolling/ up the sum. . . ." But the means are defective: there is
no ready-made language for the poem. Williams pictures the poet
as a dog, "sniffing the trees," no hero, just an ordinary fellow.
(The dog sniffing trees, marking them with his urine, and so on,
marks off a territory, defines a subject.)

> just another dog
> among a lot of dogs.   (3)

The poet is a lame dog; the sound ones have run out on more
normal "quests" ("after the rabbits," material success—or, the
safe traditions and prestige offered by Europe to poets like Eliot
and Pound). The poet of *Paterson* may not be the best of the
bunch, but he's the only one who hasn't run off. He has the territory, for what it's worth.

A semilogical transition ("For . . .") leads Williams into what
Martz considers a "wry echo of Eliot's 'East Coker,' "[1]

> For the beginning is assuredly
> the end—since we know nothing, pure
> and simple, beyond
> our own complexities.   (3)

When knowledge does come, it will be knowledge of "our own
complexities," the beginning from which the quest started. The
progress will have been circular.

And yet, Williams goes on to argue, "there is/ no return."
(Though the "end" can only be self-knowledge, we cannot return
to the same "self" from which the quest proceeded; in returning
we find ourselves changed by the knowledge acquired in the in-
terval.) This introduces the poem's central analogy, man and city
together constituting an "identity . . . an interpenetration, both
ways." A man's identity is not separable from that of his place,
or "city." Whether he likes it or not, he participates in the character of his city, and the reverse is also true. This identity and

---

[1] Martz, p. 143. Martz suggests that *Paterson* may be a "deliberate counterpart" of *Four Quartets*, "the eternal Pelagian's answer to the doctrine of
original sin."

"interpenetration" is explained by a quotation from Santayana used later in the poem, in which cities are said to be "a second body for the human mind, a second organism, more rational, permanent and decorative than the animal organism of flesh and blood. . . ."[2] Here the interpenetration of man and city illustrates the way in which the act of synthesis ("Rolling/ up!") unites different and even opposite things. The idea of a "man" is inseparable from the idea of "city," and so, for instance, the concepts "ignorance" and "knowledge" overlap and reinforce each other. The language here suggests something like the Hegelian synthesis of opposing principles, or even a mystical union of opposites; but the paradoxical "identity" is here perhaps simply a warning against confidence in fixed categories. Ignorance and knowledge are interlocked, but not symmetrically:

> In ignorance
> a certain knowledge and knowledge,
> undispersed, its own undoing. (4)

Ignorance contains a "certain" knowledge—a freshness of perception, say, that may be lost with experience; and "knowledge" may lead to its opposite by failing to "disperse" itself, that is, by rigidity and a failure of expression.

Williams parenthetically describes what happens to "undispersed" knowledge in the image of a seed ("packed tight with detail") gone sour and lost in the flux, while the mind, "distracted, floats off in the same/ scum)." The seed here is the *potency* of knowledge, rendered impotent by the failure of distribution (by faulty "sowing").

The subject is the poet's attempt at a synthesis ("Rolling up, rolling up heavy with/ numbers") and his attempt to avoid simply repeating what has already been done. He has the advantage of ignorance, if he will accept it as an advantage. The image of "the ignorant sun/ rising in the slot of/ hollow suns risen . . ." suggests the freshness of coming onto the scene for the first time, in unawareness that one is participating in a cycle. If the sun rising is simply a recurrence, then there can be nothing

---

[2] *The Last Puritan*, quoted by Williams at the outset of Book Three.

new; but the new sun's "ignorance" allows it to start fresh—and
it's true that what it sees differs from anything seen by previous
suns. Translated into human terms, the course of the sun presents
the paradox "that never in this/ world will a man live well in
his body/ save dying—and not know himself/ dying. . . ." "Dying"
is the final act of synthesis, and in Book Four it will be associated
with the completion of the poem and the poet's lifework.

In the process of synthesis lies a danger to the poet; he is
warned to "beware lest he turn to no more than/ the writing of
stale poems . . ." (4). Those who do so have "minds like beds
always made up. . . ." (Here a suggestion of the *sleep* of Paterson
the giant, from which the poet attempts to rouse him, and of the
sleep of death: the stale poets are already "dead.") To write a
stale poem is an act of caution or a sign of disability; the poet
is "unwilling or unable" to carry out the search for "rigor of
beauty," a search requiring the ignorance of a new sun, hot and
bright still, though previous suns are now "hollow."

At the outset, then, Williams anticipates much of the later argument of the poem.[3]

The continuous natural process of division and regathering,
now represented by the metamorphosis of water, indicates what
the poet must do in attempting to offer a synthesis:

> divided as the dew,
> floating mists, to be rained down and
> regathered into a river that flows
> and encircles.   (5)

There is a continuous oscillation between what Williams calls
"mathematics" and what he calls "particulars," between (say)
the multiplicity of things experienced, and the mind's attempt to
order them. (But the movement back and forth also produces a
progress, the eventual synthesis.) The river as image for continuity and renewal will appear again late in the poem, when
Williams addresses "My serpent, my river!" (193), preparing to
juxtapose instances of death with a celebration of the birth of
the poem. Here at the outset the river represents that whole

---

[3] The Preface to Book One (3-5) seems to have been composed quite late
in the writing of *Paterson*.

which the poem's particulars (like the "dew" and "floating mists") will constitute.

SECTION 1

The first section of Book One opens with a sketch of the landscape around Paterson, stressing the harmony and natural abundance of the region, and introduces some of the meanings Williams associates with his three main geographical personifications: the city, the river, and the "low Mountain" nearby.

Though the giant Paterson is fixed and unchanging, he animates the innumerable particulars who inhabit him. The giant's dreams—the meaning of life in that place, in submerged mythic form—enter the desires of the people. These thoughts or dreams are powered by the river. The subtleties of the giant's "machinations" draw "their substance from the noise of the pouring river," and these subtleties in turn "animate a thousand automatons." This elemental machinery is the secret of the place, invisible even to the people who inhabit the area, and who are "automatons" in part because their lives derive from that of the giant, in part because they are "unroused," unaware of what gives them life ("their sources") and of "the sills of their/ disappointments. . . ." The introductory account of the giant Paterson, associating the giant's sleep with the people's unawareness, prepares for the role of the poet, who will attempt to articulate the giant's reveries, rousing the people, as best he can, by "defective means."

The great central theme of the poem will be the poet's attempt to give voice to the life of this place; now the slogan "no ideas but in things" states a supporting notion, the means that will be used to that end.

> —Say it, no ideas but in things—
> nothing but the blank faces of the houses
> and cylindrical trees
> bent, forked by preconception and accident—
> split, furrowed, creased, mottled, stained—
> secret—into the body of the light!   (6)

Williams himself explained the slogan to mean that "The poet does not . . . permit himself to go beyond the thought to be dis-

covered in the context of that with which he is dealing: no ideas
but in things."[4]

The trees have acquired their various shapes as "preconcep-
tion" (innate character) and "accident" worked together; each
tree has come into a public existence, particularized—bent,
forked, split, and so on, each in its own way. What the poet starts
with, then, is something that has already been shaped and damaged by forces like these, and that is in a sense obvious, though
uninterpreted as yet. Central to this passage is Williams's belief
that there is a "poem" that every person is trying to communicate: a rare presence, of which the true poet "catches a rumor."[5]
The "blank faces" are expressionless, uninterpreted; they are "secret" until the poet interprets them, bringing them by means of
language "into the body of the light!" The blankness of the houses
is referred to again (on 38), where Williams describes the convent
of St. Ann. These are aspects of that which needs a language—to
bring out its secret meaning.

The Passaic River originates above the city "from oozy fields/
abandoned to grey beds of dead grass,/ black sumac, withered
weed-stalks,/ mud and thickets cluttered with dead leaves," and
pours in above the city to crash "from the edge of the gorge/ in
a recoil of spray and rainbow mists" (6–7). Zabriskie's commentary is useful: "The Passaic River, which, like the city, is central
to the poem, rises in the southern Watchung Range, in the same
general region as the Raritan, which flows southeast. Before the
glaciation of New Jersey, the Passaic and Raritan were nearly
parallel rivers to the sea. However, the last glacier, and the
morainal material it dropped, blocked the Passaic and forced it
to seek another outlet, determining its present devious northward course. In this blockage, Passaic Falls and the bend around

[4] The explanation of the phrase "No ideas but in things" (which occurs
again on 9) appears in Williams's *Autobiography*, p. 390. The passage beginning "Say it . . ." and concluding with "rainbow mists" had originally
been part of the short poem "Paterson" (*Collected Earlier Poems*, pp. 233–
235), parts of which are used later (on 9 and 27–28). The version in *Paterson*
omits a few lines. The phrase "No ideas but in things" was also featured in
the second stanza of "A Sort of a Song," where some of *Paterson*'s themes
are stated: "—through metaphor to reconcile/ the people and the stones./
Compose. (No ideas/ but in things) Invent!/ Saxifrage is my flower that
splits/ the rocks" (*Collected Later Poems*, p. 7).

[5] *Autobiography*, p. 362.

Paterson were created. . . ." At one time, Zabriskie points out, the "wild romantic beauty of the Falls drew many visitors," and the Falls were considered a spectacle to rival Niagara; but now, "neglected, except for the water power they produce, in shabby surroundings, and now more inaccessible than they were a century ago, the Falls are a continual reproach to the city and state."[6]

The river—noise, an unremitting forward rush—suggests to Williams the search for a "common language"; (the river in a way *is* the common but cryptic language which the poet hopes to decode and reply to). After describing the course of the river and the crash of waters "from the edge of the gorge" Williams comments parenthetically:

> (What common language to unravel?
> .   .   combed into straight lines
> from the rafter of a rock's
> lip.)[7]   (7)

In his *Autobiography* (p. 392) Williams explained the significance of the Falls: "The Falls let out a roar as it crashed upon the rocks at its base. In the imagination this roar is a speech or a voice, a speech in particular; it is the poem itself that is the answer." So the roar of the Falls *calls for* an answer; there is a challenge to the poet. The combing of the waters from "a rock's/ lip" suggests the poet's role in giving order and significance to

---

[6] Zabriskie, pp. 202, 208.

[7] These four lines are almost identical with the opening of "Paterson: The Falls," *Collected Later Poems*, p. 10. ("Paterson: the Falls" appeared in *The Wedge*, 1944, pp. 18–20; the passage "What common language to unravel..." had appeared in *The Broken Span*, 1941, [no pagination].) In "Paterson: the Falls" Williams had sketched some of the main themes of *Paterson*, including the Evangelist's sermon and the role of Alexander Hamilton. Early *Paterson* material includes some extensive quotations from that poem, or from earlier versions of the poem. When Williams chose to omit much of it he presumably did so not because he had abandoned the original plan but because he chose to present the same notions differently, some of them in prose, for instance. One earlier version of this material includes after the phrase "—Say it, no ideas but in things—," this passage: "and factories, crystallized from its force/ stand like ice about the chimney rocks/ : the water/ even when and though frozen/ still whispers and moans—/ And in the brittle air/ a factory bell clangs, at dawn, and/ snow whines under their feet . ." The "crystallized" factories is a detail from the short poem "Paterson"; the rest is from "Paterson: the Falls."

the multiple and chaotic. The act of combing as an image for the poet's ordering of particulars reappears later in the poem.

The poet's reply to this riddle or challenge will be an attempt at "marriage," here indicated in a direct statement of the analogy between man and city:

> A man like a city and a woman like a flower
> —who are in love. Two women. Three women.
> Innumerable women, each like a flower.
>
> > > > But
> only one man—like a city.[8]   (7)

The layout of the place—a city, set in the midst of nature—suggests the way in which a man (imagination, active intelligence, the poet himself) must come to terms with (master, absorb, understand) a woman or women (the particulars of a world). The city, no matter how many elements it contains, forms a unity. The poet must fuse the disparate elements of his experience into a unity by finding the right language for it. The poem is to be a love story—a kind of metaphorical polygamy, as Paterson is called upon to "marry" (both as husband and as minister) all the women who appear in the poem. Since the poet's subject matter is multiple and diverse, it can be thought of as "innumerable women." If the poet is successful in what he is attempting, the result will be a modern recreation of the order and beauty of the primal landscape, a "marriage" of the local and contemporary to the age-old and elemental. The poet is asked to minister at a "marriage" like the one that wed the primal Paterson to the primal Mountain.

Several methods are at work in this stretch: the description of the river's course is straightforward and fairly literal, its symbolic significance emerging easily; the rhetorical question about language suggests a way of interpreting the river—the question is abrupt, slightly enigmatic; and the statement about the man and the woman is a direct and portentous way of laying claim to a large-scale analogy.

The next passage, an extract from a letter, gives a quick ironic

[8] A slightly different version of the passage beginning "A man like a city" was published in *The Broken Span* (1941) along with some other material intended at that time for *Paterson*. This material, a group of sketches, was entitled "For the Poem Patterson" [*sic*]. (See Wallace, A 22.)

illustration of the theme Williams has just stated hopefully: "A man like a city" and so on. A lady asks Dr. P. to return her poems. The tone is polite irritation; the woman's feelings have evidently been hurt. This is the first of a series of letters from the lady-poet ("Cress"), passages of which are shuffled in among other things in the first two books of *Paterson*. Trapped by the city, the woman has sought out Dr. P. as a human resource and ally; he has not responded. While he persists with his own work, the woman's letters criticize his enterprise with increasing bitterness. The woman's letter is an instance of what Williams calls "divorce." The poet's inability to respond underlines the difficulty present in his attempt to "marry" the world of the present day. Before she is finished, Cress will be allowed to make a strong case against what she considers the aestheticism and isolation of Dr. P., and in favor of a direct immersion in the realities of the city.

> Besides, I know myself to be more the woman than the
> poet; and to concern myself less with the publishers of
> poetry than with . . . living. . . . (7)

Paterson's thoughts are compared to the waters (7–8). In Williams's scheme, Zabriskie points out, "as the waters of the Falls drive the electric motors of the factories, as they once drove the undershot water wheels; so do they drive the thoughts of the sleeping giant, Paterson. . . ."[9] "Jostled," the waters "interlace, repel and cut under,/ rise rock-thwarted and turn aside/ but forever strain forward." Sometimes they strike an eddy "and whirl, marked by a/ leaf or curdy spume, seeming/ to forget ." They encounter obstacles, work their way around them, "Retake later the advance and/ are replaced by succeeding hordes/ pushing forward. . . ." They keep coming, and on hitting the bottom, "All lightness lost, weight regained in/ the repulse," they are driven by a fury of escape to "rebound/ upon those coming after." The waters have their own leaps and recoveries; their movement is varied, but the general direction and force of the Falls remain more or less constant. An image for the way in which consciousness proceeds: there is unremitting advance, fury, rebounding, and a resulting *unity*.

[9] Zabriskie, p. 208.

In his account of the personified topography, resumed at this point (8), Williams turns to the "low mountain," emphasizing the beauty and abundance of the place. In the elemental landscape, the mountain is Paterson's wife, the feminine principle of the poem and in turn the "source" of the many women who appear in the poem (who also are his "wives"). Here Williams describes the mountain as a woman dressed in natural finery ("farms and ponds, laurel and the temperate wild cactus,/ yellow flowered . .."). "The Valley of the Rocks" mentioned in the description is (to quote an early guide) "the name of a picturesque level at the bottom of the precipitous wall to the east of the Cataract."[10] As part of her costume the mountain wears "pearls at her ankles": a detail supported by prose on the discovery of a pearl in a mussel taken from Notch Brook near Paterson, and on the accidental destruction of a large pearl when its shell was boiled open. The destruction of the pearl states quickly a new theme: destruction of the rich promise of the locality as a consequence of ignorant commercial exploitation.

Williams now toys for a moment with the personification of Paterson: (*a*) as a person much like himself, and (*b*) as a giant whose "thoughts" are particular people ("Mr./ Paterson has gone away/ to rest and write. Inside the bus one sees/ his thoughts sitting and standing").[11] The poet attempts to understand the "mathematic" of his relation to these people, Paterson's "thoughts." The people are "incommunicado," lack a voice; the equation ordering their interrelationships is so complex that it's "beyond solution":

> yet
> its sense is clear—that they may live
> his thought is listed in the Telephone
> Directory—   (9)

In an earlier version of this passage the following appears after "Telephone Directory" (and before "And derivatively"):

[10] Van Derhoven, p. 23.
[11] The passage belongs to Williams's early conception of *Paterson*: like the passages on 9 and 27–28, it is quoted from "Paterson," *Collected Earlier Poems*, pp. 233–235.

> . .   the streets divide it
> into squares and the squares
> into history, horizontal and perpendicular

> —And Singac, the Backbone: buried in the ground whence
> it shows, holding the Little Falls draped smoothly over it
> cropping up there   .

On 10 Williams begins to provide his locale with a mythic past complete with monsters and miracles, as if to say, "yes, even here in the pastless United States, an epic is possible, with all the trimmings." Among the early marvels of the area was a "monster in human form," a dwarf whose head was as large as his body. The account of the dwarf (Pieter Van Winkle) seems to have been taken from Barber and Howe, *Historical Collections of the State of New Jersey*, with very slight modifications. From earlier versions it appears that the passage from Barber and Howe was involved in Williams's plan for the poem from a very early stage. Williams uses several of the Van Winkles in the poem—possibly intending the Rip Van Winkle story to reinforce the theme of Paterson as "sleeping giant." (William Nelson tells the story of how Washington Irving got his character's name from a member of the Van Winkle family.) As Ralph Nash points out, Pieter the Dwarf becomes for Williams a "sardonic symbol of himself as poet."[12] In the last part of Book Four there are references to the dwarf's grave, and an account of the murder of John S. Van Winkle and his wife (187–188). In an early draft (Buffalo MS) for the beginning of *Paterson*, Williams tries to get the poem under way by means of a dialogue, part of which concerns this description of the dwarf. One of the speakers comments: "a paralytic hydrocephalic or waterhead. Why don't we use our own language like the Greeks?" The other speaker then explicitly identifies the dwarf as "the genius of the Falls."

In still another version, Williams interrupted the account of the dwarf with this comment in verse, in which the bitter amuse-

---

[12] Nash, p. 196. The description of the dwarf, quoted by Williams from Barber and Howe, p. 407, is also given by Nelson, p. 100, where it is attributed to Surgeon James Thacher. The dwarf, as Thirlwall notes, is an instance of Williams's deliberate use of the "fantastic" in *Paterson*; see Thirlwall, pp. 268, 273.

ment at one of nature's tricks carries over to the figure of the poet:

> . . not his element.   Perhaps he was
> intended to be a burrower or to float in
> the sea or hang like a gall from an oak
> twig.   (Buffalo MS)

Like the hydrocephalic dwarf, the Falls were a natural "wonder," as was the huge fish caught in 1817 (prose account on 10–11).[13] The people are looking for a wonder; in *Paterson* a leaderless mob will make its appearance on various occasions—to watch a dangerous feat, or an execution. And the poem itself is to be a "wonder," though Williams is uneasily aware that it may simply be a spectacular failure.

In the meantime, while the indifferent populace admires these "wonders," they let the elemental beauty of the place slip from them.

To the early settlers the Falls were a natural wonder, worth traveling to see; they were also, potentially, a source of waterpower, and this potential led Alexander Hamilton to imagine at the site of the Falls a large national manufacturing center: the future city of Paterson. Hamilton now appears for the first time, briefly, in a prose passage (10) recounting the rapid growth of Paterson as a mill town by the middle of the nineteenth century, and analyzing the heterogeneous population it attracted.

Williams has now established the Falls in several ways: as part of the original landscape, as an object of wonder to the people, as a source of waterpower (and hence the pretext for the industrialization of the region and the force drawing immigrants to Paterson in the nineteenth century), as an analogy for the course of the poet's thoughts, and as the propounder of a challenge or riddle.[14]

---

[13] I have not identified the source of the prose account of the fish. The newspaper article "The Monster Taken" is referred to by Longwell, pp. 58–59. Nelson and Shriner (I, 142) includes some of the account.

[14] At one time Williams included (for 11) the ten lines from "Paterson: the Falls" beginning "and pickerel . . ." and concluding "there: the rocks silent." This passage was followed by "They begin!" In revision, Williams replaced elements from the earlier poem (in which the argument is stated pretty directly) with prose on Hamilton, the fish, and so forth, in which reference to the poem's main themes is oblique.

Now we are at the Falls, watching the sunlight playing on the spray: the famous "rainbow" of the Falls, "formed by the reflection of the sunlight through the mists and floating wreaths of spray which ascend from the water, as they come foaming and dashing over the precipice."[15] Williams's description catches the violence and beauty of the spectacle.

The rainbow spray, perceived as a "flower," becomes the flower who is Paterson's wife (or one of them). The passage on 11 described a beginning, full of promise, but one that is unfulfilled because there is no language:

> They begin!
> The perfections are sharpened
> The flower spreads its colored petals
> wide in the sun
> But the tongue of the bee
> misses them
> They sink back into the loam
> crying out. (11)

The poet is pictured as a bee—Williams's metaphorical elaboration of the poet as "honey-tongued." His job is to carry pollen from flower to flower, in this way "marrying" his people as a minister does. Those flowers that are missed by the "tongue of the bee" die unfulfilled; we watch them "sink back into the loam."[16]

Some of these particulars (people, the thoughts of the giant—and of the poet) are said to try to escape; they go to the "Coast without gain." Now they are pictured as waters, strands of the Falls. They "fail," as Mrs. Cumming and Sam Patch fail a few pages later. Language has failed them, and they die "incommunicado." Either they do not know the words "or have not/ the courage to use them ." They are like:

[15] Van Derhoven, p. 21.

[16] Sister Bernetta, tracing the metamorphosis of the female/ mountain principle in *Paterson*, comes at the present passage from a slightly different angle; her interpretation is worth quoting: "The Park is her head, the features of which have been carved by the Passaic out of the colored rocks. A few pages later this image is blended with that of a flower to which Williams has previously in the poem compared the woman. But no bee carries fertilizing pollen to the heart of this flower; instead it sinks back into the ground, wilting, disappearing, destined for sterility instead of fruitful marriage" (Quinn, p. 97).

                    —girls from
          families that have decayed and
          taken to the hills: no words.
          They may look at the torrent in
                    their minds
          and it is foreign to them.   .   (11–12)

The phrase "foreign to them" implies that the poem will introduce people to their own lives (interpret for them "the torrent
in/ their minds").

The poet's search for a principle of unity and for a language
now appears obliquely in two passages, one a stretch of prose on
the Ramapo Mountains and their inhabitants; the second a verse
passage recalling a picture of an African chief and his wives.

The inhabitants of the Ramapos exemplify the miscellane-
ousness and meagerness Williams found characteristic of American local culture. These people, the so-called Jackson or Jackson's Whites, provide an extreme instance of the working of the
melting-pot principle in American history: a principle already
touched on in the analysis of Paterson's population (10). It is a
collection of uprooted people. First, remnants from the Tusca-
rora tribe, compelled to move to New York after savage battles
in the south ("Violence broke out in Tennessee . . ."): the Tusca-
rora women, children, old men, and a few others had elected to
remain in the Ramapos, at least for a time. These people were
joined by others for whom the mountains provided sanctuary:
Hessian troops, some of them albinos, deserting from the British
army; and women who had been brought from England to serve
the sexual needs of the British troops in New York City. (The
label "Jackson's Whites" evidently derived from the name of the
man who had procured the women.) At the close of the Revolutionary War the women—and their "brats"—were simply released
from the stockade where they had been quartered; most of them
escaped to the western shore of the Hudson and, together with a
few soldiers and Tories, made their way into the mountains. The
last main element in the racial blend consisted of escaped Negro
slaves. "This conglomerate manned the early iron furnaces,
brought in the lime and burned the wood to make the necessary
charcoal."[17]

[17] The quotation is from Williams's notes (Buffalo MS). The prose on

This racial aggregate is set off against two other presences: (*a*) the primitive setting—the forest of butternut, elm, and so on, a river in which trout slithered "among the shallow stones," and (*b*) the aristocratic beauty of a colonial estate, "lovely Ringwood," with "its velvet lawns," a beauty reminiscent of Old World culture.

The significant phrase "two phases" appears near the beginning of the passage: "If there was not beauty, there was a strangeness and a bold association of wild and cultured life grew up together in the Ramapos: two phases," that is, one the so far meager efforts at a local culture at home in the New World setting, the other our attempts to transplant culture from England and the Old World.

These phases had been the subject of an important essay, "The American Background," first published in 1934. America had begun with many promises of a "related culture," a living culture rooted in local conditions, but these beginnings had "stagnated," lacking "money to make them mobile." In the meantime, "wealth took the scene, representative of a sort of squatter spirit, irresponsible because unrelated to the territory it overran" (*Selected Essays*, p. 149). The result was the dominance of what Williams called a "secondary culture," derivative from Europe, represented at its best by the great art collections of wealthy men like Morgan. One cannot ignore a Morgan collection: "Its illuminated manuscripts alone, dating from the fifth century, must make us humble and raise our aspirations to the heights." But the importation of art objects didn't touch our real cultural poverty: "But neither can a region afford not to have lived. It must be understood, while we are looking, that great art, in all its significance and implications, in all its direct

---

12–13 is undoubtedly Williams's own, based on notes he had taken, apparently with the idea originally of writing a passage of verse about the Jackson Whites. One earlier version (Yale MS) shows Williams revising his notes in the direction of the version finally used. Williams's sources include, probably, the Federal Writers' Project's *New Jersey: A Guide to Its Present and Past* (New York, 1939), pp. 505–506, and possibly a short book by John C. Storms, *Origin of the Jackson-Whites of the Ramapo Mountains* (Park Ridge, 1936). The summary above supplements Williams's sketch with a few details from Storms's study. On the subject of the Jackson Whites the reader may consult Brewton Berry, *Almost White* (New York, 1963), pp. 23–27.

application to our moment, has used great wealth merely as an instrument, and that the life and vigor of every primary culture is its real reason for being" (*Selected Essays*, p. 160).

The argument that a region must "live," and the critique of America's local culture, appear in various forms in Williams's work, in *White Mule*, for instance, and in the well-known poem beginning "The pure products of America/ go crazy—."[18]

> and young slatterns, bathed
> in filth
> from Monday to Saturday
>
> to be tricked out that night
> with gauds
> from imaginations which have no
>
> peasant traditions to give them
> character

The young Elsie, rescued from her surroundings by an agent, "reared by the state and/ sent out at fifteen to work in/ some hard-pressed/ house in the suburbs" expresses "with broken/ brain the truth about us." This is the truth about us because we have never successfully fostered a "primary" or "related" culture here. The poet of *Paterson*, attempting to find a language for his subject, is in effect attempting to make up for this cultural deficit.

The prose on 12–13, then, describing life in Ramapos, illustrates the incoherence and inarticulateness of our local culture. Later in the poem, Phyllis, the tough young nurse of Book Four, will come from the Ramapos; and the "Old World" principle in our culture will be represented by the wealthy Lesbian, Corydon.

In "The American Background" Williams cited Jefferson's Monticello as an instance of a successful fusion of the two main elements in American culture. In *Paterson* the poet attempts such a fusion.

---

[18] "To Elsie," *Collected Earlier Poems*, pp. 270–272. In an earlier version of *Paterson*, Book One, Williams has his female speaker say, "I come from the most degraded stock." This speaker, who is not defined very clearly in the first book, is presumably equivalent to Phyllis, or roughly so.

Another subject implicit in this passage is the violence characteristic of American history, as Williams touches on various clashes from which the groups forming the Jackson Whites had been precipitated: the Revolutionary War, battles with Indians, and so on. George Washington appears here because he had come "up from Pompton for rest after the traitors' hangings." An earlier draft had contrasted the reassuringly quiet scene at Ringwood with the violent events of the area's history:

> Certainly you would say under these calm trees—
> There's no violence here: rapine, harlotry,
> disease and abandonment—
> engrafted on the wild. Hamilton, violence at
> his birth, drawn toward violence, to die also
> by violence. Violence in the earth. Iron
> lightnings from the earth. Thunderbolts of steel—
> dug by the primitives, by slaves—enkindled
> by strange fires, illicit, unrecognized—the
> Jackson Whites—and the first horseman of
> his day sleeping at the Mansion—Ringwood—after
> the executions at Pompton—   (Buffalo MS)

Williams's point is that it's an American tradition to ignore the violence of our origins.

The final paragraph, dealing with the way in which the Barbados were settled by Irish, sold as slaves, continues the theme of transplantation of culture and language. The logic for including this information here is in part one of verbal association: the area in which the Jackson Whites had originally settled was called New Barbados.[19]

Now Williams abruptly moves to an African scene he remembers from *National Geographic*, nine wives of an African chief, lined on a log "in a descending scale of freshness": a glimpse of a principle of order, continuity, and possibly of revitalization. Here there is uniformity and orderliness, contrasting with the helter-skelter way things have developed in the Ramapos. The chief's first wife is a version of Paterson's first wife, the mountain. Her "careworn eyes" are "serious, menacing—but unabashed" (13). Williams begins to suggest the symbolic role she

[19] The last paragraph follows pretty closely a passage from Seamus MacCall's biography of *Thomas Moore* (London, 1935), p. 94.

will take on in the next section (21), where she reappears as the source of the poet's inspiration—a mysterious and dangerous force located in the midst of things.[20]

Confronted by the challenge of multiplicity, to which the glimpse of the first wife may offer an answer, Williams now pictures his own enterprise and its risks in terms of two deaths associated with the Passaic Falls. The first is that of a Mrs. Cumming, who fell from a point above the Falls while visiting there with her husband in 1812.

Williams quotes an old-fashioned prose account, commenting:

> A false language. A true. A false language pouring—a
> language (misunderstood) pouring (misinterpreted) without
> dignity, without minister, crashing upon a stone ear.   (15)

"Without minister" is a pun: Mr. Cumming was a minister. The woman's death is divorce of a kind. The language of the old account is unable to save Mrs. Cumming.

The source of Williams's account is Barber and Howe (pp. 412–413), and, ultimately, a historical work entitled *Alden's Collections*; Williams at one time gave a title to the prose passage: "Mrs. Sarah Cumming from Alden's Collections" (Yale MS, title scratched out). Another typescript (Buffalo MS) seems to show that Williams had tried a version of his own before deciding simply to use the old account. Among Williams's notes to himself for changes in Book One is this one indicating the direction it was taking: "Include various notes, somewhat in full on Patch (his *acts*) Mrs. Cummins [*sic*], personal notes—odds and ends etc. *Cut* the long early Paterson bit to sharper figures. End with the monastery in the country as compensation or correlative of the city and its draggle" (Buffalo MS).

An early version of this passage indicates how Williams was thinking about his material. After the account of Mrs. Cumming's death, Williams had this in verse:

[20] The manuscripts show that Williams had at one time a single long passage on the subject, before deciding to break up his treatment and introduce the subject briefly here. This long passage on the first wife is associated in the Buffalo manuscripts with material (including the preacher's sermon) separated from it in the published version. Much of what we read now in section 2 seems to have been written long before the present arrangement of *Paterson* into books and sections.

What was that cry? What was that fall?
Nobody saw her. It was, or was it?
the laughter of the waterfall—a true
language she could understand,

. . . .

Or was it nothing in the blood but
an emptiness that drew her in? a language
she could understand—   (Buffalo MS)

Then "A false language. A true . . ." (15).

The second death is that of the famous Sam Patch, a resident
of Paterson who had earned a national reputation for his spectacular leaps from high places, starting with the Falls of the
Passaic, to be killed, finally, in a leap from the Genesee Falls near
Rochester.

Unlike the tragic fall of Mrs. Cumming, Patch's first leap was
deliberate (though stimulated by alcohol) and successful. Williams identifies his own "Paterson" with Sam Patch, successful
and cocky, in a mock advertisement printed on 15 (an advertisement once intended as the opening or title page for *Paterson*).[21]

THE GRRRREAT HISTORY of that

old time Jersey Patriot

N. F. PATERSON!

(N for Noah; F for Faitoute; P for short)

"Jersey Lightning" to the boys.

As "Faitoute," Paterson is the man who "does it all" (the man
of many wives, major responsibilities, and so on); as Noah, he
survives the flood (death and the flood of texts in Book Three);
"for short" ends a characteristic Williams series, the last term
shooting out of line. "Jersey Lightning" is a New Jersey applejack
cider, noted for its potency.

[21] Buffalo MS. An account of Sam Patch's leap was at one time part of
verse reminiscences on early days in Paterson—the long reminiscent passage
(very early) that Williams was to use in Book Four, section 3 (Yale MS). His
main source for the career of Sam Patch, followed very closely, is Longwell,
pp. 36–39. A few details (e.g., the reference to the pet bear) may have come
from E. M. Graf's *Short Sketches on Passaic County History* (Paterson, 1935),
pp. 17–20.

Patch "became a national hero in '28, '29 and toured the country / diving from cliffs and masts, rocks and bridges—to prove his / thesis: Some things can be done as well as others." And this thesis, in a way, is what the poet intends to prove. After an account of Patch's successful leap (15–16), Williams plays with another of his slogans:

> There's no mistake in Sam Patch!
>
> > The water pouring still
> from the edge of the rocks, filling
> his ears with its sound, hard to interpret.
> A wonder!   (17)

The man who leaps from the Falls becomes an interpreter of it, like the poet.

Patch is a type for the poet, taking a risk, ultimately to fail. In *The Great American Novel* Williams had toyed with the theme of "taking a leap," in a sketch describing a boy trying to decide to jump twelve feet into the water (pp. 57–58; *Imaginations*, pp. 206–207):

> He had never dived from such a height in his life. He had climbed up there to dive and he must dive or yield. What would he yield? At least it was something he did not intend to yield. He tried his best to imitate the others, he stood on the edge and plunged. It seemed to him that he plunged. As a matter of fact he dropped over the edge with his body bent almost double so that his thighs hit the water with a stinging impact, also the lower part of his belly, also the top of his head. He did not feel certain of himself for a moment or two after rising to the surface. That was about enough. Memory began to fill the blank of his mind.

One subject in *Paterson* is the difficulty of distinguishing between the "leap" or deliberate risk necessary for any great enterprise and the "fall" of someone from carelessness or despair or lack of skill. "To fall," in a characteristic Williams play on words, means "to fail." To leap is to take the necessary chance, and by dint of courage and skill, to survive. This is the secret of Patch's successful leap. A man is going to "fall" sooner or later anyway; life itself is a "fall."

We are meant to be conscious always of Williams struggling to get the poem written: the poem has a deliberately achieved air of desperate improvisation. When Patch fails, he suggests the fate Williams fears for himself: will he himself fail this time? Patch's skill (or luck) is equated with the poet's skill—his language. The key concept in the report of Patch's death is Williams's addition: "Speech had failed him. . . ." On November 13, 1829, Patch was to leap 125 feet from the falls of the Genesee River. A crowd gathered, and Patch "made a short speech as he was wont to do." To Williams this suggests his own situation: "What could [Patch] say that he must leap so desperately to complete it? And plunged toward the stream below." Something went wrong, and "instead of descending with a plummetlike fall his body wavered in the air—Speech had failed him. . . ." After Patch hit the water the crowd was silent. His body was not recovered until the following spring, when it was found "frozen in an ice-cake" (17), another obliquely thematic detail, since to be "frozen in an ice-cake," like sinking back into the loam, is to be lost because of a failure to be articulate. Discussing Williams's use of Sam Patch in *Paterson* as "one of the negative aspects of the man-Paterson symbol," Frank Thompson commented: "When Patch makes his leap, he suddenly becomes important on another level: he has shown the consequences of a false language. The fact that the verbal reality he represents is false becomes, for the moment (and for the poem), more important than the fact that he is a man."[22]

The next section consists mainly of ruminations on themes introduced in the first section.

SECTION 2

Having described the topography of the area around Paterson, and having indicated some of the main features of the "elemental character" of the place, Williams proceeds to reflections on his own role, picking up and elaborating some of the terms of the

[22] "The Symbolic Structure of *Paterson*," *Western Review*, XIX (Summer 1955), 289. Joseph Slate argues that in emphasizing the bridge from which Patch leaped, constructed by a certain Tim Crane, Williams was alluding to Hart Crane's *The Bridge* ("William Carlos Williams, Hart Crane, and 'The Virtue of History,'" *Texas Studies in Literature and Language*, VI [Winter 1965], 486–511).

first section. The poet's responsibility is to give a voice to the
voiceless particulars of his own world, to rescue by means of language those who would otherwise "go to the coast without gain."
If the poet can find a language by means of which to convey the
meaning of these lives, he will in a sense save them from death,
as Homer rescued Achilles. But Williams's concern also refers
to his own fate, since the failure to find a language will also be
the failure of the poem and, in a sense, his own death. At this
point in the poem he is Sam Patch, but a Sam Patch who has not
yet failed.

As he considers his own situation, Williams introduces the
term "divorce," which in this section refers specifically to the
state of knowledge "in our time." The universities compart-
mentalize knowledge and prevent it from circulating freely; as a
result there is no living source from which the people can draw
what they need. Cut off from what would sustain them, they live
and die in isolation, without ripening.

Williams pictures a bud lying "tight-curled" on the pavement,
divorced from its source and from its "fellows." The bud serves
as emblem for the isolation and arrested growth of individuals in
a society that lacks a living culture; and it can represent other
kinds of separation, including the separation of one field of
knowledge from another.[23] In terms of the metaphorical marriage
of Paterson to many women (who are "like flowers"), the bud is
one of Paterson's wives, but divorced from him.

As an alternative to a culture marked by divisions and imbalances, Williams locates a hidden "source," an elemental presence,
akin to the elemental character of the area around Paterson. It is
the "first wife" in the *Geographic* picture mentioned in the first
section. (The implied identity of the older wife in the *Geographic*
picture with the "low mountain," Paterson's wife, is explicit in
some of the earlier versions of this section.)

The development of the argument is tentative and slow, as
the poet tests his still unclear notion of what he can do against
his clearer notion of the imperfections of his material.

---

[23] A related meaning is suggested by Sister Bernetta: "Beauty is spoiled
by severance from the springs of its life—the bud upon the pavement, divorced from its fellows, symbol of all those who revolt against wholeness,
who refuse to embrace what would save them" (Quinn, p. 113).

"There is no direction." The poem has a method but no destination:

> Whither? I
> cannot say. I cannot say
> more than how. The how (the howl) only
> is at my disposal (proposal) : watching—
> colder than stone   .   (18)

The river's noise presumably accounts for Williams's playing with sounds.

Like the river's noise, the green bud challenges "our waking." The roar of the river reminds the poet of the river-like course of life, hence of his own mortality, arousing a fear of going "to the coast without gain." ("Forever in our ears [arrears]"—we are behind in doing the job; death makes the matter urgent.) The green bud, an instance of unfledged desire, "irresponsible, green," stands for the poet's world as it presently appears to him. The bud "falls," as Patch and Mrs. Cumming did. The absence of coherence and ripeness in his material tempts the poet to give up; so does the awareness of death, tempting him to "sleep." The river's challenge to "our waking" includes both a challenge to get on with the job and a temptation to give it up.

The green bud concept carries over into a description of two young girls, one of whom picks a willow twig, holds it in the air and exclaims "Ain't they beautiful!" She announces—gives birth to—the spring ritual, Easter. The parenthetical exclamation "(or eels or a moon!)" seems to involve a kind of visual "rhyme": what the girl admires might be any of these things; their shape (and significance) is similar; and there is a hint of sexual symbolism. The girls, like the green bud, illustrate "unfledged desire." The girl's pleased exclamation is itself an instance of an inadequacy of the language, and several pages later Williams indicates that what she cries aloud is (in effect) "Divorce!"—that is, the divorce of learning from the people. The air in which the girls move is described in language suggestive of the action of waters at the edge of the Falls. The girls weave "about themselves, from under/ the heavy air, whorls of thick translucencies." Their "clear hair dangling" resembles the movement of the Falls. The association with the river identifies the girls with the flowers who go "to the Coast without gain"; they are mortal, they lack a language.[24]

The springtime scene causes Paterson to consider his own relation to the "ground." He's not a "robin nor erudite"—that is, he doesn't migrate, returning to the same spot each year, as the robin does (to sing the same song), nor does he repeat himself like a scholar. Or, if he does, the ground itself has changed. The exclamation "Indians!" is a reminder that the locality once supported a different culture.

> Why even speak of "I," he dreams, which
> interests me almost not at all?   (19)

The poet (as the dreaming giant Paterson) is not interested in the poem as a claim to personal identity and distinction, as an assertion of what an "I" can do. (The poet has his job almost by default: the other dogs ran out after rabbits.)

We are still clearly at the beginning of the job. The poet has not yet fixed on a theme, yet he already knows something about the theme that will emerge:

>   The theme
> is as it may prove: asleep, unrecognized—
> all of a piece, alone
> in a wind that does not move the others—
> in that way: a way to spend
> a Sunday afternoon while the green bush shakes.   (19)

The language here used to describe the still undiscovered theme is close to that which a page or so later will describe the sycamore branch that becomes a symbol for the source of the poet's inspiration. The branch moves in its way—moved by a wind that does not move the other branches in the same way. Wind—inspiration, but also the "male" force of the poet, the "indifferent gale: male . . ." that causes the juniper bush (image for the poet) to

[24] Among the earlier readings of this passage are two of particular interest. In a version in the Yale library, the line reading "(or eels or a moon!)" reads "or/ eels or fish." The second reference to the girls (22) appeared at one time in this form: "Two sisters, tied together—(separately) in a bow— from whose open mouths/ Easter is born—crying aloud, Divorce!" (Buffalo MS).

tremble "frantically." In one version the juniper on the embankment was an unidentified bush: "a short, compact bush/ not to be botanically identified."

To discover his subject the poet must be patient, unobtrusive, simply "spending a Sunday afternoon." He has the job of finding new and difficult connections among a "mass" of so far unrelated particulars. The "new ground" is a mild pun; the poet will find a new *basis* for these interrelationships, but the ground is also America, the New World. The words "an assonance, a homologue" suggest a search for unnoted resemblances and connections, no matter how slight, and hence (perhaps) for groupings to replace the obsolete categories of the universities. In dealing with the varied and not-yet-related (the "disparate"), the poet's job is to "clarify/ and compress."

The grammar is unclear. The poet hopes to "clarify and compress" the disparate and also perhaps the river, which is now "curling, full"; and he hopes to do this "as a bush shakes/ and a white crane will fly/ and settle later!" These images for the poet's work indicate that despite the urgency there can be no hurry about it. But the summer (of the poet's maturity?) may not come. The crane settles (and the suspended statement completes itself with the phrase) "in the shallow water!"

Implicit here is the poet's decision to go on living and working though death tempts him. The search for beauty has kept him going, but so far the search has been fruitless.

> The thought returns: Why have I not
> but for imagined beauty where there is none
> or none available, long since
> put myself deliberately in the way of death?   (20)

The tone is not desperate so much as impatient. He knows that the promise of beauty has kept him alive, but he knows that he may have been kidding himself. Here again an echo effect: "Stale as whale's breath: breath! Breath!" The language, imbedding the old categories, is stale; the gasp for breath becomes a cry for inspiration.

And Williams returns to Patch and Mrs. Cumming as exemplars of his own possible fate. Patch made a courageous, maybe foolhardy, attempt to leap the Falls, and finally died as the result of taking a chance. Mrs. Cumming's death was accidental, or perhaps a suicide. No one "saw" her fall (though her husband was standing nearby), presumably because no poet was there to "redeem" her death by means of language (20). Two deaths: both corpses "silent, uncommunicative."

The parodic bird call, "Only of late, late!" suggests the poet's sense of his own danger, as though he has barely escaped, or barely seen the way to escape, the fate he associates with Patch and Mrs. Cumming. Like them, he is in danger of going "to the coast without gain." Now he begins to perceive the source of his breath (inspiration) clearly, as if though clear ice—ice like that in which the body of Sam Patch was encased when finally recovered. (Another bird call: "Clearly!"—the poet as robin begins to sing. . . .)

THE POET'S SOURCE

There is a sycamore at the edge of the Falls; Williams describes one branch of it carefully, so as to show it at once distinctly itself, with its own movement, and as part of the whole tree (21); he then refers back to the chief and his wives in the *Geographic* picture (first mentioned on 13–14).

The mottled sycamore branch is a particular, separate, moving in the wind according to its own laws, yet not isolate: connected to the tree (as the first wife firmly straddles the log). The branch singled out by the poet sways less than the others, "separate, slowly," and "with giraffish awkwardness." So also

> the first wife, with giraffish awkwardness
> among thick lightnings that stab at
> the mystery of a man: in sum, a sleep, a
> source, a scourge   .   (21)

The woman's old thighs grip reverently the log that "all of a piece, holds up the others." The log supports the first wife and the others, just as Williams's elemental Paterson supports transient particulars. ("Butterflies settle on his stone ear" [6]). The African scene is orderly yet strange ("her varnished hair / trussed up like a termite's nest . . ."), suggestive of unfamiliar danger. The poet pays attention, recognizing his own dependence on the principle embodied by the sycamore branch and by the chief's eldest wife: "alert: begin to know the mottled branch/ that sings ."

The poet's source is "certainly NOT the university," which is

> a green bud fallen upon the pavement its
> sweet breath suppressed: Divorce (the
> language stutters)
>
> unfledged: (22)

The university is one of the forces to blame for the present condition of the language.

Now Williams picks up the statement that had broken off on 21 ("... the mottled branch/ that sings ...") with "While/ the green bush sways: is whence/ I draw my breath ...," explicitly identifying the branch as the source of his inspiration.

Having identified the latent presence which is both his source and theme, Williams compares it to a flower and to a hunted wild animal.

> Which is to say, though it be poorly
> said, there is a first wife
> and a first beauty, complex, ovate—
> the woody sepals standing back under
> the stress to hold it there, innate
>
> a flower within a flower whose history
> (within the mind) crouching
> among the ferny rocks, laughs at the names
> by which they think to trap it. Escapes!
> Never by running but by lying still— (22)

The "flower within a flower" has a history, which mocks our attempts to name it. It can be pictured as a wild and dangerous animal, with its own cane-brake ("by its den in the/ rocks, bole and fangs"), camouflaged ("canes and stripes/ blending") and thus able to escape by lying still. It grins (ugly: "beauty defied"), knowing that it eludes our categories ("not for the sake of the encyclopedia"). Its breath stinks, and if we should approach too closely this breath would "fell us."

> The temple upon
> the rock is its brother, whose majesty
> lies in jungles—made to spring,
> at the rifle-shot of learning: to kill

and grind those bones:[25]   (23)

Williams's subject is the elusiveness of particulars—or of the beauty resident in particulars, conceived not in isolation but as having a history and a ground. The elusiveness appears as a wildness, like that of an animal that knows how to conceal itself by blending into its surroundings but will also fight when attacked. To impose preexistent categories is to trap or shoot the wild creature. That which the poet is seeking will elude our categories, and, if cornered, it will spring and kill. (In this passage the university, the encyclopedia and the "rifle-shot of learning" are roughly equivalent terms.)

The association of the history of the first beauty with the "temple on the rock" suggests a spontaneous awe before the unsponsored beauty of the world, an awe that is at the basis of primitive religious feeling.

The elusiveness of this essential beauty leads Williams to an enumeration of events marked by subtle metamorphoses and by the shading off of one form into another:

> These terrible things they reflect:
> the snow falling into the water,
> part upon the rock, part in the dry weeds
> and part into the water where it
> vanishes—its form no longer what it was.   (23)

[25] The main argument of this long passage, and many of its details, go back to an early stage of the poem's development—to a time before Williams had settled on the arrangement of *Paterson* into four books with three sections each. At one time the passage beginning "which is to say" led into "Sunday in the Park" and the preacher's sermon. As Williams worked on this passage he added new material (including much of the prose), and blocked things out differently. What should be noted is the close tie-in (still implicit, though not so obvious in the final version) between the argument here (22) and the "Park" theme of Book Two. One early version (Buffalo MS) has a *city* at the center of each flower; the *history* lies in the mind "as a tiger among rocks"; the temple that springs at the rifle shot of learning is killed—"killed by learning."

The phrase "these terrible things" evidently refers to the metaphors just employed to suggest the way in which the "history" escapes our categories. What follows is a descriptive list, suggesting the pathos of the various fates of particulars falling at random, and providing instances of events that our fixed concepts are unable to handle: a bird alighting, a daisy bending to the wind, "the pitiful snake with its mosaic skin/ and frantic tongue . . . ," and so on. From an image of snow falling (its fall akin to the roar of the Falls) Williams goes on to picture "the whole din of fracturing thought/ as it falls tinnily to nothing upon the streets . . ." (23). The streets here no doubt signify the everyday world, against which thought falls and noisily breaks itself.

The enumeration concludes:

> Pithy philosophies of
> daily exits and entrances, with books
> propping up one end of the shaky table—
> The vague accuracies of events dancing two
> and two with language which they
> forever surpass—and dawns
> tangled in darkness—   (23)

Books prop up the table—a precarious makeshift balance in our everyday "philosophies" for coming to terms with the world's subtleties. Events are characterized both by vagueness (they merge into other events, and into the whole pattern of experience, lacking clear boundaries) and by "accuracy," (they are what they are, no doubt about it). Or: events are "accurate" in themselves but vague in that they do not appear entirely to the mind. They can't be categorized. If this is so, what can the poet hope to do? The descriptive list itself provides part of an answer. If the poet has an eye for detail and can find the right word, he can capture the event itself in his poem, and this pairing of language and event can be described metaphorically as a "dance," though, even at best, events will surpass the language used to describe them.

The poet's relation to his material is problematic, since events refuse to conform neatly to his language. "No ideas but in things" is still an operative principle, but a thing is not a concept. The grace and fluidity of the things Williams has just described are instances of precisely those qualities in the world which elude our thought.

On 24 the topic of marriage and that of the elemental giants come together in a love scene, in which Dr. Paterson speaks to a woman, momentarily attentive to the presence of "the giant whose apertures we/ cohabit. . . ." The giant's thoughts are the stream, and the speaker and the woman are "isolated in the stream," so that there are "three alike" (including the giant). As they sit and talk, "with long lapses of silence," the speaker is conscious of "the stream/ that has no language, coursing/ beneath the quiet heaven of/ your eyes."[26] And the quiet heaven of the woman's eyes "has no speech." While the man speaks to the woman, the silence itself "speaks of giants"

> who have died in the past and have
> returned to those scenes unsatisfied
> and who is not unsatisfied, the
> silent, Singac the rock-shoulder
> emerging from the rocks—and the giants
> live again in your silence and
> unacknowledged desire—   (25)

The notion is that of a resurrection, the giants coming to life as the elemental human passions present in the woman's silence and in her "unacknowledged desire." (Singac is the name of a place west of Paterson where the river bends.)

A dance or marriage now is implicit in references to air touching water, "brother/ to brother" but separate:

> . . . touching as the mind touches,
> counter-current, upstream
> brings in the fields, hot and cold
> parallel but never mingling. . . .   (25)

The play of the wind over water becomes a symbol for the mind's action. The mind "brings in the rumors of separate worlds"—that

---

[26] One earlier draft includes this interesting passage: "we sit and talk,/ you resemble the queen, Anna Bolein [*sic*]/ you look at me with a look born of/ the stream coursing within" (Yale MS). The woman would resemble Anne Boleyn in being one of a series of wives. The stream coursing within: a fairly direct reference to the "river of life" motif.

of air and that of water, as illustrated by "the birds as against the
fish" and

> > > > the grape
> to the green weed that streams out undulant
> with the current at low tide beside the
> bramble in blossom, the storm by the flood—
> song and wings— (25)

Air and water are dissimilar principles, "parallel but never
mingling"; the air carries "water-drops/ and snow." So, the implication goes, mind touches the world but never in fact becomes
mixed with it.

The air-water theme continues, as Williams describes a sea-
plane landing in the bay at Port au Prince, Haiti. This is Williams visiting a place associated with his family—the first trip he
and his wife had taken by air. In the *Autobiography* he wrote:
"At Port au Prince, Haiti, an hour later, it was blowing half a
gale. We cut into it but the waves were high. When we hit the
first one hard! we rebounded fifty feet into the air, then down,
up and down again. All in brilliant sunshine along a green mountain to our right, immaculately primitive." The poet's Uncle
Carlos had fled in the 1870's "from this city of small low houses"
before "the revolutionists coming in at the far end of the street."[27]
(The poet is identified with the refugees in the Ramapos.)

The hard landing in the "land-locked/ bay" continues the
series of landings and encounters of the elements: the bird alighting, thought falling on the streets, and so on.

A sudden shift in the argument now takes place, as Williams
turns his attention to the "back streets" and their inhabitants.
The logic would appear to be this: Williams has been dealing
with the mind's relation to external reality, a relation defined by
the image of air moving over the water. Now he considers the

---

[27] *Autobiography*, pp. 313–314. The last phrase, quoted from the *Autobiography*, is practically identical with the last line and a half of the account
in *Paterson*. (The date of his uncle's flight is given in the *Autobiography* as
the "early 1880's.") Another detail from the stopover in Haiti appears in
an earlier version of the passage, which concludes with these four lines:
"waiting for the gray-haired/ President to board his special plane together/
with his blond secretary and we were forbidden/ to go ashore—" The President and his secretary appear in Book Four, section 3 (p. 224).

reality that comprises his own "given": the stunted lives of people living in a modern city.

This is first illustrated by a letter from a man ("T."), telling about the work he does around the house, and about his sister "Billy," eccentric and bossy, always wanting to "lay blame."[28] There's a mother with a crippled head, obsessed with fire.

These are Paterson's thoughts, his people. "They fail, they limp with corns" (27). A woman tells someone, presumably Dr. P., about her husband, who (she fears) means to kill her: "He comes in after midnight,/ I pretend to be asleep." An instance of latent violence in the context of "marriage."

The verse immediately after this (27) is partly unexplained detail (a grocery list: "A quart of potatoes, half a dozen oranges,/ a bunch of beets and some soup greens"), partly comment, with advice by the poet to himself never "in despair and anxiety" to forget to "drive wit in, in till it discover/ his thoughts, decorous and simple. . . ."[29] This is advice about the characterization of Paterson: "*His* thoughts" are the thoughts of the elemental giant Paterson, in which despair and anxiety are balanced by decorum and simplicity. Despair and anxiety are the poet's natural re-action to the world. Yet the thoughts of the giant with whom he identifies himself are "decorous and simple," and the poet's job is to locate and reveal them without disguising his own despair and anxiety.

At this point the poet is forced by a "delirium of solutions" into back streets "to begin again": acrid smells, a yelping dog and "the expressionless black navel" of a woman mourning love's deceit together illustrate what must be made whole.

[28] Evidently a postscript to a letter sent to Williams, enclosing a poem. Here, as often with the prose, Williams's earlier version gave considerably more of the original (Yale MS).

[29] In one version the grocery list passage appears in this form, suggesting its original significance for Williams: "Sermonize them: a quart of potatoes, half/ a dozen oranges, a bunch of beets/ and some soup greens; Look I have a new set/ of teeth. Why you look ten years younger—/ You played beautiful! What then?" At this point appeared two lines, scratched out: "Read aright, it is the rape of that/ raw faced, bow legged girl that is forecast" (Yale MS). The seven-line passage beginning "But never . . ." is taken from "Paterson" (*Collected Earlier Poems*, pp. 234–235), as is the line "So in his high decorum he is wise."

> They are the divisions and imbalances
> of his whole concept, made weak by pity,
> flouting desire; they are—No ideas but
> in the facts   .   .[30]   (28)

The poet cannot escape from these "divisions" and "imbalances": they are entailed by the program of starting from "things."

The section ends with a letter from E. D.,[31] among other things accusing Williams of separating the "book" from the man who wrote it. Like the "Cress" letters of Book Two, this serves to characterize the poet and to register objections that Williams is willing to let stand. E. D.'s critique has to be included among the "facts."

SECTION 3

Section 3 begins quietly. The season is late winter or early spring, and there is a thaw. For the moment, the poet is alone:

> How strange you are, you idiot!
> So you think because the rose
> is red that you shall have the mastery?
> The rose is green and will bloom,
> overtopping you, green, livid
> green when you shall no more speak, or
> taste, or even be. My whole life
> has hung too long upon a partial victory.   (30)

The striking paradoxical image of a huge "livid" green rose that threatens to overtop and survive the poet seems to take up the divorced "green bud" of the preceeding section, but with the important difference that the divorced bud offered no promise of "blooming." The livid green rose "will" bloom—has not yet

---

[30] Modified slightly from the conclusion of "Paterson," *Collected Earlier Poems,* p. 235.

[31] Edward Dahlberg. ("T.J." in *Paterson I* and in the four-book version; changed to "E.D." for the volume including *Paterson V.*) An earlier version in the Yale collection includes several paragraphs prior to the ones actually published, in which Dahlberg wrote that he abhors busy people, and went on to say that he frankly doesn't know what Williams is saying when he puts the past into "a frozen theorem."

shown its full potential. And it will stay green—not follow the
natural course of things, to reach maturity and then die. The language of this passage anticipates that of the poet's prayer at the
end of Book Two, section 2:

> The world spreads
> for me like a flower opening—and
> will close for me as might a rose—
>
> wither and fall to the ground
> and rot and be drawn up
> into a flower again. But you
> never wither—but blossom
> all about me.   (75)

In the prayer, Williams addresses a Deity ever present in the
changing world, which is compared to a rose that opens and
closes, withers and dies—to become a flower again. This Deity is
the principle that sustains itself through these changes. The rose
illustrates the world of natural change, and defines the poet's
place in it, since the world will "close" for him, just as it now
spreads itself before him.

Generally in *Paterson* the rose is used to represent the world
outside the poet. If that is its significance here, the argument
seems to be that the poet can never have the upper hand, since
the world (in essence) is eternally green. In that case, the livid
green rose would not be the world of the present, but the world
as eternally young.[32] The *red* rose of the beginning of the passage might in that case be the deceptive maturity of the world
encountered.

Or the paradoxical (nonliteral) greenness of the rose may refer to the fertility of the imagination, which wins out over the
literal. A reading close to this is suggested by Sister Bernetta, who
points out that the woman of the poem has now been changed
again "into a flower": "He starts by alluding to woman in her
character of rose carved out of the red rock, destined to remain
after that nine-months' wonder, Paterson the man, or even the
city itself, has vanished." In this interpretation the passage is

---

[32] Peterson (p. 37) interprets the "rose" as the world of the present: "Yet
if the world of the present—that is, the 'rose'—is 'livid green,' at least it *is*
a rose rather than a bud."

said to emphasize "the permanence of art, which will outlast the artist."[33]

In any case, the poet at the outset of this section is conscious of his own mortality, and uses the rose as symbol for something that will outlast him. Even livid and green, he reminds himself, the rose will win out. His whole life so far has "hung too long upon a partial victory." What seems to be another voice adds: "But, creature of the weather, I/ don't want to go any faster than/ I have to go to win." (The poet, like a flower, depends on the local weather; must therefore be patient, though he wants to "win.")

Williams places Dr. P. in particular surroundings: in a room on a cold day, probing his ear with a hairpin, listening to the snow dripping from a cornice, perceiving a woman's face in the linoleum, and so on. There is an anticipation of seasonal rebirth, already suggested by the blooming of the (metaphorical) rose. The probing in Paterson's ear has symbolic force: a page later Williams comments, "of/ earth his ears are full. . . ." There is no sound (that is, for the moment, perhaps, he fails to hear the riddling challenge of the Falls). His thoughts soar:

> to the magnificence of imagined delights
> where he would probe
>
> as into the pupil of an eye
> as through a hoople of fire, and emerge
> sheathed in a robe
>
> streaming with light. . . .   (31)

In this mood, such daydreams of heroic accomplishment seem possible: "What heroic/ dawn and desire/ is denied to his thoughts?" His thoughts are trees, streaming with rain, from which "his mind drinks of desire." A song expresses this mood— a song by a (sycamore) tree in praise of maturity (its youth a "contemptible twig. . . . A mere stick that has/ twenty leaves/ against my convolutions)" (31–32).[34] The speaker is half amused at his own self-satisfaction. The tree celebrates its own maturity, triumphing—for the moment at least—over the "contemptible twig" of its youth. (This praise of maturity may also be the voice

---

[33] Quinn, p. 101.
[34] One draft has "The Sycamore" as a heading for this passage (Yale MS).

of the "first wife," symbolically associated with the sycamore
tree in section 2.)

> Let it rot, at my center.
>   Whose center?
> I stand and surpass
>   youth's leanness.
>
> My surface is myself.
>   Under which
> to witness, youth is
>   buried. Roots?
>
> Everybody has roots.   (32)

That is: there is no need to go scratching after roots as Eliot and
Pound had done.

The mood changes abruptly, as the song is followed by the
poet's bitter remark that "We go on living, we permit ourselves/
to continue—but certainly/ not for the university. . . ." Presumably the university comes under fire at this point because Williams's effort to do his job reminds him of the forces working
against him. The university is made up of clerks, forgetful of
their obligations, and "spitted on fixed concepts like/ roasting
hogs, sputtering, their drip sizzling/ in the fire."

The prose at the bottom of 33, evidently someone's observation
of Dr. Williams himself at work, seems intended to continue the
opening scene of Dr. P. in his office—preoccupied, trying to re-
move a label from a mayonnaise jar while the patients wait. This
is a reminder of the multiple character of Paterson's concerns,
and a look at Paterson *thinking*.

The stasis in society continues to be the subject of 33–34,
where Williams presents some contrasts. The abundance (ex-
travagance) of such-and-such a rich man's estate, "in time of general privation," is contrasted with Cornelius Doremus's will
(34), which William Nelson had given as an example of the
modest personal requirements of a well-to-do person of the early
eighteenth century.[35] The natural abundance of the place (as

[35] Nelson, p. 386. (The same will also appears in Nelson and Shriner, I,
138–139). One earlier version of *Paterson I* contained at this point other
material similar to the Doremus will.

established in the first section), is set off against what we now
have, a civilization largely unsatisfactory because of what Williams sees as a failure of distribution. In an earlier version the
Doremus will was followed by this comment on defenders of
the present economic system:

> And their answer is likely to be
> that bananas are today as common
> up-state as apples. And telephone rates
> have dropped 75% in half a century
> . . . . .[36]   (Buffalo MS)

In Williams's view of present-day American society, money
and knowledge stay at the top; the small towns and the lower
classes are deprived; and the universities, disguising and protecting the special interests, continue to fragment knowledge in
order to maintain the present stasis:

> They block the release
> that should cleanse and assume
> prerogatives as a private recompense.
> Others are also at fault because
> they do nothing.   (34)

(An earlier version of the passage had argued that the obstruction
of knowledge made "surgery" necessary.)[37]

Williams's reference to people assuming "prerogatives as a
private recompense" is followed (35) by a long prose account
about catching eels and fish from the mud of a drained lake
bottom.[38] "The whole bottom was covered with people, and the
big eels, weighing from three to four pounds each, would approach the edge and then the boys would strike at them. . . ."
Williams may be using the account as an analogue for the ex-

---

[36] In that version the passage "Who restricts knowledge?" is almost the
same, but there is an interesting association of the blockage of knowledge
with the blocking *gates* at wealthy estates.

[37] "If knowledge were not obstructed/ surgery need not be resorted to/
and present transitions might be affected/ less painfully. . . ." (Yale MS).

[38] According to Zabriskie, p. 213. "Dundee Lake is the site of the miracle
of the fishes in Book I"; the lake was made by a dam in the nineteenth century. (Williams is quoting from an article in *The Prospector*, "Draining the
Lake at Lakeview.")

ploitation of America's natural abundance; one paragraph in
particular must have appealed to him:

> Those who prepared the nets were not the ones who
> got the most fish. It was the hoodlums and men who
> leaped into the mud and water where the nets could not
> work that rescued from the mud and water the finest load
> of fish. (35)

The account concludes with a scene of men hard at work with
sticks, beating the eels to benumb them, using "lights on shore
and lanterns over the mud" all night long.

Paterson is said to be "moveless" and envious of

> the men that ran
> and could run off
> toward the peripheries—
> to other centers, direct—
> for clarity (if
> they found it)
> loveliness and
> authority in the world— (36)

These, of course, are writers like Eliot and Pound who had believed in the promise of a "springtime" outside of themselves,
in a *place* where they might go to achieve "clarity" and acquire
authority. (From Williams's point of view the "centers" which
they sought lie outside, on the periphery. . . .) Williams has just
made it clea*r why* he might envy this line of action, since he saw
and felt strongly the flaws of his own headquarters. Paterson is
unable to pick up and leave; and Williams uses his own identification with Paterson to suggest the *inwardness* of his own
search. The springtime for which other men sought was something he saw "within himself—ice bound"

> and leaped, "the body, not until
> the following spring, frozen in
> an ice cake." (36)

Here again, the death of Sam Patch suggests the poet's awareness
of his own possible failure.

Now the poet confronts himself with the present-day city of Paterson: the industrial city, the ravished park, the polluted river. Prose: a man's body lodged between logs hanging over the precipice; "a very large number of visitors. . . ."[39] (One of the motifs here: people coming to stare at a wonder—as they will come, in Book Four, to see a man killed). The man's body caught among the logs, the "river red," introduces the "sea of blood" motif to which Williams will return at the end of the poem: the poet himself, taking a risk, will die symbolically when the poem concludes (or "fails"). Verse: the river polluted, "Half the river red, half steaming purple/ from the factory vents."

> What can he think else—along
> the gravel of the ravished park, torn by
> the wild workers' children tearing up the grass,
> kicking, screaming? A chemistry, corollary
> to academic misuse, which the theorem
> with accuracy, accurately misses . .   (37)

Because the universities have gone wrong, this is what we have.

"What can he think else"—Paterson's thoughts are confined to the actual lives of workers and their children, and for a moment he reflects on what this amounts to: "their mouths eating and kissing,/ spitting and sucking, speaking; a/ partitype of five ." The mouths perform these five functions. Nothing "escapes" the eyes of the workers' children—neither sex nor death. In the meantime the factory runs on, the silk spinning accompanied by "a music of pathetic souvenirs," among these souvenirs a comb and nail file ("to/ remind him, to remind him!") and pictures of "himself" between two children, "all returned/ weeping, weeping". . . . The silk spinning, of course, refers to industrial Paterson ("the silk city"); the souvenirs refer to someone's death— the death of a worker (it could be the man whose body

---

[39] Quoted almost verbatim from a long account in *The Prospector*. A man named Grogan had taken a boat out on the river in a dangerous current. The boat shot over the dam above the Falls proper. An earlier version includes the full account (Buffalo MS). Still another version (Yale MS) omits the prose passage here; this seems to mean that the passage was added later to prepare for the verse at the bottom of 36, which in that version began: "What then does he think—?/ half the river red."

was caught in the crotch of the logs), perhaps symbolic of the impending "death" of Paterson.

The widow remarries—she has "a vile tongue/ but laborious ways, driving a drunken/ husband . ."

> What do I care for the flies, shit with them.
> I'm out of the house all day.   (37)

The same indifference pollutes the streams. Williams comments:

> Into the sewer they threw the dead horse.
> What birth does this foretell? I think
> he'll write a novel bye and bye .   (37)

This is a comment on "naturalism" and of course on the naturalistic element in Williams's own program (perhaps his own novels). The dead horse may be "fertile"—or it may simply foretell the birth of flies.

At this point Williams attributes two voices (minds) to Paterson:

> P. Your interest is in the bloody loam but what
>   I'm after is the finished product.
>
> I. Leadership passes into empire; empire begets insolence; insolence brings ruin.
>
> Such is the mystery of his one two, one two.   (38)

The poet who loves his raw material is set off against the poet carefully finishing his work: P.'s statement is a quotation from Ezra Pound, but it also represents Williams's own desire for "mastery." (Later, in Book Four, Williams returns to the question of "empire"; see 179.)

A passage from the *Autobiography* (p. 119) is worth quoting in this connection. Williams, visiting Paris, had been oppressed by the Comédie Française: "To them the meaning of art is skill, to manipulate the parts to produce an effect diametrically opposed to my own values, my lack of skills forced to proceed without them."

And "so" (driven perhaps by the "mystery of his one two, one two") Paterson drives out "among the rest" to visit the suburbs. It is a search for beauty in unpromising material. Next to a rhu-

barb farm, "the convent of the Little Sisters of/ St. Ann pretends
a mystery." The architecture irritates him; the building seems
a counterpart for the poor man's part of the city:

> Things, things unmentionable,
> the sink with the waste farina in it and
> lumps of rancid meat, milk-bottle tops: have
> here a tranquility and loveliness
> Have here (in his thoughts)
> a complement tranquil and chaste.   (39)

In this way Paterson's thoughts provide an orderly "complement"
for the disorder and ugliness in the lives of the city poor—just
as the red brick convent provides a complement for the city.
The poet escapes from material ugliness by ordering what he
sees into a kind of beauty; this will be Williams's subject again
in Book Two.

At this point Paterson is said to shift his change, and there is a
playful reference to Paterson the giant: prose describing the
earthquake of 1737.[40]

The section ends with a simile—thought compared to a snail
clambering

> ... upon the wet rocks
> hidden from sun and sight—
> hedged in by the pouring torrent—   (39)

In that way "thought" is shut in from the world and "unknown
to the world,/ cloaks itself in mystery—"

Meanwhile, supporting the rock and the water that "thrives
there" is "the myth," "Earth, the chatterer, father of all/ speech."

So the first book ends with a glimpse of this concealed and
mysterious figure who supports all the things of the poet's world
and all the terms of his poem. It is "earth" itself, a giant akin

---

[40] Barber and Howe, p. 50. This is given as one of a series of "Remarkable
Occurrences." An earlier version (Buffalo MS) has three earthquakes rather
than one; two are from Barber and Howe, and the third seems to be someone's personal account: "I was a child but I can remember clearly all that
took place. It would begin with a low rumbling in the distance. . . ." (Reminiscences of Williams's mother? Part of the account goes like this: "The
people thinking the island would go down had fled the city at the bay's edge
and gathered together at the highest point, on Gunpowder hill. . . .")

to (and in part identifiable with) the giant Paterson. "Earth,"
the place, fathers it all, holds it up—but is shrouded there, concealed even from the poet, though the poet senses the giant's
presence.

Book Two

SUNDAY IN THE PARK

To present the "modern replicas" of the elemental character of the place, Williams has Dr. P. spend an ordinary Sunday at Garret Mountain Park. There the people of Paterson go to relax after a week's work; and Dr. Paterson, as one of them, walks around the Park, observing them and reflecting on the challenge that confronts him. Gradually he ascends the summit, from which he looks out over the city, catching a glimpse of the forces that have made the city what it is. Metaphorically, the walk in the Park is a love scene, Paterson visiting his woman, the Mountain. A kind of ceremony takes place, as the modern crowd unknowingly participates in an age-old festival of love, but a festival disguised and thwarted by the modern setting.

In the second section Paterson witnesses an open-air sermon, not very well attended, in which a Protestant preacher named Klaus Ehrens tells the story of his life to show that material wealth does not bring happiness. In Williams's terms the preacher's sermon is true enough, a just critique of the drive for economic gain that has dominated American history; but the preacher himself fails, since he has no terms (no "language") for wedding the people to the place. By implication the sermon deals with what happens to the religious impulse in modern industrial society, and Williams interrupts it with prose fragments indicating Hamilton's role in making America a manufacturing state, and with material criticizing the Federal Reserve System. The sermon also continues the "ceremony" of the opening section; section two ends with a prayer, the poet's "Address to the Deity," an expression of that religious awe before the world which is absent from the sermon and from Hamilton's plans for harnessing the powers of the new country.

In the third section, Paterson returns from the summit as night falls, and his walk down is used as the occasion for a meditation

on defeat and the recognition of defeat. A dialogue takes place—
possibly a continuation of the love scene of Book One, section 2.
"He" and "She," Dr. P. and a woman, Paterson and the elemental
landscape, come together for a marriage that would be, presumably, the proper termination for the day's ceremonies. But
the marriage also fails. The poet is either unable to "marry," for
lack of a language, or else he uses the absence of a language as his
excuse for refusing. He marries "with empty words." At the end
Paterson heads for the Library, where he will search (unsuccess-
fully) for the language he needs.

SECTION 1

The manuscripts show that Williams conceived the first section,
or parts of it, as a "Saturnalia," and in one or two of the earlier
versions he quotes (for 52) the refrain from *The Vigil of Venus*,
"Tomorrow may loveless, may lover tomorrow make love," possibly influenced by the interpretation of Allen Tate that had
emphasized the poet's hope of finding his "voice" on the occasion
of the festival of love.[1] Though Williams omitted the line in
the published version, the notion of a Vigil of Love is implicit.

The modern ceremony of love is both a continuation of an age-
old festival and a debasement of it. Insofar as the elemental religious passions of love and awe still appear in this American
Sunday, to the poet it is a moving occasion. The ceremony fails,
however, because of those forces in America which have prevented, and still prevent, the marriage of the American people
to the land, and because so far no poet has come along to bring
about the marriage.

Williams once characterized the subject of Book Two as "the
reaction of a sensitive person to the show of force," and went on
to discuss at some length what he had intended in the first section:

---

[1] In Tate's introduction to his translation of *The Vigil* (Cummington,
Mass., 1943) he paraphrased the poet's question, "When shall I, he says, like
Philomela the swallow suffer violence and be moved to sing?" adding "It is
this unexpected and dramatic ending that makes, for me, what were otherwise an interesting ritualistic chant, one of the finest of lyric poems." Among
Williams's notes, this one: "Chapultepec: Grasshopper Hill/ Crowds walking up and down—the multiple/ Saturnalia, mother of the drama—and
dance" (Buffalo MS).

This is just about as good as I can do. It is a contrast between the vulgarity of the lovers in the park and the fineness, the aristocracy of the metrical arrangement of the verse. I do have measure here, but the very subject hides it from the uninitiated. . . . I was impassioned when I wrote Part II. I had just been out on the mountain. I was always concerned with the plight of the young in the industrial age who are affected by love. It's a classic theme because a tragic theme—because love is much thought about and written about. It's tragedy when it is realized by an artist and comes out in a form like this. I love the impassioned simplicity of young lovers. When it's thwarted, and they don't know it's thwarted, then the vulgarity is lifted to distinction by being treated with the very greatest in art which I can conceive.

It's easy to miss, but the whole theme of *Paterson* is brought out in this passage, the contrast between the mythic beauty of the Falls and Mountain and the industrial hideousness. But they haven't been able to lick us. To escape as an artist, to escape from the scene would be a defeat for me. But I will not be licked; so in this scene love has triumphed. If I as artist had separated myself from the scene, it would be a defeat. But I have not. I have made myself a part of the scene. I must be an artist in my own bailiwick—despite the conditions which make it hard. That is why this scene brings it to a head . . . every artistic world has a secret motivation. When the world asks: "Gee, doc, what does it all mean?" they respect me, not as a doctor, but because of this world which they don't understand—an elevated world which they know exists and which they would see manifested in me— a world which scares them because it is above them. They can meet me, but there is something about me that makes them uneasy.

In this passage I have gotten some of this in words. The construction is subtle but expressed in commonest terms. The arrangement is not common. I have always tried to lead an elevated life, which they respect even if they don't share it. So I must make it apparent to them.[2]

The opening section, then, attempts to present the tragic dignity of the lovers in the park, their tragedy caused by the "industrial hideousness" of the region. Love is the subject of various particular scenes. The crowd of people, for instance, "makes

[2] Conversation of April 8, 1954, quoted by Thirlwall, pp. 276–277.

love" to the Park: the rock is "stroked" by their clambering feet. Stirring up grasshoppers as he walks out across the fields, Paterson remembers a carved grasshopper from Mexico, which becomes a symbol for the permanence of what art can achieve; the poet's act of "invention" is a form of love. The same idea appears in a scene that Paterson notices on his way to the rampart: a man affectionately combing the hair of a newly washed collie bitch—the combing suggestive of an artist at work, the beautiful animal a type for Venus. And the age-old human passions that underlie both the pleasure of the Sunday crowd and the artist's work appear suddenly in the spontaneous dance of an Italian woman, Mary, which expresses the religious significance of the occasion; the "source" of her dance is in a world beyond history; its meaning is clear only to the poet. While "love," in one form or another, appears in these various instances, Williams insists on the actual "divorce" visible in the industrial landscape; and a story of divorce appears in letters from Cress, the lady-poet, who attacks Dr. P. for his attempt to keep his distance from her.

At work in the first section are three groups of terms, all governed by the idea of an age-old festival debased by the modern setting.

1. The present scene, "love" doing the best it can in the setting created by modern industrial society; the woman's letters, representing a failure of love, and also a challenge to the poet by the "real" world to participate on its terms; the "amnesic crowd . . .": the multiplicity and latent violence of the people as "great beast";

2. The background of this scene, a background including what Williams saw as the primitive character and destiny of the area, and the elemental energies of Mary and the peasant from a film by Eisenstein (58); also, the economic forces that have worked to make the place what it is today;

3. The poet himself, examining his material, fussing with it, searching doggedly for a new formal principle by means of which to order it and render its significance; this also is "love," and promises a durable victory, as represented by the carved grasshopper which, though "lost and covered/ with ash," lives on.

Williams begins the section with a reference to the symbolic marriage of Paterson and the Mountain. The city/man goes to visit his wife.

> The scene's the Park
> upon the rock,
> female to the city
>
> —upon whose body Paterson instructs his thoughts
> (concretely). (43)

The rock is hard, definite, concrete—as are the particulars from which the poet must start: "No ideas but in things."

Paterson walks, climbs a footpath, enjoys the view, looks around at the other people—ordinary working-class Americans on a holiday, nothing elegant about them—the same people Williams had described years earlier in a poem touching on industrial strife in Paterson:

> . . the ugly legs of the young girls,
> pistons too powerful for delicacy! .
> the men's arms, red, used to heat and cold,
> to toss quartered beeves and .[3] (44)

Together these people comprise the "great beast" of Hamilton's antidemocratic fears. In a sense they are also Paterson himself—they add up to the city, the modern replica of Paterson the giant.

These girls with ugly legs are the poet's "flower of a day!"—the poet's subject matter and mistress, the "flower" of the poem, beautiful (potentially) and transient. The crowd, and the poet himself, are seen as "over-riding/ the risks . . . ," a reference to the danger and cost to the poet of his "love." Paterson looks back at the towers, "beautiful but expensive"—literally so, but also suggestive of the cost of beauty, the price that the poet must be

---

[3] This description of the people is taken from the Queen's speech in "The Strike," a section of "The Wanderer: A Rococo Study," which appeared in the early collection *Al Que Quiere!*, pp. 75–87. (The passage used in *Paterson* can be found in *Collected Earlier Poems*, p. 7.) As Sister Bernetta points out, the Queen's speech anticipates a theme central to *Paterson* (Quinn, pp. 128–129). A later detail, small birds attacking a crow (46) also picks up a motif from "The Wanderer" (see Thirlwall, p. 258).

willing to pay for the beauty he may or may not achieve. An
electrical analogy (Paterson as the "positive/ in spite of all")
brings in a new pun on "ground": the ground is dry, as in *The
Waste Land*, but also the "ground" for an electrical current.

As Paterson walks he looks around at the setting—thickets, a
"scattering of man-high cedars," and so on. The shallow rooting
of these trees and shrubs becomes an emblem for the cultural
soil: "(so close are we to ruin every day!)"

As if to insist that this scene is literally a man walking before
it is anything else, Williams inserts a textbook account of what it
is to walk. In earlier versions Williams quoted the account at
some length, simply by pasting in a page. The textbook passage,
broken up, was to provide a frame for the account of what Paterson saw and the inferences he drew; this frame still appears in the
word "walking," repeated several times during the section.

Now (45) Williams introduces a second main subject, in the
form of a passage from one of Cress's letters: that is, something
that Dr. P. has on his mind as he walks through the fields, and
to which his walk is in part an answer.

The letter presents an instance of "divorce." The lady-poet,
befriended by Dr. P., now quarrels with his attempt to keep her
at a distance. He has evidently asked her to stop writing to him.
Her letters continue to appear throughout Book Two, fragments
placed in the midst of other material, and the longest quotation
serves as the conclusion to Book Two. It is a short one-sided
espistolary novel; Dr. P. never directly replies. At one time Williams planned to include two sizable letters from "C" as an "in-
terlude," separate from the actual books of *Paterson*; he gradually
came around to the plan of breaking up the letters and inserting
passages within the body of the poem. In one early version of
Book Two Williams included a passage in verse, in which a
woman spoke:

> My love, my love why have you forsaken
> me? In every face, I see your image
> cast (and lost)! she cries in anguish
> from the stones
> on which their feet slip as they climb,
> laughing and calling out.
>   Wait for me! (Buffalo MS)

This complaint of the Park—of the "elemental" symbolized by the stones—seems to have given way, in revision, to passages from the woman's letter. This suggests that the woman's letter is being used in much the same way, roughly as a "complaint," in which the poet's world accuses him (justly?) of desertion.[4]

Cress's insistence on the value of life—her own life, the direct experience of "real" life—makes her a spokesman for the poet's world and subject matter. She is a Muse of sorts, offering herself to a reluctant poet. She writes of a "damming up" of her creative capacities (caused by her failure with him), of a "kind of blockage, exiling one's self from one's self . . ." (45). She can't believe that Dr. P.'s ignoring her letters was "natural"—and so the "whole side of life" connected with those letters has taken on for her "that same kind of unreality and inaccessibility which the lives of other people often have for us" (48). The "damming up" metaphor suggests the course of the River/ Falls (as does her reference to "some surface crust of myself . . . finally congealed into some impenetrable substance"). Later (64) we learn that Cress can communicate with only one person, Dr. P., and that she fears she will "never again be able to recapture any sense of [her] own personal identity" (76). This way of talking about herself was made to order for Williams's scheme.

The woman's letter breaks off and the poet comments, parodying Elizabeth Barrett,

<blockquote>How do I love you? These! (45)</blockquote>

---

[4] The manuscripts show extensive revision of this material, and Williams's attitude toward "Cress" may have changed as he revised; this is hard to say. In one version a passage from the woman's letter was followed by this comment:

<blockquote>And as always, Beauty, is still preserved
by poverty and loneliness in a woman.—
(that makes her speak) as a poet
—or a city: in a backwash of the times
This is no figure.</blockquote>

<blockquote>Investigating, prying— (Buffalo MS)</blockquote>

(Above "Beauty" was something in handwriting, not legible.) This comment was followed by the passage beginning "Which is to say . . ." (from the second section of Book One), then by material not used in the published version, then by "That the poem . . ." (Book Two, section 3).

As if to say: look at the poem, where my "love" appears in the description of Sunday in the Park.

Paterson hears the "indeterminate" voices of the crowd, sees the people in small groups moving away ("filtering off") along the bypaths. He has nothing to do, no business, but to listen "to the water falling," though here, far from the Falls, there is no sound of it but that brought by the wind (by "spirit"). It is the Falls in his mind, the sound of ongoing life (with its riddle and challenge) to which he listens; these people are also strands of the Falls, and he listens to them. The italicized question and answer calls attention to his apparent idleness, to the absence of a "career." In Europe the question would be different.[5]

The prose on 46 gives historical continuity to the modern Sunday crowd, and serves as another reminder of the violence latent in the mass (or in the society that has produced the mass). The German Singing Societies of Paterson used to meet on Garret Mountain, but one day in 1880 a nearby property owner, William Dalzell, became angry because they walked over his garden, and he shot a man to stop them "from crossing any part of his grounds." The group of singers, enraged and transformed into a mob, chased Dalzell and burned the barn in which he was hiding; they would have lynched him. . . .[6] The incident illustrates a dialectic—people vs. property owner—that operates in several key passages, for instance in the story of Lambert, the antiunion capitalist of section 2. Dalzell, like Lambert, appears as one man fighting for his property rights against the mass: hence (ironically) a "poet," one against the many, as the next passage (small birds attacking a crow) bears out.

> Signs everywhere of birds nesting, while
> in the air, slow, a crow zigzags
> with the heavy wings before the wasp-thrusts
> of smaller birds circling about him
> that dive from above stabbing for his eyes[7]   (46)

The image reappears in Book Four, where "all the professions"

---

[5] Referred to in notes as the "Temple incident" (Yale MS).

[6] Here again Williams is using *The Prospector*, quoting almost verbatim from an article on "The Garret Mountain Riot."

[7] See n. 3, above.

are pictured as attacking the poet (191). The detail, then, something Paterson notices as he walks through the park, also takes its place among the poet's reflections on his dealings with the people.

The people as a disorganized "mass" is one key term in this stretch; uncultivated nature is another. Paterson's walk brings him into an uncultivated field, "stubble and matted brambles/ seeming a pasture," but no signs of labor. As he walks along, some grasshoppers start up, "a flight of empurpled wings"; and this sudden flight jars from his memory the image of a carved grasshopper, discovered at Chapultepec, "grasshopper hill," in Mexico City.[8] The carving is said to tumble from the core of the poet's mind, the mind pictured as a "rubble-bank disintegrating beneath a tropic downpour." The tropic downpour is another equivalent for the Falls in Paterson's mind, this time leading to a flash of discovery, analogous to the literal discovery of the old Aztec carving. Garret Mountain Park itself becomes for the moment "grasshopper hill!"—a place where discoveries are made. The wings of the grasshoppers are transformed into "couriers to the ceremonial of love!"—Cupids. And Paterson's mind is compared to the carved grasshopper, a "red stone carved to be/ endless flight ." (49). Love is said to be "a stone endlessly in flight"; though "lost and covered/ with ash," it falls from the undermined bank and comes to life: "begins churring!"

The carved grasshopper demonstrates the power of art to give durable shape to the artist's love for his world. It is the record of an act of love, something permanent yet always in flight.

> The stone lives, the flesh dies
> —we know nothing of death. (49)

In an earlier typescript Williams had compared the head of the carved grasshopper to that of a bull:

---

[8] A photograph of the carved grasshopper to which Williams presumably refers has been published in Bart McDowell, "Mexico's Window on the Past," *National Geographic*, CXXIV (Oct. 1968), 493–521 at p. 517, photographs by B. Anthony Stewart. It appears in the illustration section elsewhere in this book.

> Head like a bull, bull-headed love the
> Babylonian . the red bull, the winged bull
> —turned insect: rescued, oversized in
> red stone. (Buffalo MS)

In the same version the carved grasshopper was said to last as long as stone will last: "—by virtue of the caress laid on/ by an undying hand." Like the bull, then, the grasshopper is associated with sexual power, and its creation is an act of love, a "caress." "Rescued" is a key notion, implicit in the published version: not only the rescue of the grasshopper, but a rescue of the elemental force of love.

The Aztec grasshopper is an instance of "Love/ combating sleep": art fighting against the sleep of death that both tempts and threatens the artist.

The mink that appears in the prose of 49–50 is a local counterpart for the grasshopper celebrated in stone. The men's attempt to shoot the mink or beat it with clubs is another instance of wanton attack on what survives of the "elemental"; it is presumably also an instance of nature's elusiveness (the mink escaped). The style of the passage illustrates our faulty invention: the Aztecs could celebrate a grasshopper, but this is how we celebrate our minks.[9]

An instance of what art can do, the carved grasshopper leads the poet to reflect on the power of invention in a passage apparently suggested by Pound's USURA sermon in *The Cantos*.[10] The poet will be unable to make things appear in the poem unless he can devise a new form, one that is appropriate to his own world. By "invention" Williams means, primarily, a new way of handling the line. If the poet can invent a new line, then he can make the actual footprints of mice, for instance, appear in the poem. But "without invention" nothing will appear.

[9] The prose is from *The Prospector*, Oct. 29, 1936: "A Mink Hunt in Main Street." Peterson, pp. 60–61, notes the connection of grasshopper and mink.

[10] Canto XLV: "With usura hath no man a house of good stone," and so on. Edgar F. Racey, Jr. discusses the main differences between these two passages in "Pound and Williams: The Poet as Renewer," *Bucknell Review*, XI (March 1963), 21–30.

>   without invention
> nothing lies under the witch-hazel
> bush, the alder does not grow from among
> the hummocks margining the all
> but spent channel of the old swale.   (50)

These are details from the scene Williams is about to describe. Williams draws analogies between poetry and science—between the new measurement of astronomical distances and the new "measure" required by the poet. A new measure will bring poetry into line with the advances of recent science. The old line (by which Williams meant traditional English measures, and iambic pentameter specifically) is obsolete, unusable. The living word used to live in the line, but is now fossilized, crumbled to "chalk."

The poet's thoughts on invention are set off against the actual scene before him, lovers in the park:

> Under the bush they lie protected
> from the offending sun—   (50)

The poet's power of invention will enable these people to appear in the poem. The park, Williams comments, is devoted to "pleasure" (sexual pleasure among people whose minds have been "beaten thin" by waste) and to "grasshoppers" (and so, to the permanent beauty that survives the poet's act of creation) (51).

The pairing of "pleasure" and symbolic wings governs the description of the lovers (50–52). It's eleven o'clock. Paterson notices "3 colored girls, of age!" who stroll by, their color "flagrant," voices "vagrant," and their laughter "wild, flagellant": these qualities dissociate the girls "from the fixed scene ." Other girls illustrate the present character of the region. "*But* the white girl, . . .": the description emphasizes a grossness and vulgarity:

> Minds beaten thin
> by waste—among
>
> the working classes SOME sort
> of breakdown
> has occurred. . . .   (51)

The boy has a sunshade over his eyes; their faces are "mottled by the shadows of the leaves." They are unannoyed and "at least here unchallenged./ Not undignified . . ." (52). That is: even as he critically observes the couple, the poet is struck by an unexpected dignity in them. It is at this point that Williams once placed the line from *The Vigil of Venus*, "Tomorrow may loveless, may lover tomorrow make love."[11] Whether or not the poet approves of what he sees, he is witnessing a festival of sorts; and he describes the lovers' actions, with mild irony, in ceremonial terms. After the couple bathes and eats a few sandwiches "their pitiful thoughts do meet/ in the flesh." And they are "surrounded by churring loves!" Gay wings (of Cupid) bear them, and like the grasshopper, "their thoughts alight,/ away/ . . among the grass."

Love as the poet's act of ordering is set over against the grossness and multiplicity of the actual scene. Williams keeps his own effort in view, as if to say: what I am doing is not an easy thing to do.

Paterson moves from the lovers to the park itself, tries to catch a glimpse of the "primitive destiny" of the place. He walks on "across the old swale," now dry—just a trace of the water that used to be there, though Indian alders mark its former presence (52). He thinks of Indians—who were at home in this country, as the Sunday crowd is not—and imagines them moving in concealment among the alders, to whoop out and capture some of the settlers. Dismisses the thought (presumably as a bad attempt at historical fiction):

> Forget it! for God's sake, Cut
> out that stuff   .   (52)

A chipmunk, "with tail erect, scampers among the stones." And Williams interprets the detail: "(Thus the mind grows, up flinty pinnacles)".

The next passage provides an image for what the poet does—a man carefully combing a dog. On a treeless knoll Paterson has noticed a "stone wall, a sort of circular redoubt against the sky." Climbing to see what's there, he leans forward to pick up what

---

[11] Followed by: "they do, their pitiful thoughts do meet/ in the flesh, asleep/ the sleepy flesh" (Buffalo MS).

appears to be a flint arrowhead "(it is not)," looks out at the "chronic hills" in the north (chronic: permanent, a reminder of the elemental landscape). In some earlier versions the hills are specifically referred to at this point as the home of the Jackson Whites. Arriving at the knoll, Dr. P. stops short: within the wall a man in tweeds is combing out "a new-washed Collie bitch," leashed to a stone bench; the man combs her deliberately until the long hair lies "as he designs, like ripples in white sand giving off its clean-dog odor." The dog stands patiently "before his caresses in that bare 'sea-chamber.' " The care and affection of the man for the dog is another instance of "love," like that of the artist who carved the grasshopper. The "ripples in white sand" introduce an association of dog and the sea to which Williams returns at the end of Book Four, when Paterson emerges from the sea accompanied by his dog, in a context suggesting a "birth of Venus."

Williams reworked the collie passage a good many times, in one version explicitly identifying the circular redoubt as a temple of Venus:

the stone, floor, stone slabs—toward which the
rubble had led—wound up steeply to that miniature—crude
temple of Venus—obedient under his touch!
                    —a dog! a bitch! a white bitch! (Buffalo MS)

(This would also be the "temple upon the rock" of Book One.) Like the Park, the collie is an aspect of the feminine principle, caressed and fondled by the artist, whose "combing" is a form of unraveling, sorting out: as the multiple strands of the Falls were to be "combed into straight lines/ from that rafter of a rock's/ lip." (7).

Williams's clean-washed collie has a counterpart, "Musty," who contrived to escape while in heat despite great efforts by the owner's friend, who apologizes in a letter explaining the incident. The pairing of Musty and the collie seems a half-comic examination of the topic of sacred and profane love: the clean-washed dog a symbol for Venus, complete with a temple, "Musty" an earthy replica, unruly and fertile. The collie has a master, a poet; Musty is looked after, not too successfully, by a female neighbor. Also: an oblique reference to the "melting pot" prin-

ciple, Musty's escape an instance of miscegenation. And Musty's
escape is a play on the notion of dogs "at large"; the section ends
with the sign: "NO DOGS ALLOWED AT LARGE IN THIS
PARK." (It may also be, I suspect, that Musty represents the
crowd, the "great beast.")[12]

Williams returns to the Sunday crowd, which now draws near,
its voices "multiple and inarticulate." Among these voices the
poet's ear "strains to catch" *one* voice "of peculiar accent," that
is, the new poetic language, expressive of the place and of these
people, a language taking its point of departure from the rhythms
and phrasing of actual American speech.

The scene is still a festival of love. The Park finds "what peace
there is," accepts the people; she is "stroked/ by their clambering
feet," as the collie is stroked by her master.

The poet's search for a principle of unity continues, as Paterson at length arrives at the "rampart," from which he commands
a view of church spires and other distant objects. A few details
establish the place, giving a sense of height and a perspective:

> Sunday in the park,
> limited by the escarpment, eastward; to
> the west abutting on the old road: recreation
> with a view! the binoculars chained
> to anchored stanchions along the east wall—
> beyond which, a hawk
> soars!

—a trumpet sounds fitfully.   (55)

The "fitful" sound of the trumpet organizes the scene: the sound

---

[12] Nash (p. 192) discusses the passage as a "commentary on the civilization's
fear of fertility":

> The comic picture of the housewife peeking between her laundered sheets
> and trying to beat off the male with a stick is also a serious commentary
> on the civilization's fear of fertility and its attempts to govern and control
> brute nature. The penitent letter, confessing that Musty has become preg-
> nant in spite of the housewife's precautions, takes its place with many
> thematic references to the dog, an animal that links the urban and pastoral
> world. . . . It is a kind of link between the Dog-as-Opponent (NO DOGS
> ALLOWED AT LARGE IN THIS PARK; "guilty lovers and stray
> dogs" . . . and the Dog-as-Companion. . . .

(The Musty letter—obviously—is one of Williams's inventions.)

carries, but intermittently. The binoculars *chained* to *anchored* stanchions are set off against the soaring hawk and the carry of the trumpet notes. The trumpet's call suggests the one voice for which the poet is listening: a clarion, a call to order. The soaring hawk represents the imagination, which achieves a clear hawk's-eye view of the region.

From the vantage point of Garret Mountain Park one can look down toward the city of Paterson and see the church spires, the gorge of the Passaic, and the baseball field on the other side of the gorge. This large view provides a glimpse into the principles responsible for what the poet sees. The secret is the force of the Falls, which has called the present scene into existence, summoning churches and factories from "the pit," and so on. And the poet's imagination (like the hawk) soars, beckoned by the "thundrous voice," the same voice that "has ineluctably called them—that unmoving roar!/ churches and factories/ (at a price)/ together, summoned them from the pit ." The price (presumably) was the destruction of the elemental promise of the place. The voice of the giant Paterson, one among many, though "moving under all" remains unheard (56). He moves about, "his voice mingling with other voices," in the early afternoon (56).

Throughout this passage Williams plays with the notion of musical "time" (first a metronome, then on the next page, the order "Time! Count! Sever and mark time!"). This is both the poet calling his material to order and (maybe) a reference to the "march" of traditional measures. The scene below has its own "Music."

> Stand at the rampart (use a metronome
> if your ear is deficient, one made in Hungary
> if you prefer)
> and look away north by east where the church
> spires still spend their wits against
> the sky   to the ball-park
> in the hollow with its minute figures running
> —beyond the gap where the river
> plunges into the narrow gorge, unseen.   (55)

Together the churches and the factories define the setting for the "ceremony of love." Institutional religion appears as an ally of the manufacturing interests. In 1947 Williams wrote to Babette Deutsch, who had asked him about his treatment of Paterson labor violence, that he had found little he wanted to say "about the labor violence which has had Paterson as its scene during the last thirty or, perhaps, hundred years. . . ."

However, in *Paterson* the social unrest that occasions all strikes is strong—underscored, especially in the 3d part, but I must confess that the aesthetic shock occasioned by the rise of the masses upon the artist receives top notice.

In Part or Book II, soon to appear (this fall, I think), there will be much more in the same manner, that is, much more relating to the economic distress occasioned by human greed and blindness—aided, as always, by the church, all churches in the broadest sense of that designation—but still, there will be little treating directly of the rise of labor as a named force. I am not a Marxian.[13]

The record of "human greed and blindness" will be a principal subject of the second section. In this section the record is implicit in what we see of the people of industrial Paterson.

As Paterson, following the other hikers, ascends to the summit, Williams singles out another instance of the elemental: "the bare rock-table," scratched by the hikers' boot-nails . . . "more than the glacier scratched/ them." In an early work Williams had used the glacier scratches on a boulder to illustrate the freshness of the very old, contrasted with the aging of historical objects: "The camouflaged cannon in the park seems ten thousand years old—or infinitely past—compared to the boulder with the glacier scratches upon it, which seems new, fresh by comparison—its secret undrained."[14]

The secret of the elemental landscape is associated with that of elemental human energies, glimpsed by the poet in a scene that Williams in his notes labeled "Wops on the Rock." As Paterson proceeds to "the picturesque summit," he comes across a group of picknickers, among them a young man playing a guitar "dead pan," the others eating and drinking. One of the women, Mary, gets up and starts to dance, challenging the others.

[13] *Selected Letters*, pp. 258–259.
[14] *A Novelette and Other Prose*, p. 49; *Imaginations*, p. 302.

> Come on! Wassa ma'? You got
> broken leg?
>
> It is this air!
> the air of the Midi
> and the old cultures intoxicates them:
> present!
>
> —lifts one arm holding the cymbals
> of her thoughts, cocks her old head
> and dances! raising her skirts:
>
> La la la la!
>
> What a bunch of bums! Afraid somebody see
> you? (57)

In this the poet perceives "the old, the very old, old upon old, / the undying: even to the minute gestures, / the hand holding the cup, the wine / spilling, the arm stained by it."

Mary dancing calls to his mind a scene from an Eisenstein film,[15] a peasant drinking from a wineskin, "laughing, toothless," the wine dribbling down his chin. Williams comments "Heavenly man!" Mary and the peasant both embody forces that society attempts to suppress, ineradicable Priapic energies that are at the basis of religious emotion, and that call into existence the "festival," of which what we now see is a stunted survival.

> The leer, the cave of it,
> the female of it facing the male, the satyr—
> (Priapus!)
> with that lonely implication, goatherd
> and goat, fertility, the attack, drunk
> cleansed .
>
> Rejected. Even the film
> suppressed : but . persistent. (58)

The release and "cleansing" of the old festival, though "rejected," still persists, and we see something of it here.

But only the poet perceives the essential element in the scene— the permanence of the "very old." In one earlier version Williams commented on the scene described: "But scholarship passes them by and can't say one clear word to the purpose concerning

[15] Evidently *Que Viva Mexico*. See Peterson, p. 73.

them except irony. . . ."[16] The meaning of the scene is spelled out
in another early version (the passage scratched out in the manuscript), where the Italian-Americans are seen as participants in
an ancient "dance":

> the flat rock implying all
> dance, the enclosed bay, the grass trampled
> (as tho' by the dance) the aimless strollers
> gaping but
>
> The old, living still the old!   Not a painting
> but living, all by a recognition, a waking!
> —and the old lives, outmoded but alive, the
> new harder, colder—but the old still lives,
> here.   (Buffalo MS)

The "recognition" and "waking" belong to the poet—a flash of
insight like one of Joyce's epiphanies.

The poet's awakening to these undying energies, and his attempt to discern the elemental features of the place, connect the
argument of this section with the discussions of the first wife and
the mottled sycamore branch of Book One. Paterson here catches
another glimpse of that principle, permanent yet elusive, which
is his own "source." In the next section, Klaus Ehrens, a Protestant and a northerner, preaches a sermon that serves as a counterpart of Mary's dance. Mary and the "heavenly man" of the film
define what is missing in the religious framework of Protestantism, and in the modern industrial society which, as Williams
sees it, gave practical expression to the Protestant attitude.

The entirety of section 1 has been a "ceremony of love,"
though no one behaves very ceremoniously. Now we are in-
structed to look down from a ledge to a love scene: a couple lying
in a "grassy den/ somewhat removed from the traffic," the woman
"desiring"; the man, who has been drinking, "flagrantly bored
and sleeping, a/ beer bottle still grasped spear-like/ in his
hand ." (59) The spearlike grasping of the beer bottle seems

[16] Buffalo MS. This is Williams's comment on what seems to be a very
early version, a passage starting out "The group of fat Wops, full of beer. . . ."
Williams's commentary helps to explain what the scene was doing there in
the first place; as very often happened as Williams revised, the scene itself
became sharper and more elaborate, while most of the direct interpretive
comment was eliminated.

an ironic play on the Mars-Venus theme; the "flagrancy" of the man's boredom carries along (again ironically) the flagrancy of the "3 colored girls," which will become the flamelike "Beautiful thing" of Book Three. Some boys look down at the pair from columnar rocks above; the couple lies as if "besieged," the boys stare down as if "from history!" and, puzzled and bored by what they see, "go charging off." (Until the boys charge off we have a kind of temple—Mars and Venus enshrined, surrounded by columns from which Cupids look down.) The boys, it may be, replace and represent the "scholars" who in earlier versions were said to miss the significance of what they see. From the standpoint of "history," as from that of childhood ("sexless"), the scene appears inconsequential.

In the background you can hear the shouting of the Evangelist, whose sermon will be featured in the second part. (A shout, not a "music.") In the foreground the woman "leans/ her lean belly to the man's backside/ toying with the clips of his/ suspenders ." Now the sleeping man is transformed into Paterson, the sleeping giant, as if resting against the Mountain; and he adds his "useless voice" to the scene:

> until there moves in his sleep
> a music that is whole, unequivocal (in
> his sleep, sweating in his sleep—laboring
> against sleep, agasp!)

                    —and does not waken.   (60)

The music that moves in Paterson's sleep, "whole" and "unequivocal," contrasts with the actual scene and defines a latent presence, an alternative. In the meantime the giant continues to animate the individuals who comprise the Sunday crowd, though they are "amnesic" (forgetful of their origin) and "scattered" (there are a lot of them, and no voice to unite them). They also are listening for a single voice, but what they hear is

                    Pleasure! Pleasure!

The crowd (also the giant) is "half dismayed" to sense the multiple voices as "its own."

The section ends with a "call to order." The poet's job is to perceive beauty in the stench and disorder of the present. The present scene may be one of "deformity," but the poet must attempt to "decipher" it. The horn or trumpet, equivalent to the giant's voice and to the language sought by the poet, is the means for translating the noise and deformity of the scene.

The crowd is marshaled to "the conveniences," where some of them (but not many) will attend the preacher's sermon. The cop directing traffic (60) is an ordering principle, hence (maybe) a figure for the poet (as the minister will be). A pun: the giant/ crowd is "relieved/ (relived)"—the people are heading for the restrooms and the giant Paterson is "relived" by the multiple crowd.

Williams describes the trees nearby, and the shallow soil trampled by the people. That is, the city (its people) is set over against what remains of the "elemental" (soil, rock and trees); one detail in particular becomes an instance of what the poet must do: "sweetbarked sassafras ./ leaning from the rancid grease." The "corrosion" and "parasitic curd" represent the chemistry worked by the poet: something added that transforms his material.

The advice (or command) to "be good dogs," enforced by the sign "NO DOGS ALLOWED AT LARGE IN THE PARK," touches on two kinds of order: a social order (not too effective, given the unruliness of the dogs and the natural passions), and the poet's regulation of his material: the poem, in a sense, is his "Park."

SECTION 2

Like the ceremony of love in section 1, the open air sermon of section 2 takes place "in the Park," that is, in the scarred landscape of modern industrial America. Williams's preacher, Klaus Ehrens, is an immigrant (evidently from Holland), a Protestant but not attached to any particular church, earnest in what he has to say, and given to a "folksy" delivery with large emphatic gestures. He had made a good bit of money earlier in his life, only to learn that money will not make a man good or happy, and he passes this lesson along to his few listeners. Williams supplements the preacher's attack on avarice with prose material touching on the economic history of this country, and thus on the background for the scene in the Park. The argument of the sermon and the supporting material can be summarized roughly as follows. Private capitalistic interests, which had received official sponsorship in the early days of the republic (specifically from Alexander Hamilton), have succeeded in turning the country into a private preserve, at the expense of the people, and at great damage to the land. So far no one has offered a new vision to replace that of Hamilton. Conventional religion, even at its best, has failed to provide such a vision; Ehrens obviously fails to provide one. In effect, the "old theology," with its focus on another world ("the empty blue"), comes to the aid of the private interests dominant in this one. If there is a hope of "salvation," it resides in the work of the poet, who (toward the end of the section) prays, apologetically, to the principle persistent in all of earth's changes.

The section opens with the cryptic announcement:

Blocked.
         (Make a song out of that: concretely)
By whom? (62)

The blockage refers on one level to the course of the river. Zabriskie points out that the last glacier "and the morainal material it dropped, blocked the Passaic and forced it to seek another outlet, determining its present devious northward course," and creating the Passaic Falls and the bend around Paterson. "The action of the glacier, blocking the river and forcing it to the falls, runs through the poem in the theme of 'Blocked' where the blockage is transferred to knowledge, power, and the poet."[17] The question "By whom?" refers to the forces responsible for the present "stasis" and for the poet's frustration. To "Make a song out of that: concretely" would be to present, in a poem, the forces "blocking" the poet; and the section will attempt to do that. "Concretely" picks up the pun used at the opening of the first section, where Paterson visited his woman to instruct his thoughts "concretely."

[17] Zabriskie, p. 202.

The two forces mainly responsible for blocking the poet are institutional religion, embodied by a "massive church"; and monopoly capitalism, represented by the few industrialists to whom certain members of the Senate are attempting to hand over "the bomb."

The passage on the "massive church" (62) was quoted more fully in an earlier version.[18] The church in question was located between Arena da San Pedro and Avila, in "a village, so stony and brown you hardly could tell it was the home of human beings." Seeing the misery and the big church, the writer had been struck by the thought that "those poor souls had nothing else in the world, save that church, between them and the eternal stony, ungrateful and unpromising dirt they lived by. . . ." This sentence, quoted by Williams in the published version, was followed in the typescript by a comment: ". . . for several years I always went to the Tenebrae services, following [the text] in Latin. . . . It always ends with the Miserere—so beautifully sung. And certainly it seems to me it always needs to be sung . . . always has and always will." For Williams, however, the massive church is not so much an object lesson in the permanence of human misery as an illustration of the association between poverty and the church. (Churches exist because of poverty, and poverty exists because of human selfishness and faulty institutions.) In the earlier version Williams had commented: "No church has anything to do with religion, all are institutions for the regulation of man in whom religious qualities exist."

The attempt to give "the bomb" (by which Williams means the resources for producing atomic energy) to a few industrialists is the first of several publicly sponsored private take-overs featured in this section. Other monopolies include Paterson's Society For Establishing Useful Manufactures (73), and the Federal Reserve System (73–74). (The prose on 62 commenting angrily on the proposed giveaway seems to come from Williams's own notes, evidently intended at one time to be turned into verse [Yale MS].)

As a result of the blockage (or "stasis") attributed to these

[18] Buffalo MS. (I have not identified the source of this prose.)

forces, the people are gypped ("Cash is mulct of them that others may live/ secure") and knowledge is "restricted." And so:

> We leap awake and what we see
> fells us   .   (62)

That is, when we "wake up" to the significance of the scene in the Park, the force of what we see causes us to despair and fail. To "leap awake" joins the idea of leaping, as Sam Patch did, and as the poet must do, to that of rousing from sleep, as Paterson the giant attempts to do (or the poet for him). The modern scene stuns the poet who hopes to discover and reveal the latent meaning of the place.[19]

The first page, then, sets up the terms in which the sermon and the prose material of this section are to be understood. With these terms established, Williams returns to the scene in the Park, where Faitoute stands looking away from "the drunken/ lovers," both now asleep. He seems about to walk out into the air (as if in despair at what he has seen):

> indifferent,
> started again wandering—foot pacing foot outward
> into emptiness   .   .   (63)

Preparing for the sermon, Williams touches lightly on images for multiplicity and unity. The figures of the crowd ("moving beyond the screen of the trees") are brought into focus for an instant by music that "blurts out suddenly"—literally, music to accompany the sermon, but also a hint of the voice or "clarion call" for which the poet is listening. Other details continue the scene from 60–61: the policeman, for instance, directs people to the conveniences. There is a joking reference to the female of the poem, the woman or women who are Faitoute's "requites," in the sign nailed to a tree: "Women" (also, perhaps, the wo-man/park is crucified).

The setting is spare: a cramped arena near the urinals; some

---

[19] These two lines were preceded in one fairly late version with four lines indicating Williams's judgment of the preacher's style: "Faulty love/ —what S. would call 'no man'/ slimes the tongue/ with eloquence" (Buffalo MS).

broken benches; "the paltry congregation"; cornet, clarinet and trombone. Williams's notes show that he once considered making a direct reference to the quasi-aristocratic past of the old "Castle," near which the preacher will speak:

Lambert castle, the lookout and pleasure spot where the Ryerson girls used to go for their great parties—fresh from painting school: now the public convenience center: where the preacher has pulled a few benches together for Sunday service—   (Yale MS)

As he starts the preacher's sermon, which will exhibit the "divorce" characteristic of our time, Williams feeds in other items touching on the subject of divorce. Most important is a passage from one of the lady-poet's letters, stating her inability to communicate with anyone other than Dr. P., and alluding to the "disastrous effect" of her failure with him (64). There is also a newspaper report of a suicide (or murder?) with love as the motive (69). An opposing motif, the artist's affectionate effort to order his material, appears quickly in a reference to the man who "walks his dog absorbedly/ along the wall top . . . ," evidently the same man Paterson had noticed in the "circular redoubt," carefully combing the hair of the collie bitch. (The dog's master, as type for the artist, is set off against the preacher.)

The sermon of Book Two, one of the earliest notions to enter the plan for *Paterson*, was based on a sermon Williams heard at Lambert Tower "sometime before the war."[20] The sermon made a deep impression on Williams, and there are many versions of it, showing signs of extensive and careful revision over a long period of time. The later versions seem to move gradually further from the content of the sermon Williams actually heard; as he reworked the sermon, he seems to have eliminated certain "realistic" details as he added allusions to the symbolic argument of *Paterson*. (The sermon of the final version is shorter and less wordy than some of the earlier versions.) It is clear, however, that Williams had conceived a symbolic role for the preacher

[20] Letter from Professor Thirlwall. Notes and typescript versions for the preacher's sermon are found in both the Buffalo and Yale collections. A late version (in the Yale collection) gives the sermon itself in a form very close to that of the published version, but with all the prose material on Hamilton and the S.U.M. presented separately.

from the outset: he had referred to the preacher in "Paterson: the Falls," the short poem announcing the main themes of *Paterson*. Some of the earlier versions show a close association between the preacher and the "first wife" passages of Book One. The final selection and arrangement of the prose interruptions seem to have taken place late in Williams's revision of material for this section.

For Williams the sermon is an attempt to do what the poet must do: that is, to reorient this country by providing an alternative to the moneymaking drive that has dominated American history so far. The preacher does in fact offer an alternative, the familiar "Christian" doctrine of treasures in heaven; but this won't do. Failing to provide a satisfactory new synthesis, the preacher becomes (like Sam Patch) a figure for the unsuccessful poet. (His failure will be the point of departure for the third section, where it is taken to mean that "no poet has come," and where a vision shows him "drowning" among the bass-wood trees.) In one of the typescripts this scratched out comment can be read:

Minister: he does not have it (the language) though his
leap is just. Cataclysmic birth: of no value unless—trivial
unless oriented.

This, then, would be the lesson perceptible in the preacher's failure: a lesson to the poet himself. (It is interesting that Williams thought of the sermon as a "leap," like that of Patch, or like the metaphorical leap of the poet.)

The failure of the sermon, then, is specifically a failure of language: "One sees him first. Few listen" (65). The preacher's harangue is a "falls" that hangs "featureless on the ear" (70).

As he is a figure for the poet, the preacher is also, ironically, a modern version of St. Francis, or a John the Baptist. These references, explicit in some of the early drafts, appear by implication in the published version. Ehrens is a St. Francis, "calling to the birds and trees"—not out of overflowing love for the created world, but simply out of failure to attract an audience. (One earlier version included this comment: "The birds & the trees listened or didn't listen—not even the dog.") As a John the Baptist he receives no support from heaven: "No figure/ from the clouds

seems brought hovering near" (65). His failure to attract an audience is symptomatic of his failure to "bring in" the particulars
of his world, to accomplish a new synthesis. Few people listen or
pay any attention, except (Williams notes at the outset) some
stray Polock, baffled by what he sees, who mutters "What kind of
priest is this?" and goes scowling off in alarm. Though Ehrens
represents no particular denomination, he is in effect a sectary—
"A Protestant! protesting . . ." (65); the theology he offers will
not suffice to "compose" the differences among American people
of various faiths and national origins.

So, though there are things Williams clearly admired about
his preacher, the man's essential role in the poem is to illustrate
failure. Williams's notes make this clear:

His humanity—his experience—his sense of proportion
his christian charity if not his christian fortitude—apart
from the complete informality of his presentation—the
lack of official sanction—rather because of it his sermon
or preaching dissociated from any church had a certain
primitive flavor—his white hair flying his foreign accent
(Holland Dutch) even—of a John the Babtist [*sic*] in the
Wilderness. All but his theology! THAT made him one
with the crowd, figuratively speaking since there was no
one much to listen.   (Buffalo MS)

The sermon is interrupted and followed by prose material of
two kinds. The first is an account of Alexander Hamilton's role
in the founding of Paterson, in which the projected city appears
as part of a grandiose project for encouraging manufactures in
this country and, indirectly, as part of a program for keeping
power in the hands of the propertied classes. The second is a
blast at the Federal Reserve System, characterizing it as the front
for a credit monopoly. Together the two sets of prose material
define and criticize the economic policies that have guided this
country since the days of Hamilton. These policies are the background for the scene in the Park.

One of Williams's main reasons for the selection of Paterson
as the setting and symbolic hero of his poem had been the belief
that it was typical of the United States—that the shape and direction given to Paterson by Hamilton clearly exhibited the shape
and direction Hamilton and his allies had given to the nation as

a whole. The prose on pages 67, 69, and 73–74 presents Hamilton's plans for the founding of Paterson as a "corollary" of his role in the struggle for the "assumption" by the new federal government of debts contracted by individual states during and immediately after the Revolutionary War. The plan for Paterson is in this way linked to Hamilton's distrust of the populace ("'a great beast,' as he saw them . . ." [67]) and to those centralizing and pro-European tendencies that Williams blamed for the failure of this country to develop a culture of its own. Hamilton had opposed the repudiation of debts as injurious to the credit of the new nation, and he knew that in order to raise money to repay the debts it would be necessary to find sources of tax revenue. Hence the program for encouraging manufactures. A closely related motive for spurring the country's industrialization was to prevent it from being victimized as a mere producer of raw materials. Williams's summary, taken mainly from a source not unsympathetic to Hamilton, presents the rationale for these plans in a more or less official manner.

As a corollary to the famous struggle for assumption lay
the realization among many leading minds in the young
republic that unless industry were set upon its feet, unless manufactured goods could be produced income for
taxation would be a myth.[21]   (69)

The apparent success of Hamilton's plans to encourage national manufactures, and the importance of Paterson in this success, appear in the passage on 74 of *Paterson*, reporting that Washington wore a coat of homespun "woven in Paterson" to the first inaugural.

Williams had strong reservations about Hamilton's program and about the accepted version of Hamilton's role, according to which his policies had saved the country from political and economic chaos. He perceived that a case could still be made for those who had opposed the new Constitution, favoring a loose federation of states, and for those who had opposed Hamilton's

21 Williams's source for the material on Hamilton and the S.U.M. was the Federal Writers' Project's *Stories of New Jersey* (New York, 1938), pp. 58–62. Parts of the chapter on Hamilton and the founding of Paterson are quoted verbatim; earlier versions of this section quoted the chapter even more fully.

attempt to make this country into a manufacturing country along European lines. It seemed to Williams, as it had seemed to "revisionist" historians of the first part of this century, that the strong central government and its good credit chiefly benefited capitalists and certain groups of property owners (among them, specifically, those who held the bonds for debts the government agreed not to "repudiate").

Charles Beard's *Economic Interpretation of the Constitution* had appeared in 1913. It was perhaps the most influential work to reinterpret the early history of the United States in terms of the economic interests of the men who made the decisions about the form the new national government would take. Whether or not Williams had read Beard's work, he would have been familiar with other works treating the alternatives that had been available. Among these was *Mainland* by Gilbert Seldes, whose judgment of Hamilton's role closely resembled that of Williams. Seldes wrote that everything Hamilton did tended toward centralization, because he distrusted the mass "and was afraid that they could gain power in the separate states." His distrust of the people motivated his opposition to large-scale repudiation of the public debt. According to Seldes, the financial system fostered by Hamilton was modeled closely on that of Europe and in no way specially adapted to the needs of the new country. "This was the beginning of a financial system already tied up with industry which was to become more and more Europeanized as time went on; so we can say that Hamilton tried to impose upon the United States, which was beginning to expand, a financial system similar to that of England, which was beginning to contract. . . ."[22]

The realities of Hamilton's plans for Paterson, as distinct from the grandiose proposal (including city plans by L'Enfant later discarded as impractical [*Paterson*, 79]) appeared most clearly in the history of the Society For Establishing Useful Manufactures. Here again George Zabriskie supplies the relevant background:

The Society For Establishing Useful Manufactures was chartered with the help of Alexander Hamilton in 1791. Although originally planned as a kind of super-company, controlling both water rights and manufacturing estab-

[22] Seldes, p. 282.

lishments, it was not long before the sale of water power (later electric power) from the Falls became its sole concern. Of the early privileges granted the S.U.M. by the legislature—perpetual exemption from county and township taxes, the right to hold property (including water rights), improve rivers, build canals, and conduct lotteries—all but the lottery provision are still in force, despite lawsuits by the City of Paterson and private enterprises, beginning with the Morris Canal suit of 1824. To this day, it is the sole proprietor of the Falls and the adjacent land.[23]

According to Harry Emerson Wildes, Paterson had been from its inception a "company town," dominated by a private monopoly: "The SUM charter clearly demonstrated New Jersey's kindliness to large-scale business; the generosity that flowered a century later in trust incorporation was clearly evident. Paterson was from the beginning nothing but a company town, six miles square, solely dominated by the SUM. . . ."[24] Williams shared this sharply negative judgment of the S.U.M., though the prose in which he presents its history conceals this judgment in part. An earlier version included this comment on the S.U.M.: "—the Society for the useful cutting of throats might have been a better name for it" (Buffalo MS). And readers of *In the American Grain* will remember the discussion of Hamilton and his plans:

> . . . to harness the whole, young, aspiring genius to a treadmill? Paterson he wished to make capital of the country because there was waterpower there which to his time and mind seemed colossal. And so he organized a company to hold the land thereabouts, with dams and sluices, the origin today of the vilest swillhole in christendom, the Passaic River; impossible to remove the nuisance so tight had he, Hamilton, sewed up his privileges unto kingdom-come, through his holding company, in the State legislature. *His* company. *His* United States. Hamiltonia—the land of the company.[25]

The second set of prose material accompanying the sermon is

[23] Zabriskie, p. 209.

[24] *Twin Rivers: The Raritan and the Passaic* (New York, 1943), p. 248.

[25] From the chapter "The Virtue of History," which takes the form of a dialogue on Aaron Burr (*In the American Grain*, p. 195).

clearly polemical. It is an attack on the Federal Reserve System, apparently emanating from a spokesman for the "social credit" movement, or some post–World War II variant.

The Federal Reserve System comes under attack because it is another "private monopoly," a monopoly to which Congress had given the power "to issue and regulate all our money" (73). Though established by the government, it is not answerable to the people and, in fact, works as a "Legalized National Usury System," serving the banking interests (74). So runs the critique. It is not of course clear that Williams means to endorse the attack by including it here; it simply appears, much as the account of Hamilton appears, without direct comment. But the attack is consistent with the overall argument of *Paterson*, insofar as that touches on economic questions, and it is consistent with Williams's attitude on such questions as expressed elsewhere. The present city of Paterson (Williams might argue) is sufficient evidence that something has gone wrong with Hamilton's schemes. What we now have, as opposed to what was promised, is a hideous industrial city, set in a landscape disfigured by our attempts to make use of it, and inhabited by a people cut off from knowledge and beauty. If we try to fix the blame for this state of things, we note inevitably the role played by large private monopolies, of which the S.U.M. is one instance. The banks (he might proceed) comprise another monopoly, protected by the agency (the F.R.S.) supposedly intended to regulate them in the public interest. In fact, the banks form the basic monopoly responsible for the other abuses. The material quoted on 73–74, then, is presumably intended to stand as a valid critique of the monopolistic forces that have dominated this country—whatever reservations Williams may have had about the theoretical basis of the critique.[26]

[26] And Williams did not have many such reservations. Like Ezra Pound, Williams was skeptical of orthodox theories of money and credit, and though attacks on usury and the banks do not figure so prominently in Williams's writings as in Pound's, his economic thought, such as it is, draws its support from some of the economists who had influenced Pound. (For a discussion of the economic ideas in *Paterson* and their relation to Pound's, see Davenport, pp. 183–190.) The attack on the Federal Reserve System quoted in *Paterson* was excerpted from a letter sent to Williams in January 1947, and from a flyer enclosed containing a speech by Thomas Edison "on the Money Subject." (Some of the language in *Paterson* therefore belongs to Edison, who

The attack on the forces in America represented by Hamilton and the Federal Reserve System explains other passages in this section, for instance, the parody patriotic hymn "America the golden!" (68) Because the monopolists have taken away from us what ought to be ours, we "take our hats/ in hand" (in mock respect, to beg). And the satirical conceit on 73, in which the American eagle makes himself small in order to "creep into the hinged egg" may refer to the founding fathers' decision to accept the framework of European capitalism.

And the song beginning "Is this the only beauty here?" refers to the world brought about by Hamilton.

> Is this the only beauty here?
> And is this beauty—
> torn to shreds by the
> lurking schismatists? (71)

Ehrens had just brought his sermon to a rhetorical climax, punctuating it with the formulary "In the Name of the Father/ and the Son and the Holy Ghost./ Amen." Is this indeed the

---

was quoted in the flyer as saying, among other things: "GOLD IS A RELIC OF JULIUS CAESAR AND INTEREST IS AN INVENTION OF SATAN.") The letter from which Williams excerpted (presumably sent out to a list of more or less sympathetic recipients) recommended three books: Arthur Kitson's *The Bankers' Conspiracy!*, Brooks Adams's *The Law of Civilization and Decay* (with an introduction by Charles A. Beard), and Charles E. Coughlin's *Money*. Kitson's book explains the Federal Reserve Act of 1913 as the result of a conspiracy; Adams (whose work preceded, of course, the "social credit" movement but anticipated some of its concerns) had described the way in which bankers like Rothschild could profit from an "inelastic currency" by creating a shortage of money in times of expansion. Father Coughlin's argument is less easy to describe. (He is best known, of course, as a right-wing opponent of the New Deal and an anti-Semite.) Williams, whose sympathies were pretty much to the left, seems to have considered "social credit" as a middle ground between the extremes of fascism and communism. (This judgment appears in a draft of a lecture in the Buffalo collection entitled "The Attack on Credit Monopoly from a Cultural Viewpoint," a lecture presumably given to an audience of social credit-ers. Among other things, Williams had claimed that the credit monopoly was responsible for blocking the fruits of the "first Revolution.")

In an interview, Mrs. Williams commented briefly on Williams's involvement with the "social credit business" (Stanley Koehler, "The Art of Poetry VI: William Carlos Williams," *Paris Review*, VIII [Summer–Fall 1964], 140). Joel Conarroe discusses the "economic motif" in *Paterson* in *Journal of American Studies*, II (April 1968), 105–115.

"Beauty of holiness?" (The poet doubts it.) Is there any beauty in the scene? The trees? the dogs? (In a sense, yes; they embody the elemental.) The women here are not beautiful—"Unless it is beauty/ to be, anywhere,/ so flagrant in desire."

> The beauty of holiness,
> if this it be,
>
> is the only beauty
> visible in this place
> other than the view
> and a fresh budding tree.   (71)

The view and the tree: images for the latent significance of the scene at large, and for the *promise* implied by the tree's fresh buds.

The tone of the passage is one of dismay and repulsion, a repulsion that the poet will have to overcome if he is to "marry" this world, but the full force of which Williams wants to register at this point.

As the sermon reaches its conclusion, Paterson stands at the parapet, from which the preacher is only one element in the scene:

> Leans on the parapet thinking, while
> the preacher, outnumbered, addresses
> the leaves in the patient trees :   (72)

(Outnumbered: that is, unable to come to terms with the *multiple*.)

From where Paterson is standing one could have seen the murderer hanged: this is John Johnson, the man who killed John S. Van Winkle and his wife in 1850. Williams plans to use this murder at the end of Book Four, partly as a symbolic death for Paterson himself. The image also brings into play the Judas motif, and in the present context suggests that someone has "murdered" the republic with money as a motive.[27]

> One kills
> for money but doesn't always get it.   (72)

[27] For the Judas motif, see Davenport, p. 187.

The sermon concludes on 73 with references to God's "bound-less resources" and to "our Blessed Lord who/ died on the Cross for us that we may be saved." It is followed immediately by prose material on the Federal Reserve System, the allegory of the eagle, and the prose introducing the S.U.M.—that is, by a bitter commentary on the setting in which the sermon has been delivered. Now the poet himself prays.

The prayer is in part a commentary on what the poet has just witnessed—on the love scene of the first section, and the sermon of the second. It brings to a close the failed religious festival of Book Two.

A prayer to whom? At one time Williams entitled this passage "Address to the Deity."[28] But it is a Deity closely identified with the world itself; it is that principle which sustains itself within all natural change—no doubt the same principle that Williams had approached so warily in the "first wife" passages of Book One. He or she is "the eternal bride and/ father," and so on: that is, none of these things, but a presence supporting and nourishing all things, sustaining the world of change and appearance. The tone of the prayer is apologetic, as though the poet's own indignation at the profanation of the Park now seems a false note. And a prayer to such a Being seems not quite the right thing: "no prayer should cause you anything/ but tears. . . ." The prayer expresses in a new form the poet's commitment to the local, this time as a religious commitment to the local "home" of the god he worships:

> Why should I move from this place
> where I was born? knowing
> how futile would be the search
> for you in the multiplicity
> of your debacle. (75)

(A Buffalo typescript shows that the word "debacle" replaces "universe"—a characteristic Williams revision.)

The individual lives and dies. For him the world opens and

---

[28] The title appears in one of the Yale typescripts; Sister Bernetta called attention to it (Quinn, p. 103); Peterson, however, objects to theistic inferences from this title (pp. 94–95).

"spreads . . . like a flower opening," but it will also "close . . .
as might a rose—." It will

> wither and fall to the ground
> and rot and be drawn up
> into a flower again. But you
> never wither—but blossom
> all about me. In that I forget
> myself perpetually—in your
> composition and decomposition
> I find my . .
>   despair!   (75)

The poet's personal identity is incommensurable with the perpetual flowering of the principle persisting through all changes:
hence "despair." But the poet's "despair," at this point, also refers back to the disheartening scene in which he has just par-
ticipated, and which the prayer terminates.[29]

Section 2, confirming the fact of "divorce" in our time and
sketching its origins, ends on the note of divorce, with a complaint by the feminine principle, here embodied by the lady-poet.
She would like to see Dr. P., but only if there can be "some little
warmth of friendliness and friendship" on his part.

SECTION 3

The Park closes at nine o'clock. Paterson prepares to walk or
drive down from the mountain. As darkness comes on, the Sunday crowd leaves the Park, no one remaining "but guilty lovers
and stray dogs"—and the poet himself, "Alone, watching the May
moon above the/ trees ." The efforts of the preacher have failed.
"No poet has come" to express the meaning of the place. The
question posed now is whether the poet can come to terms with
what he has seen. Will he consent to "marry" the world as he
finds it? And even if he does, since the language is inadequate,
will he be doing any more than marrying "with empty words?"

---

[29] An earlier version (Buffalo MS) had ended in this way: "You blossom all
about me/ to my delight in that I forget/ myself perpetually—." Still another
had this: "Do you think, Sir/ that we shall succumb? without/ knowing?
More?/ Ah remember, remember me/ the stones cry and turned to/ look
at those passing."

A voice warns him that unless he *invents*, he and his kind will disappear, blotted out forever by "pulpy weeds." As he hears this warning he "almost falls": that is, either takes a chance and fails, or gives up and dies. At length, "pursed by the roar," Paterson flees to the Library in an attempt to escape from the unremitting challenge of the Falls, and to search in records of the past for the language he needs.

The subject of this section, then, is the poet's reaction to the defects of the world in which he finds himself, and his assessment of what is demanded of him on behalf of that world. The failure of the preacher's sermon means that so far no one has offered satisfactory terms for interpreting the present world. The religious impulse, thwarted by the forces of modern industrial civilization, can no longer provide a living "myth"; or, rather, those who claim to speak for religion can no longer do so. Lacking a language, the preacher is unable to do the job he attempted, no matter how earnest he may be. The poet now finds that it's up to him to do what the preacher has failed to do: he sees visions of what will happen if he fails. Though Williams had a pretty clear idea of what the poet is called upon to do, he meant for his character to have doubts about the quality of his material and about the language available. What now takes place is a postponement; though urgently warned to "marry," Paterson attempts to make an escape, hoping to prepare himself by a study of the past.

Section 3 is in part the poet's bleak review of what he has seen during the day. He has witnessed a failure, and he knows it—a degraded festival of love, followed by an unsuccessful sermon to an almost nonexistent audience. The failure of the sermon is a failure for the poet; the preacher is a "poet" of sorts, and he has spoken in an attempt to do roughly what the poet must do— "answer" the modern, provide a vision that can replace the vision of Hamilton. This was more than he could do. As he considers the preacher's failure, Paterson's mood is close to despair.

Williams uses the coming of night to represent a moment in a man's life, the beginning of the downhill course, of the "descent" into old age, a point at which the man mentally revisits the scenes of earlier defeats. To think over events of the past is to acknowledge defeat; and yet, as Williams argues, this very ac-

knowledgment offers the hope of a victory. Indeed, the act of
retrospect (even a negative retrospect) constitutes victory of a
kind. It is a way for the mind (and art) to win out over "life,"
with its defeats.

But "life" is given the last word, in such a way as to call into
question the value of what the poet does. Immediately after a
statement of the failure of invention "in our day," Williams
quotes from one of Cress's letters, telling Dr. P. that he might as
well toss his literature and everyone else's into a garbage truck,
as long as people "with the top-cream minds and the 'finer' sen-
sibilities" use these minds as means of "ducking responsibility
toward a better understanding of their fellow men, except the-
oretically—which doesn't mean a God damned thing" (82). And
the section ends with Cress's long indignant critique of Dr. P.'s
enterprise as a kind of aesthetic exercise, irrelevant to the plight
of actual human beings.

The governing logic of the section appears at the outset in
the poet's admonition to himself to "Look for the nul/ defeats it
all/ the N of all/ equations" —that is, the poem's "night" and
everything it may represent, including the poet's doubts about his
world and about himself. The negative principle, whatever it
may be, is invisible ("past all/ seeing"); and it destroys history
and memory ("the death of all/ that's past/ all being .") The
language used here suggests a metaphysical search—not only a
search for but the expectation of finding a "nul" at the basis of
all things. It is not, perhaps, an assertion that a "nul" does underlie all existence; rather, it expresses the poet's willingness to
confront the underlying blankness, if that's what it is, as he must
face any fact. The search for the negative principle is a step that
the poet must take if he is going to accomplish anything. He can
only continue with his own business if he can in some way accept
his defeat; specifically, he must accept the failure of the festival
of love and the sermon.[30]

The advice to search for the nul is countered by a quiet affir-
mation offered in the form of a rhyming proverb:

---

[30] A somewhat different reading is given by Peterson, pp. 100–102.

> But Spring shall come and flowers will bloom
> And man must chatter of his doom   .   .   (77)

Later, after speaking of the need to know the "dregs" as well as the clear air, Williams has the poet "win a war" simply by going home to write ("obscurely to scribble") (85).

At this point nightfall and Paterson's "descent" from the summit are used together as vehicles for a man's thoughts on reaching the age of self-doubt and retrospect. This is the well-known "descent" passage, the argument of which had been anticipated by a passage in *Kora in Hell.* "In middle life the mind passes to a variegated October. This is the time youth in its faulty aspirations has set for the achievement of great summits. But having attained the mountain top one is not snatched into a cloud but the descent proffers its blandishments quite as a matter of course. At this the fellow is cast into a great confusion and rather plaintively looks about to see if any has fared better than he."[31] The "descent" is a descent past the middle of one's life and by this logic also a descent to revisit scenes of the past. The accomplishment of memory, then, is in part an avowal of failure, in part a compensation for actual failures:

> For what we cannot accomplish, what
> is denied to love,
> what we have lost in the anticipation—
> a descent follows,
> endless and indestructible   .   (79)

The passage is a consolation, a reflection on the power of the mind to transform loss into gain. The descent has permanence ("endless and indestructible"), and it is a form of restitution, something given in recompense "for" the loss of this and that. In this way the mental revisiting of earlier failures allows for the opposite of despair: ". . . a new awakening :/ which is a reversal/ of despair." The mind wins out.

Because the sun has gone down, there are no shadows: "Love without shadows" is now possible, a love without passion and contingence.

---

[31] *Kora in Hell*, p. 25; *Imaginations*, p. 43.

> Love without shadows stirs now
> > beginning to waken
> > as night

advances.[32]   (78)

The poet's reflections on defeat also bear on the failure of the religious festival, which now comes to a close as a car leaves the park, scattering gravel (79).

Paterson can still hear (in his mind) "the pouring water!" Dogs and trees together "conspire to invent" a world that is "gone"—the sounds and odors of nature suggest to the poet the elemental setting, now lost. (The present scene is dark, and one is free to imagine another.) The preacher has failed, and the Park reverberates with the news that "No poet has come." The sermon stank:

> Variously the dogs barked, the trees
> stuck their fingers to their noses. No
> poet has come, no poet has come.
> —soon no one in the park but
> guilty lovers and stray dogs .

> >   Unleashed!   (79)

The stray dogs are "unleashed"—and the poet feels himself freed from the day's restraints:

> Alone, watching the May moon above the
> trees   .   (79)

Closing time: a sense of release and solitude, and of something ominous in the oncoming darkness. The people dress and prepare to leave the Park—"The 'great beast' all removed/ before the plunging night, the crickets'/ black wings and hylas wake ."

---

[32] The "descent" passage had a special technical importance for Williams, to whom it came to seem a "milestone" in his metrical development. "One of the most successful things in [*Paterson*, Book Two] is a passage in section three of the poem which brought about—without realizing it at the time of the writing—my final conception of what my own poetry should be; a passage which, sometime later, brought all my thinking about free verse to a head." He felt that the "variable foot" concept was implicit in the passage (*I Wanted To Write a Poem*, pp. 80–83).

(The "plunging" night may involve a pun on "leap"—associated with despair, with the "nul.")

A prose interruption: just as something was missing from the preacher's sermon, something was "missing" from the unspecified work referred to at the bottom of 80. Like the sermon, evidently, a synthesis that failed: instead of a calm bell "tolling the morning of a new age . . . ," the sound of a door loose on its hinges.[33]

Williams's judgment of the preacher was spelled out more clearly in a much earlier version, which emphasized the preacher's *banality*; in that version Faitoute, though "impressed," finally rejects the preacher and leaves the scene. The following passage, apparently intended to precede the preacher's sermon, includes some of the language used by Williams in the third section of the published poem (80):

> As the preacher talks he comes conscious by
> moments, rouses by moments, resents his
> interference with the air in the trees, the offense
> of his dull wittedness, his banality—Then
> is impressed. Finally rejects him and goes.
> Gets in his car. Drives to the edge of the falls.
> Smells the flat river water.[34]   (Buffalo MS)

The reference to driving to the Falls does not appear in the published version, where the scene at the edge of the Falls seems to take place only in Paterson's mind. (But this is perhaps not certain.) The "rejection" of the preacher occurs (residually—not clearly) on 80.

Paterson "ponders" the sermon.[35] The poem is (in idea at least) "the most perfect rock and temple, the highest/ falls," and Paterson is disheartened to find it "so rivaled"—that is, by the preacher's sermon. The preacher, or poet, appears as "in disgrace,"

---

[33] The first part may be a quotation; the "slow complaining of a door loose on its hinges" is presumably Williams's own comparison—it was at one time part of a verse comment on the prose here (Yale MS).

[34] This passage was followed by:

> . Between listening stares off into the northeast
> Omsk! . . over the city. Recalls the history and what should
> be written. From a Parapet: The dog

(At this point Williams led into the preacher's sermon.)

[35] In one manuscript the passage beginning "That the poem . . ." has this caption: ": FROM HERE ON HE PONDERS THE SERMON."

forced to borrow from "erudition" the terms of his language,
failing, trying again—in an attempt to form (Ezekiel-like, from
"his bones") a vision above the world. The city, which is the
scene above which the poet's vision would rise, is characterized
as "invisible, thrashing, breeding/. debased." As a result of
the breakdown in the distribution of knowledge, the city is "reversed in the mirror of its/ own squalor,"

> debased by the divorce from learning,
> its garbage on the curbs, its legislators
> under the garbage, uninstructed, incapable of
> self instruction   .   (81)

The university goes its own way, continuing the fragmentation
of knowledge, while the city, separated from learning, continues
to debase itself.

The poet turns away from the city: "a thwarting, an avul-
sion :" (81).

All this restates the "divorce" theme, which now appears in an
image of uprooted flowers:

> —flowers uprooted, columbine, yellow and red,
> strewn upon the path; dogwoods in full flower,
> the trees dismembered; its women
> shallow, its men steadfastly refusing—at
> the best   .[36]   (81)

The Park, mutilated by the Sunday crowd, provides these analogues for the isolated people of the modern city—people including, no doubt, Cress and Dr. P. ("steadfastly refusing").

Divorce also characterizes the language. The words lack style;
there are no scholars; and Williams describes the words (or the
scholars?) as objects in the river, mastered and submerged by its
flow.

> .   or dangling, about whom
> the water weaves its strands encasing them
> in a sort of thick lacquer, lodged
> under its flow   .   (81)

[36] In an earlier version of the passage on 80–81, one that in general is
more explicit and less cryptic than the published version, Williams had this
line on the women and men: "its women brainless, its men moneymakers"
(Buffalo MS).

Perplexed and discouraged, but still attempting to discover a meaning in the scene, Paterson is "caught (in mind)/ beside the water" (81). ("In mind": he is still in the Park, but imagines himself a few miles away, standing at the edge of the Falls.) He looks down and listens, but still can discern no "syllable" in the confused uproar, no means to express the meaning of this place, or the turbulence of his own thoughts. Though "untaught," he strains to hear, shaking "with the intensity/ of his listening ." As he strains, he is comforted by "the thought of the stream," "its terrifying plunge, inviting marriage—and/ a wreath of fur ." That is, he is tempted to take a chance, to "leap"—or to give up.

The day's festival, no doubt, should have led to the consummation of a "marriage," and an invitation to marriage now appears in a dialogue between Faitoute and a woman who represents the modern "replicas" as well as the "insistence of place." "She" comments:

> Stones invent nothing, only a man invents.
> What answer the waterfall? filling
> the basin by the snag-toothed stones? (82)

The poet must "invent." The setting, the place itself, will not do the job for him. How does he propose to give an answer to the waterfall? He replies in terms that for Williams are true enough: "Clearly, it is the new, uninterpreted, that/ remoulds the old, pouring down ." (82) But "She" reminds him that such remolding has not taken place in our day.

The advice or warning to "invent" is followed by two visions of the consequences of the failure to articulate.

First, the preacher (*Le/ pauvre petit ministre*), swinging his arms (as he did in the sermon) is seen to drown "under the indifferent fragrance of the bass-wood/ trees .": a vision of the would-be poet blotted out for lack of invention. The minister's sermon had illustrated the fact that "It has not been enacted in our day!" (Now the preacher's group leaves the Park, Williams commenting that the kids, bored by the sermon, ought at least to get a kick out of the light truck scooting down the hill.)

A second vision discloses more exactly the sense of what Pater-

son has seen: a dwarf, "hideously deformed," is transformed into
a strange treelike form, his roots trampled by the crowds "as by
the feet of the straining/ minister," sparrows singing from his
eyes, his fingers sprouting leaves. This is a vision of the poet overcome by his material, having failed to articulate the secret "meaning" of the place. The dwarf's voice is that voice which Paterson
has been straining to hear.

> His ears are toadstools, his fingers have
> begun to sprout leaves (his voice is drowned
> under the falls)   .   (83)

The poet is warned to sing his song quickly,

>   . . . or
> not insects but pulpy weeds will blot out
> your kind.   (83)

That is, he and the people for whom he speaks will undergo the
fate imaged by the metamorphosis of the dwarf.

The woman speaks urgently:

> Marry us! Marry us!
>   Or! be dragged down, dragged
> under and lost.   (83)

The poet "all but falls . ." The temptation to fall is associated
with advice to "marry." And he does marry, but "with empty
words," feeling that it would be "better to/ stumble at/ the
edge/ to fall/ fall/ and be/ —divorced/ from the insistence of
place" and from the other insistent demands required by his attempt to interpret the Falls. Sister Bernetta summarizes this
action: "He pauses once more to look down at the Falls, trem-
bling with the strain of trying to decipher the language of the
torrent. The moment is perilous. Like Patch at the Genesee
Falls, Paterson is drawn towards destruction by the terrifying
plunge of the waters. . . ."[37] For Paterson to leap at this point
would be (in terms of the symbols provided by Sam Patch and
Mrs. Cumming) simply a way of letting go, a shortcut to failure
and death.

[37] Quinn, p. 111.

> and leaped (or fell) without a
> language, tongue-tied
> > the language worn out   .   (84)

This is both marriage (with the stream) and "divorce" with a vengeance. Since the job of interpreting the roar of the Falls seems hopelessly difficult, the poet, in a mood akin to despair, is tempted to take a crazy risk, unprepared, or simply do away with himself.

In one version (evidently a fairly late version, since it resembles in most respects the published text of this passage):

> He almost falls! catches himself and is
> less amazed. Patch plunged in—but too
> stupid to care.   (Yale MS)

(Other drafts had "too drunk to care.")

The account of the poet's "fall" (or near fall) is followed by a cryptic reference to the dwarf:

> The dwarf lived there, close to the waterfall—
> saved by his protective coloring.   (84)

The dwarf is "saved" when the poet almost falls; he belongs to the place (as the "Genius of the Falls") and the place conceals him—as the "first wife" was concealed in the second section of Book One.

The woman advises Paterson to go home and get to work, to "compose" and be reconciled with his world, "it is/ the only truth!" To "compose is also (by a pun) to "reconcile" and "yoke" —the pun is explicit in an earlier version (in which the dwarf and poet are identified):

> At last, the dwarf gets a meaning
> Go home and write, compose. If you don't
> nobody else will—they are all
> running away or dying (to please).
> —compose, compose their differences—
> accrete, fertilize, draw in.   (Yale MS)

The reply, "Ha!" seems a skeptical rejection of the advice to accept his world; presumably it is the poet who now says "the

language is worn out," offering this as an excuse for not acting.
The woman's voice accuses the poet of having abandoned her
(more or less as Cress does in her letters); and then "at the magic
sound of the stream" she throws herself upon the "bed" (pun
on stream-bed) in a "pitiful gesture" (offering marriage) that is
lost among the words.

The words are these:

> Invent (if you can) discover or
> nothing is clear—will surmount
> the drumming in your head. There will be
> nothing clear, nothing clear .[38]   (84)

The confused noise of the Falls ("the drumming in your head")
is set off against the potential clarity of the poet's invention. The
Falls, here again, expresses the demand of the place to be made
articulate, but it also expresses the persistent course of life (pulse-
beat, the course of blood—leading eventually to a "sea of blood"),
a violent and obscure (uninterpreted) flow; and again (as on
7–8) it suggests the course of unremitting *thought*—which also
demands a language.

Paterson "flees": in a note to an earlier version Williams speci-
fied that he fled "to the library." That is, he turns to records of the
past for assistance—for the language that will enable him to come
to terms with the present. But the roar pursues him: he carries
it in his mind.

Now the movement is quick and disrupted; a few meanings
for the fragments on 84–85 can be suggested. The scholarly meet-

---

[38] In the same earlier version quoted above, these lines read:

> Invent, discover or nothing clear
> will surmount the drumming in your head.
> Nothing clear. There is nothing clear,
> He fled! pursued by the roar.

These phrases appear in various combinations: "give us blood," "honor us
with metaphor" (Buffalo MS). In some of the earlier versions, the poet is
begged to "give blood" by means of metaphor to the women (particulars,
flowers, and so on). The poet's work appeared as an act of transfusion,
giving blood (restoring life) to particulars in danger of dying—as, in the
"tongue of the bee" passage (11–12) the poet's words prevent the flowers
from sinking back "into the loam."

ing at Princeton may be another form taken by the "roar": to Williams, presumably, a babble of voices (like that of the Sunday crowd), in need of a poet to provide a unifying language. When Faitoute grinds his heel "hard down on the stone:" it seems a way of saying good-bye to the Park; the weather report (moderate weather promised for the next day) indicates that night is not permanent. The short dialogue ("Me with my pants, coat and vest still on!" and "And me still in my galoshes!") continues the love scene, the galoshes a joking reference to the stream.

The poet shouts advice to himself:

> A man is under the crassest necessity
> to break down the pinnacles of his moods
> fearlessly —
> to the bases; base! . . .   (85)

The pun on "base" is clear enough: what supports our highest moods (and victories) may be something we hesitate to acknowledge; but we can't reascend without coming to terms with this "base" element. The key to recovery is action—the act of writing:

> From that base, unabashed, to regain
> the sun kissed summits of love!
>
>   —obscurely
> in to scribble   .   and a war won!   (85)

The hint of a victory to come by dint of "scribbling" is corroborated by the poem that follows—a "song written/ previously," in the structure of which Paterson now finds something "of interest." The poem returns to the scene of the descent: darkness, no disturbances, a latent force of "voluptuousness," a night propitious to the poet's act of love.[39] The next two lines complete the coming of night, and associate the celebration of feminine beauty with the approach of death:

> Her belly . her belly is like a white cloud . a
> white cloud at evening . before the shuddering night! (86)

[39] One of three poems for *Paterson*, Book Two, published in the *Partisan Review*, XV (Feb. 1948), 213–216. The others were "Signs everywhere of birds nesting . . ." and "The descent beckons . . ." (Wallace, C 398).

Despite the promise of a victory, Cress as devil's advocate is given the last word, as Book Two concludes with a long passage from one of her letters, complaining of Dr. P.'s coldness.[40] Her main point is that she has actually lived (seen and lived through poverty and degradation, taken chances), while Dr. P. insists on keeping his distance from life, and on turning everything into literature. The woman represents the claims of the "real world," demanding something better than to be turned into poetry. (Or she is a Social Muse, refusing to honor the poet's commitment to formal beauty.)

You've never had to live, Dr. P.—not in any of the by-ways and dark underground passages where life so often has to be tested. The very circumstances of your birth and social background provided you with an escape from life in the raw; and you confuse that protection from life with an *inability* to live—and are thus able to regard literature as nothing more than a desperate last extremity resulting from that illusionary inability to live.   (91)

Dr. P. must face not only the force of the woman's complaint but his own uneasy feeling that she may be in the right. Is the poet's "love" of his material simply a form of aestheticism?

Williams borrowed the woman's signature—"La votre/C"—from *Troilus and Criseyde*. In a letter to Marianne Moore, he had praised Chaucer's skill in having Cressida sign her letter in that way, speaking of "a metropolitan softness of tone, a social poetry"; he must have had these qualities ironically in mind in having "Cress" sign her letter in this way.[41] In another letter (to Horace Gregory), Williams explained and defended his inclusion of the "long letter" as something "subtly relevant" to his subject: "The purpose of the long letter at the end is partly ironic, partly 'writing' to make it plain that even poetry is writing and nothing else—so that there's a logical continuity in the art, prose, verse: an identity. . . . But specifically, as you see, the long letter is

---

[40] The passage quoted above from an earlier draft, ending "accrete, fertilize, draw in" was followed by this note: "Note: Use *all* her letters. *She* has the last word. P.S.—run on completing the story. End with the post card 12/6?/ etc." (Yale MS).

[41] *Troilus and Criseyde*, Book V, 1631. Letter to Marianne Moore, *Selected Letters*, p. 233.

definitely germane to the rest of the text. It is psychologically related to the text—just as the notes following the *Waste Land* are related to the text of the poem." The difference, he continued, was "that in this case the 'note' is subtly relevant to the matter and not merely a load for the mule's back. That it is *not* the same stuff as the poem but comes from below 14th St. is precisely the key. It does not belong in the poem itself any more than a note on—Dante would. . . . And, if you'll notice, dogs run all through the poem and will continue to do so from first to last. And there is no dog without a tail. Here the tail has tried to wag the dog. Does it? (God help me, it may yet, but I hope not!)"[42]

By the tail trying to wag the dog, Williams seems to have meant the attempt by the feminine principle (which ought to be "passive") to get the upper hand. The letter embodies a threat and challenge, but its presence here does not mean that the threat defeats the poet. Whether he is defeated remains to be seen. Though he offers no answer to Cress, Williams undercuts the letter with this much irony: the attack on the poet's aloofness ends up—in a poem.

[42] *Selected Letters,* pp. 265–266.

Book Three

THE LIBRARY

Book Three considers the poet's relationship to the past, and to the literary tradition in particular. The Park had been the setting for a ceremony that failed, apparently for the lack of a language, and at the end of Book Two Paterson had fled to the Library both for respite against the "roar" of the present, and for assistance. The books, however, do not "abate" the roar in Paterson's mind. And the whole of Book Three examines the question of whether the books offer anything that the poet can use. The answer implied by the events of Book Three is that the poet can't afford to think of himself as continuing the work of the past, as belonging to a "tradition", but must accept the fact that his own age makes entirely new demands, and go on from this recognition to invent a form that will be appropriate to his own "given." Works of the past are like fossil shells—beautiful paperweights. This line of argument is roughly the same as that which Williams developed in a number of lectures and essays.[1] Even though we may look back at a few of the very greatest works of the past, works in which a poet (Homer or Villon, for instance) succeeded in capturing the living voice and hidden meaning of his own people, we do not use these works as models but as signs of what must be done anew for our own place and time.

The main action of Book Three is simple enough. Paterson goes to the Library and reads more or less at random about the past of his region, hoping that in the past he can discover terms for understanding his own world. While he reads, he dozes and his mind wanders, so that his effort to gain inspiration from the past shades over into an effort to give life to the past. His imagination "pursues" the spirits from the past. The Library comes to seem a grotesque cemetery, confining the spirits of those writ-

[1] Especially "An Approach to the Poem."

ers who had entered (mistakenly) in search of warmth and fellowship. The books are tombs, and in visiting the Library the poet
himself risks "death"—entrapment and castration by the forces
of tradition. But, reacting against the staleness and rot of the library, Paterson, in a half-waking dream, pictures "Beautiful
thing," living beauty, violent and destructive of traditions and
old categories. She is that beauty which poets now dead once loved
and celebrated; but we cannot seek her in their works, since they
contain only an echo of life. (Nor is she "in" the present, except
insofar as a poet succeeds in drawing her out.) To embody this
concept of living beauty, Williams presents two Negro women—
one of them drunk, caught up in local gang fights, her nose
finally broken; all this to emphasize the unpredictableness of
present beauty, which refuses to appear where our traditions
locate it.

The scene in the Library, then, dramatizes the poet's attempt
to use the past, and ends with his recognition that the past cannot
supply what he needs. This recognition and the poet's escape
from the Library lead into the fourth book.

Within and around the simple story of Paterson's trip to the
Library are a number of events used more or less "allegorically"
to describe the mind's action, its relation to the world (and to its
inheritance from the past), and the effect of death on what the
mind creates. These allegorical developments are based on three
natural catastrophes that struck the city of Paterson in 1902. In
that year nearly half of Paterson was destroyed—first by fire
(February 8 and 9), then by flood, when the Passaic River over-
flowed its banks (March 2), and later by a "freak tornado" that
"devastated a part of the city unaffected by either the previous
fire or flood."[2] Williams adjusts this order of events, starting with
the cyclone ("winds" from the books), devoting the second section
to the fire (which at length razes the Library), and ending with
the flood. Both the wind and the fire are treated as positive forces.
Wind, by an etymological pun, is spirit or inspiration; fire is the
power of imagination, at once destructive and capable of trans-
forming what it touches. The flood, on the other hand, plays

[2] Zabriskie, pp. 214–215. An account of the three disasters appears in
Nelson and Shriner, II, 505–508, Williams's probable source for some of
the details.

essentially a negative role. It is death, and therefore by Williams's logic the creator of "tradition." The flood quenches the fire and creates from the ashes a new soil that Williams pictures as an infertile, "pustular scum." The poet will not live long enough to see whether this soil may at length become fertile. And so the third book ends as Paterson watches with horror the effects of the flood, considers his own situation, shouts "Let me out!" and leaves the Library.

SECTION 1

Prefacing Book Three is a quotation from Santayana's *The Last Puritan* that restates the connection between man and city, suggesting some of the terms at stake when Paterson enters the Library.

Cities, for Oliver, were not a part of nature. He could hardly feel, he could hardly admit even when it was pointed out to him, that cities are a second body for the human mind, a second organism, more rational, permanent and decorative than the animal organism of flesh and bone: a work of natural yet moral art, where the soul sets up her trophies of action and instruments of pleasure.   (94)

Santayana's metaphor in praise of cities indicates one way in which Williams intended his identification of Dr. P. and the city of Paterson. Ideally, the city is continuous with nature and with the human mind; it is a "second body." And the sketch of a man to whom this metaphor was incomprehensible supports Williams's view of the "Puritan" mentality. Implicit here, as Glauco Cambon notes, is a reference to Lewis Mumford's *The Culture of Cities*. A passage from Mumford's book anticipates one of the main subjects of *Paterson*: "When the city ceases to be a symbol of art and order, it acts in a negative fashion: it expresses and helps to make more universal the fact of disintegration. In the close quarters of the city, perversities and evil spread more quickly. . . ."[3] The scene of *Paterson* is a city acting "in a negative fashion."

[3] *The Culture of Cities*, (New York, 1938), p. 6; Cambon, p. 193. Among Williams's notes to himself for Book Three, this one: "The Last Puritan: Look up quotation 'The City' & copy out for use later" (Buffalo MS).

The first section of Book Three opens with a lyric in praise of
the locust tree in bloom.[4] How much does it "cost" for the poet
to love the locust tree? In a sense, of course, the poet pays for
beauty with his own "life-blood": he pays "A fortune bigger
than/Avery could muster" (95). The "cost" also refers to the
economics of writing. The economic forces hampering the poet
have already been touched on; the subject is treated more elaborately later in Book Three, and in the second section of Book
Four. Given a society indifferent to his work, the poet must be
willing to make sacrifices comparable, for instance, with those
made by Madame Curie.

Having indicated at the outset the "heavy cost" of the poet's
quest, Williams returns to his symbolic narrative. Paterson has
been led to the Library by "A cool of books" (95). The Library
seems to offer an end to his isolation, or at least a temporary
respite from the noisy present; it is a quiet alternative to the
incessant roar of the Falls. An earlier draft had stated Paterson's
hopes in this way:

> To drown the roar, ~~stopped at~~ the library
> for peace, searching the old town for relief
> the provincial quiet for a clue to the
> resolution of that turmoil—Snow falling,
> the lights on a Christmas eve for peace.
> A meaning, a meaning? What did they know
> and feel that we do not know? The falls silenced,
> by the summer drought, burnt out—
> stillness? Gesturing—ingrown.   (Buffalo MS)

Paterson has turned to his "own mind" because he has had no
luck in roaming the "back streets"—looking for beauty in the
things of his own world:

> Spent from wandering the useless
> streets these months, faces folded against
> him like clover at nightfall, something
> has brought him back to his own
>
>   mind .   (96)

The meaning latent in the poet's world is still withheld from

---

[4] Williams doubtless had in mind two of his early poems entitled "The
Locust Tree in Flower," *Collected Earlier Poems*, pp. 93–94.

him, almost (the clover image suggests) as if by some deliberate action "against him." Here the streets represent the external world in its male aspect, whereas the Park had embodied the female.

The act of entering the Library seems an almost desperate groping for alternatives, at a time in the poet's life when he is dissatisfied with what he has tried so far, and frightened by the persistence of his own thoughts, which now seem to do no more than beat out the rhythm of his own course toward death. The challenge to the poet reappears in a version of the "Falls" metaphor. In his mind, "a falls unseen"

> tumbles and rights itself
> and refalls—and does not cease, falling
> and refalling with a roar, a reverberation
> not of the falls but of its rumor
> 　　　　　　　　　unabated.　　　(96)

This passage links the notion of driving, sleepless thought with that of blood coursing through the brain until the man dies: a kind of physiological allegory, in which the mental falls is associated with blood, the "dark bed" equivalent to the "sea of blood" toward which the waters of life are headed. The reiteration of the roar is "unwilling to lie in its bed/ and sleep and sleep, sleep/ in its dark bed." The mind refuses to let up and simply accept death. The riddle of the Falls continues to propound itself, and evidently will continue to do so until the poet can fashion a reply.

It is summer; the cataract will soon be dry. As another version had it:

> Summer! It is summer　.
> of which
> 　　　　so much
> 　　　　　　　was expected
> I am restless
> consumed with regrets.　　　　(Yale MS)

The trip to the Library may allude to Williams's attempts to come to terms with this country's past, as in *In the American Grain*. The poet is searching for a usable tradition, and Williams

presents this search metaphorically as an attempt to derive "spirit"
from the writers whose works are now lined up on the shelves
of the Library. The spirits resident in the books may offer Paterson a clue to his own difficult quest—provide, metaphorically, the
wind to carry his imagination out on its search. The hoped-for
action of winds from the books restates the etymological pun on
in-spiration; books enclose the spirits of the men who wrote them,
and may breathe "spirit" into the poet who reads them. The
"seeking" of the imagination is pictured as the search and play
of a hawk, who has good eyes and gets a good overall view of the
scene spread out below (the city). A visit to the past, then, may
give the poet inspiration and a perspective for viewing the difficult present. Such at least is the hope.

> For there is a wind or ghost of a wind
> in all books echoing the life
> there, a high wind that fills the tubes
> of the ear until we think we hear a wind,
> actual .
>
> to lead the mind away. (95–96)

As we accept the wind's power over us, the mind perceives a trace
of the beauty for which it is seeking: "a scent, it may be, of locust
blossoms" (96), a quiet force, drawing the mind toward it.

The wind of the books may be a deception, though. We *think*
we hear an actual wind. And in fact Paterson's hope will be frus-
trated. Paterson enters the Library and begins to read.

From here on Williams feeds into the poem fragments of material about the local past, stray facts Paterson notices in newspapers and works of local history. Immersing himself in the past,
he is moved by the reality of the past and by the finality of its
disappearance. Good or bad, these things existed and exist no
longer. The uninterpreted fact that "The last wolf was killed
near the Weisse Huis in the year 1724" is first of all simply something that Paterson notices as he begins to read. But it belongs
with other facts illustrating the destruction of the primitive environment; and it exhibits the "civilizing" drive of the people
who settled the area. (The wolf is also, perhaps, another manifestation of Paterson's symbolic dog.)

As he pictures Paterson groping through this historical material, Williams invokes the violent forces that are to "blow" and "bring down": "Cyclone, fire/ and flood."[5] To these forces, Williams says "So be it!"—as though in recognition that violence and destruction must precede and accompany the work of the imagination.

> Run from it, if you will. So be it.
> (Winds that enshroud us in their folds—
> or no wind). So be it. Pull at the doors, of a hot
> afternoon, doors that the wind holds, wrenches
> from our arms—and hands. So be it.   (97)

The pun on "breath" recurs:

>   Sit breathless
> or still breathless. So be it. Then, eased
> turn to the task. So be it :

Paterson looks at old newspapers, where he finds records of deaths: "a child burned in a field,/ no language"; two others, a boy and girl, "Drowned/ wordless in the canal." The boy and girl, clasping each other and "clasped also by the water," illustrate the marriage theme; the drowning also refers back to the love scene of Book One, section 2, in which the lovers are caught in the "torrent":

> We sit and talk, sensing a little
> the rushing impact of the giants'
> violent torrent rolling over us, a
> few moments.   (24)

Again, as in the case of Sam Patch, a death by drowning is associated with the failure of language. The newspaper accounts of deaths are used to reassert the notion that the people of this place can be "rescued" only by the poet. Random events, old objects: "The Paterson/ Cricket Club, 1896. A woman lobbyist." The "So be it" chorus continues, as if to say "OK, these things used to be, let them pass." (Williams's listing of items from the past calls to mind a passage in "Old Doc Rivers" where the speaker,

---

[5] At one time it appears that the passage "Blow! Bring down!" was intended as a conclusion for the entire poem. (A page in one of the Yale typescripts had the title "Conclusion" scratched out.)

looking over old medical records, is struck by how many of the old occupations are no longer followed.)

The
old Rogers Locomotive Works. So be it.
Shield us from loneliness. So be it. The mind
reels, starts back amazed from the reading .
So be it.   (98)

(The drownings, the local millionaires and other items here had been the subject of articles in *The Prospector* in 1936—and so had the Library fire.)

"Shield us from loneliness." This passage restates Paterson's reason for entering the Library; the Library is "sanctuary to our fears." But as the past does come to life, the mind "starts back amazed"—amazed at what it means for these things to have existed here. Countering the violence of this recognition is a "vague outline, speaking":

Gently!   Gently!
as in all things an opposite
        that awakes
the fury, conceiving
        knowledge
by way of despair that has
        no place
to lay its glossy head—[6]   (98)

One item in particular catches Paterson's attention: the story of (Catholina) Lambert, a successful immigrant from England,

[6] The passage beginning "Gently! Gently!" is from "Patterson [*sic*]: Episode 17," first published in *New Directions in Prose and Poetry*, 1937; (*Collected Earlier Poems*, pp. 438–442). (See Wallace, C 245.) The poem began "Beat hell out of it/ Beautiful Thing," the opening passage comprising an image evoked "by a colored girl beating a rug in the yard of the Episcopal rectory in Rutherford" (Thirlwall, p. 262). The rest of "Episode 17" deals with a gang fight involving "guys from Paterson" and "guys from Newark," during which the girl's "flogging" of the rug takes place to "the beat of famous lines/ in the few excellent poems/ woven to make you gracious . . ." (pp. 441–442). Most of the "Beautiful Thing" episode appears in Book Three of *Paterson*, spaced in with other material. It takes up again on 104 ("And as reverie gains . . ."), then (in the third section), 126–128 ("But you!/ —in your white lace dress"). But not all of Williams's treatment of the theme comes from the earlier poem.

whose "Castle," a prominent Paterson landmark, is now to be razed. Williams dwells for a moment on Lambert's career (he was a self-made man who fought against the unions) and on his building. Lambert's "castle" had been a deliberate anachronism, an attempt to fight against the present by asserting one's right to the dignity and privileges of an old order. Hence (perhaps) it is a counterpart of traditionalism in literature; there is a paradox, of course, in the fact that Lambert would not have enjoyed in England the privileges he claimed and defended in this country:

> —the old boy himself, a Limey,
> his head full of castles. . . .   (99)

According to Zabriskie, "Lambert's fortune was destroyed by his antiunion attitude, which in the end made his mill holdings valueless. After his death the Castle and the Mountain became county property. At one time, the Castle served as an orphan asylum; later, the county started to raze the entire structure, but stopped after a wing had been torn down. At present, the Castle is the headquarters of the Passaic County Park Commission and the Passaic County Historical Society."[7] When the narrative of Lambert's career touches on his fight with the unions, Williams feeds in a bit of prose—a man reminiscing about the early days of the union movement in Paterson: "Rose and I didn't know each other when we both went to the Paterson strike around the first war. . . ." (This prose was apparently excerpted from a letter from a friend who had read *Paterson*, Book Two.)[8] Another instance of change: the contrast between the early days of the labor movement and its later success and institutionalization: "And look at the damned thing now." Like the account of Lambert, a reminder of the violence latent in modern industrial society.

The proposed razing of the Castle also illustrates the mass's

----

[7] Zabriskie, p. 212. There is a description of the building in the Federal Writers' Project's *New Jersey: A Guide to Its Present and Past* (New York, 1939), p. 355.

[8] In an earlier version Williams quoted a bit more, including this opening sentence: "Your Paterson, Book II should sell because it hits the semi-documentary groove. Rose and I didn't know each other . . ." (Yale MS).

tendency to destroy what it does not know how to value. For them the building is "in-/ comprehensible; of no USE!"—and they plan its destruction. The castle is an assertion of individual taste, therefore doomed.

The best "artifact" in Lambert's structure consisted of some of the windows—"translucent/ laminae of planed pebbles." Best because most authentic: they were not imported but came from the locality. And to Williams their transparency suggests the virtues of the poem itself:

> The province of the poem is the world.
> When the sun rises, it rises in the poem
> and when it sets darkness comes down
> and the poem is dark   .

With darkness lights appear; a man reads:

> and lamps are lit, cats prowl and men
> read, read—or mumble and stare
> at that which their small lights distinguish
> or obscure or their hands search out
>
> in the dark. The poem moves them or
> it does not move them.   (100)

The poem participates in the real world, a natural object like any other; but this participation also suggests that if the poem is good, things will behave in it as they do in the real world. Men will read the poem, and perhaps be moved by it: a natural action, like any other—like the lighting of lamps or cats prowling.

BEAUTIFUL THING

The action at this point is crucial. As he reads, or "seems to read," Paterson is "oppressed" by a "roar of books" and his mind begins to wander. His search among records of the past now gives way to a kind of waking dream in which he gropes for meaning in his own mind. As Williams put it in an early plan: "He seeks an interpretation of the Falls—that obsesses him—in reading, in books—but finds it not in the books but in his mind that wanders as he reads."[9] This "interpretation" appears in the poem as "Beautiful thing," a force opposed to the "staleness" of the Library. She is "—a dark flame,/ a wind, a flood—counter to all staleness."

Paterson's half-waking glimpse of "Beautiful thing" leads into a vision in which the Library appears as a prison "immuring" the spirits that had come here "for respite." The argument implicit in Paterson's vision of "dead men's dreams" in the Library can be paraphrased roughly: attracted by the safety and "light" offered by a tradition (or simply by the totality of work that has already been done), the writer accepts its protection and guidance only to find that he has entrapped himself. He wants to escape; but it's not certain that he can. He can be pictured, say, as a moth, flown in from the night.

[9] The rest of the page is worth quoting. It obviously dates from a time when Williams had many of his themes worked out, but had not settled on the final arrangement of parts. He seems to have expected to end the poem with the "solving of the riddle," presumably at the end of what is now Book Three. Later, of course, he rearranged these themes, and the Curie material (for instance) was moved to the fourth book:

Thinking over the sermon in the park.
The enigma posed.   Riddle in the Greek or Joycian sense.
The language, the language: the Falls

The history of SUM—
     begin, also, the history of the place.
The Curie: radium lecture

Psycho-somatic : the mind and body as it listens for the
     language—the search goes on and becomes more confused.

First mention of the 2 murders—Van Winkle (for money)
                              Adriance etc.

              give notes, first notes, of both—fairly full
                         (but *not* the outcome of either.
     Continuation of the various letters: end some of them.
The mind.   Variation of the sermon: letters of the colored girls.
The search: where to search?
     The solving of the riddle.
          /
        /
     end abruptly. Stop.   (Yale MS)

>   Flown in from before the cold or nightbound
>   (the light attracted them)
>   they sought safety (in books)
>   but ended battering against glass
>   at the high windows.[10]   (100)

This vision, of course, touches on Paterson's own possible fate;
it is also a way of regarding the books of the Library. Books "enclose" the spirits of the men who wrote them, or the beauty they
once sought. Confining the spirits within walls, the Library dis-
arms them and prevents them from acting. Only to the poet's
imagination does the "Beautiful thing" live at all.

The Library, then, becomes a symbol for the forces in society
that mean to capture the poet and tame him:

>   The Library is desolation, it has a smell of its own
>   of stagnation and death   .   (100)

As we enter, something like surgery is performed on our wits;
and if we don't "translate"—bring the past to life on our own
terms—we will "remain a castrate."

>   . . . (a slowly descending veil
>   closing about the mind
>   cutting the mind away   .
>
>   SILENCE!   (101)

SILENCE, the Library motto, had been used in an earlier version
(Buffalo MS) to signify a conspiracy of silence. The traditionalism embodied by the Library will attempt to prevent the poet
from acting.

Because of this, Faitoute's search for meaning is a risky operation, and Williams presents its dangers in terms suggested by
Odysseus's descent into Hades. An earlier version had this:

---

[10] Among the drafts for Book Three is a passage explicitly identifying the
"dead men's dreams" as bats: "Dead men's dreams pad the ceiling, unable,/
wanting to escape ~~again to life,~~ horrid/ chattering,/ a squealing of bats ."
(Yale MS).

> a descent into a
> hell. There, awake, he dozes in a fever heat, the
> cheeks burning with his blood, loaning blood to the past
> amazed—risking life: (Yale MS)

The poet recognizes that his own death will come "too soon"; the sea is death: "O Thalassa, Thalassa!/ the lash and hiss of water/ . . . How near it was to them!/ Soon!/ Too soon ."

The vision continues, as Paterson's mind now "joins" the other spirits, flying with them under the ceiling of the library building, "battering/ with the rest against the vents and high windows." He attempts to bring it back, but it "eludes him." The other spirits turn upon it

> as furies,
> shriek and execrate the imagination, the impotent,
> a woman against a woman, seeking to destroy
> it but cannot, the life will not out of it) .   (102)

The passage describing the shrieking furies took this form in an earlier version:

> and shriek as furies
> and execrate the imagination, woman against woman
> —seeking to destroy it: a library of books—decrying
> all books that feed the mind, calling them bolsheviks
> all books are the enemies of bars and battens, of
> closets and closed doors: hating books—and shutting
> them away: the library.   (Yale MS)

The meaning of the scene is clear enough. It is a struggle by the dead spirits of the past to destroy Paterson's imagination; for the moment, at least, the imagination survives. In the earlier version Williams had opposed the "library of books" to the living books "that feed the mind." The published version twists this a bit, as the swarm of violent fury-like creatures becomes a kind of living library:

> A library—of books! decrying all books
> that enfeeble the mind's intent
>
> > Beautiful thing!   (102)

It is not entirely clear who is "decrying" these books. Presumably in the published version it is the imagination or "Beautiful thing" that speaks out against the books that "enfeeble." Thirlwall quotes this from Williams's notes: "the enfeebled mind, weary of travelling the rivulet of print between top and bottom of page, But you would think that, with effort, one ought to be able to keep one's mind down on pages and pages of verse."[11]

The Library institutionalizes the poet's fear of going it alone, and will deprive him of the power to act. Can he continue to study the past without succumbing to the Library's deadness? Maybe. It's not so much the past that endangers him, as the forces of what Williams calls "stasis." The Library plays two roles in this action. It is the repository of what remains from the past, of what used to be alive, and what the imagination can still perceive as living. But it is also that which destroys life. The spirits who inhabit the Library may or may not belong to men who are now literally dead; the point is that they have accepted a form of death by agreeing to the Library's conditions. They are allowed to survive, but at the cost of impotence.

The account of the struggle between the "furies" of the Library and the imagination gives way to a stretch of prose describing an incident from Dutch colonial history. Some soldiers had tortured and killed some Indians, who had been accused, unjustly, of killing two or three pigs. One brave, cruelly wounded, asked permission to dance the "Kinte Kaye"—but he received "so many wounds that he dropped dead." The episode is part of the past that Paterson is trying to recover—something he is reading about in the Library. It exemplifies the effect of the Old World on the New; our "sources" are polluted by injustices like this one. And Williams's notation of Indian customs at the end of the passage touches on the destruction of "related" culture in this country.

They made money of sea-shells. Bird feathers. Beaver skins. When a priest died and was buried they encased him with such wealth as he possessed. The Dutch dug up

[11] Thirlwall, p. 307. He points out that this is presumably a quotation from Ford Madox Ford.

the body, stole the furs and left the carcass to the wolves
that roamed the woods.[12]   (125)

The digging up of the carcass is one of several exhumations in
the poem; here it signifies the despoiling of the Indian's heritage.

The passage touches on the "related" culture formerly present,
the Indian practice of "making" money of seashells contrasting
with the moneymaking of Lambert or Hamilton. The contrast
is reinforced as Paterson's mind wanders to a scene illustrating
the debasement of the ceremony of marriage: a man about fifty,
pushing back a cap (in gold—Volunteers of America), tells Dr. P,
"I got a woman outside I want to marry, will/ you give her a
blood test?" In an earlier version the passage was considerably
longer, and included these lines:

> Listen Doc
> see if you can't hurry it up. I want
> to get it over with as soon as possible
> I'll do what I can.   (Yale MS)

Now the poet wants to escape the Library's foulness—the life-
less clutter of books, and the stench of the past. The foulness is
also historical America, including the unjust killing of the Indians and the destruction of the primitive cultures of the New
World. But to escape it (he is warned), he must "embrace" it
(103); the embrace, perhaps, will transfigure and redeem it.

The main terms have been established, and the rest of the first
section can be summarized briefly. Still in the Library, Paterson

---

[12] This prose appears to be an amalgam from two sets of notes now in the
Yale collection. The first set was entitled "Indians *Dance of Death* circa
1644." (Williams was collecting information about various Indian rituals.)
The passage beginning "They made money . . ." comes from another set of
notes on the Indians who had inhabited New Jersey. The atrocity referred
to in the prose took place toward the beginning of "Governor Kieft's War."
An earlier version of this passage included more about the Indians; the
passage on making money of seashells appeared in verse, and there was
other material on the Lenapes, including the "War Song of the Lenapes."
There was also, at one time, a passage describing an Indian sacrifice involving dogs.

dozes and lets his mind wander. Records of the past have failed him, and he finds himself again confronted by the unpleasant facts of the present, described as a "swill-hole of corrupt cities." Someone asks Dr. P. whether he still believes in "the people," the Democracy? The subject becomes the poet's desperate mood, brought about by his judgment of the world in which he finds himself. The challenge to him, or the "riddle" that he must solve, still refers to the necessity of finding a language for this place and its people. The effort required is comparable with Madame Curie's "saintlike" effort to extract radium from pitchblende. It is the extraction of a "radiant gist" or "stain of sense" from the ore of everyday reality. Can the poet hope to do this? He is tempted to give up the attempt. In his discouragement death appears to him in an attractive form, offering to supply the "missing words." Dr. P.'s reverie now turns to alternatives to the life he has actually lived; what if like Toulouse-Lautrec he had spent his "nights in a brothel"? The question brings to his mind what Toulouse-Lautrec had witnessed and recorded—an elemental "fact," analogous to volcanic lava, which cools to the useful stone out of which "we build our roads." (A reminder that art connects with dangerous energies.) The reverie moves on to stray facts about Williams's family, brought to light in the hope that the simplicity of an earlier day may illuminate the present for him. But this continuation of the search into the past is fragmentary and inconclusive. At this point he is advised, or advises himself, to "Quit this place" (the Library), and the section ends with a restatement of the "wind" theme, this time in a literal account of an actual tornado, followed by images for Paterson's quest as the soar of a hawk and Sam Patch preparing to leap.

This is the gist of the argument developed between 103 and 112. A few of the details call for further comment.

Harry Leslie, the tightrope walker (103), is a figure for the poet—skillful, taking a chance, impersonating. Walking the tightrope also provides an image for the poet's giddy awareness of time: "the being taut, balanced between/ eternities." For the poet to "embrace the/ foulness" of historical America, as he knows he must do in order to win his release from it, means

taking a risk like that of a tightrope walker. This restates the
Sam Patch motif, and Williams implies a reference to the mass
of people who come to watch the performance. An earlier version, in which verse was used, included this comment:

The "dead heads"   cheered—   (Yale MS)

Among Williams's notes is one listing "Tight rope" as the proposed theme of this section.[13]

A note in the Yale collection lists three themes that are sub-
sidiary to the "over-all wind theme" of this section. These are "1.
the woman disclad; 2. conspiracy; 3. the flower."

The idea of a "conspiracy" against the poet appeared earlier
in the vision of spirits in the Library. I am not sure that the
"flower" theme appears in the published version of section 1,
though it may be implicit. The "woman disclad" now appears
(104–106) in a celebration of "Beautiful thing," beginning immediately after the third bit of prose on Harry Leslie. The
"women disclad" motif explains the dialogue in which Dr. P.,
"haunted" by the woman's beauty and the "quietness" of her
face, urges her to undress, "quickly, while/ your beauty is attainable." (The poet attempts to strip the "appearances" from
the present in order to perceive its latent beauty.)

The "Beautiful thing" episode concludes with Dr. P., weeping,
saying "Let's take a ride around, to see what the town looks like"
(105). To ride around the town is to continue the imagination's
search, pictured earlier as the hawk's flight over the city.

The poet is asked on 108: "What can you, what can YOU hope
to conclude/ —on a heap of dirty linen?" The question is clarified
by the continuation of the "Beautiful thing" narrative in section
2, where the Doctor is directed to a woman, lying in a basement,
her "long/ body stretched out negligently on the dirty sheet"
(125). The sardonic question on 108 means, roughly: does the
poet really expect to discover "beauty" in this unpromising
material?

The "Beautiful thing" passage leads into material on a "mar-

---

[13] Buffalo MS. Williams is paraphrasing an article that appeared in *The
Prospector*: "Harry Leslie Crossing Passaic Falls, August 4, 1879."

riage riddle"—that is, again, the question of how the poet can "marry" the material of this world. The answer to the "riddle" (107) is the "voice": again, presumably, the language latent in what the people here actually say, but discoverable only by the poet. When Williams asks "Is there no release?" he means: Will no poet come along to locate and display the language by means of which this place's meaning (and beauty) can be expressed? The essential language, still unreleased, is "unfaltering" and "new."[14]

The poet, however, is discouraged about the possibility of isolating that voice.

> Give it up. Quit it. Stop writing.
> "Saintlike" you will never
> separate that stain of sense.   (108)

The saint here is Madame Curie, who will be an analogue for the poet. The "stain of sense" is a metaphor based on the "stain" in a retort that led to the discovery of radium. Beauty, or the "poem," or the language, is radium to be separated from the inert mass (pitchblende). It is a job requiring insight and a "saintlike" patience. Pitchblende, then, is metaphorically equivalent to the "heap of dirty linen" representing the poet's world.

Williams typed across the page in one typescript: "Curie, the image of our age: boiling down the pitch-blende for that stain of radiance" (Yale MS). Later he shifted most of the material on Madame Curie to Book Four, section 2. The metaphorical references to radium here are residues of the earlier plan, serving in the published version as anticipations.

As Williams sketches the mood of the poet who fears that he will never solve the riddle, he plays off the "hope" of the poem against the thought of death (109). The poem, if successful, will be an answer to death—can stare "death in the eye" (106). But death is also an alternative to the poem. An earlier version of the material on 109 had this:

[14] In one version, the riddle appears in this form: "What language/ could allay the thirsts of our own throats?/ What winds lift us past defeats? What floods/ bear us away? What fires to compare/ with those fires :" (Yale MS).

> If the poem fails me—then?
>
> Death, kind death come
> and relieve me of this burden
>
> . in the pitch-blend [*sic*]
>
> the radiant gist   .[15]

Tired and discouraged, Paterson gives his mind over to "Irrelevant Recollections" about his family—a couple of pages of such recollections in most typescripts, a couple of lines in the published version.[16]

> There was an earlier day, of prismatic colors : whence
> to New Barbadoes came the Englishman   .
>
> Thus it began   . (109)

"New Barbadoes" is a name for the area around Rutherford, and the "Englishman" is Williams's father. One of the items included in the unpublished versions was a business letter from his father on the subject of shipping "fine fresh turtles." To describe the presumably simpler and clearer days "whence" his father came, Williams borrows a phrase that Marianne Moore had used to describe mythic Eden: it was a day "of prismatic colors." (This notion is picked up a page later in another context: "Let the colors run   .") What "began," it seems, was Williams himself— or the life of his family in New Jersey, and hence his identification with the place.

One version stated the motive for these recollections directly:

> How to recover that quality, of clarity and directness?
> An era ended.   (Yale MS)

The point, of course, is that the poet cannot recover those qualities (if indeed they were ever present). He must do his work in an "era" not marked by clarity and directness.

"Cost," on 109, is associated with death. What the poet pays for

---

[15] Yale MS. From "If" to "burden" is scratched out.

[16] "Irrelevant Recollections" was the heading scribbled at the top of this page in one of the Yale typescripts. Among the other material once included here was this about "Mestre": "a Catalan, who/ came to her when my father/ died/ and lent her money to buy a few/ fine things, a few shirts . . ." (Buffalo MS). (See *Autobiography*, p. 35.)

beauty is his own life. At the same time, the economics of "cost" and "poverty" are matters of fact, knowable—and relevant to language and poetry. So "cost" refers to the economic realities affecting the poet. At one time this passage included explicit references to Henry and Brooks Adams, men who had foreseen the consequences for the arts of the economic principles operative in this country. The passage beginning with "the fact" read:

> the fact
> of poverty is not a matter of argument.   the poverty
> of the mechanical output of letters, the costs
> always the costs.   (Yale MS)

From "the poverty" to "costs" is scratched out in the manuscript.

Toulouse-Lautrec makes his first appearance on 110; he will figure prominently in the fifth book. In his essay on *Paterson*, Thirlwall reports that Williams "had been attracted to Lautrec by the painter's ability to turn the gross into beauty." Here the celebration of the French painter supports Paterson's attempt to extract the "radiant gist" from inert material. The pretext for the reference to Lautrec is that Paterson tries "another book," presumably a book about the painter. Picking up the book is an attempt to "break through/ the dry air of the place" (the Library).

What Toulouse-Lautrec witnessed (110) and "all religions/ have excluded" seems to be simply sexual passion. This force transforms itself into "—a stone/ thrust flint-blue/ up through the sandstone/ of which, broken,/ but unbreakable/ we build our roads ." Williams is thinking of the volcanic power that creates lava, which cools to become a utilitarian object—material for road-building. An earlier version described trap rock, "cold now, of which roads are made/ but hot then, and flowing" (Buffalo MS).[17]

In the *Autobiography* Williams referred to Toulouse-Lautrec: "It is my instinctive affection for these 'lost' girls that is the best part of me—and them. I loved them all. Like Toulouse-Lautrec (who had the advantage of his deformity), I would gladly have

[17] In that version Williams made a connection between the "flint-blue" volcanic stone and "the blast of St. Pierre" that wiped out remaining members of his mother's family in the year that he received his medical degree.

lived in a brothel (of them) for the warmth (extracurricular) and the comfort to be derived therefrom." Williams had in mind certain of the young women he had known, "some of them wealthy," with no employment—"like myself, in one sense, which explains my affection for them."[18]

The speech that appears in the midst of the Toulouse-Lautrec material seems an attempt to define the language.

> Say I am the locus
>   where two women meet
>
> One from the backwoods
>   a touch of the savage
>   and of T. B.
>   (a scar on the thigh)
> The other   —   wanting,
>   from an old culture   .
> —and offer the same dish
>   different ways.   (110)

The speaker here must be the "voice." If so, this is a restatement of the argument developed earlier in connection with the Jackson Whites: the poet's need to yoke together the two great incomplete cultural tendencies of this country. Here the speech can be interpreted in this way: the language for which the poet is searching exists at the "locus" where these two cultural principles (two "women") come together. Both offer the "same dish"—both express the unchanging elemental energies.

On page 111 Paterson is advised to abandon the Library and to "Go where all/ mouths are rinsed: to the river for/ an answer." The river is presumably life itself.

The literal violence of the tornado (111–112) "counters" the dead air of the Library. (So also, by implication, did the volcano responsible for the "flint-blue" stone mentioned above.) The cyclone embodies the reality of "spirit," as distinct from the winds of the books. A few details confirm the cyclone's literal power, then the violence of the cyclone gives way to a wind at the Falls, supporting the red-shouldered hawks that in summer "ride and play" in the updraft. The hawks as symbols for the poet's imag-

---

[18] *Autobiography*, p. 224. Williams made similar comments in his interview with Walter Sutton (*Minnesota Review*, I [Spring 1961], 309–324).

ination merge into "the poor cottonspinner," Sam Patch, who looks down, preparing to leap. This is also Paterson, searching among books, "the mind elsewhere/ looking down/ Seeking."

That is: the search continues, but now it is a "real" wind that carries Paterson out on his search.

SECTION 2

The Paterson fire of 1902 now serves as the basis for an account of what the imagination does to the materials of the past and present. The action of Paterson's mind, as he sits in the Library, is described as a violent conflagration, destructive yet also in a sense "creative," since it transfigures what it destroys. The central event is Williams's description of an old bottle, mauled and reshaped by the flames, and so gaining a new "distinction." The description shows that the poet can "beat the fire at its own game." The symbolic action of the fire is supported by an old account of an Indian ceremony in which the celebrants shut themselves in a tepee filled with smoke from tobacco and heated stones. The old ritual serves as another analogue for the poet reading in the Library; he approaches the works of the past ceremoniously, attempting a kind of "communion" with the spirits of the men who wrote the books. The pun on wind and breath as "in-spiration" appears again, as Paterson in the ceremonial hut "breathes in" the acrid fumes from the books. In the meantime, as the poet watches the progress of the fire attacking the city, he celebrates its work in a mood combining excitement and resignation. He is conscious of possible failure—destruction unredeemed by beauty—and of the price he must pay for the poem.

Identified with the action of the fire—"intertwined with" the fire—is a vision of "Beautiful thing," the symbolic dark female figure introduced in the first section. "Beautiful thing" is the beauty latent in the world of the present, and therefore the poet's proper "beloved" and subject matter; she is also the poem itself, or that which *lives* in the poem: an irreducible presence—"Let them explain you and you will be/ the heart of the explanation" (123). She is another form taken by the woman of *Paterson*: the permanent mountain who is also the "first wife" of the African chief and the lady-poet of Dr. P.'s correspondence. Here she is embodied by a Negro woman whose legs had been scarred by whippings, and by another one whose nose was broken during a New Jersey gang fight. Associated with the primitive and violent, the woman's "flagrant" beauty opposes the quiet of the library. The section ends with an amalgamation of the woman and the fire, both forces "counter to all staleness"

—a flame,
black plush, a dark flame.   (128)

Fire can also embody a principle opposed to beauty. The fire that burned the works of Sappho, for instance, opposes the "fire" of her poems.

The opposition between beauty and authority, much on Williams's mind when he was writing Book Three, appears directly in the lecture, "An Approach to the Poem," which argued that there had been no "basic formal invention in poetry" since the Middle Ages, though the world of thought or mind "has gone through countless mutations." Behind this fact Williams thought he perceived various "interests," which had reason to prevent the necessary advance. "The Poem, formally, has been left behind. And interests (unnamed—economic, tribal, metaphysical, sociologic—group seizures) perhaps retrograde, recessive at least—have wanted it so, and want it and keep it so—normally! The *line*—the poetic line—is the seat of this stasis."[19]

In a late draft for Book Three, the second section begins with a direct statement of the "counter to authority" motif. The poem itself is counter to authority, making possible a coexistence that the real world does not permit. Both "Ugolino and Ariel" dwell in the poem, but they could not "live for us" without the framework of the poem, which serves as "a barrier between them and authority." And further, "The poem/ exists only under condemnation by authority:/ a smoldering fire" (Buffalo MS).

The beginning of this section deals with society's attempt to suppress the poet, and the price he must pay as a consequence.

[19] "An Approach to the Poem," p. 65.

By "cost" Williams means the effort and sacrifice, the cost to his own life, willingly paid by the poet in exchange for the beauty of the poem. But he also has in mind cost in another sense: the present economic system fails to support those whose job it is to write. In a short passage made up of two-line units, Williams associates fire with writing: "They have/ manoeuvred it so that to write/ is a fire and not only of the blood." The conditions surrounding the writer are also a fire—a "destroying fire." (". . . the writing/ should be a relief,/ relief from the conditions/ which as we advance become—a fire, / a destroying fire.") "They" are the unnamed interests referred to in the lecture, but also the mass of people, fearful of beauty.

Fearing the poet, they try to disarm him, sometimes by an easy indifference to what he does ("How *do*/ you find the time for it in/ your busy life?" [114]). The present order has nothing to fear from the poet as long as he can be kept in his place. His place, apparently, is on a library shelf, where he cannot act.

In an earlier version, after the patient—puzzled and indifferent—asks Dr. P. what the poem means, Williams had this reply and sequel:

> I can't tell you
> : Paterson lifts
>
> the stones of his memory and shivers
> —and the sludge of his veins
> stirs vaguely
>
> the expense is such—that is their
> chief weapon—the expense of time—
>
> Time is Money: this they say is an
> economic age—malice and dread.[20]   (Yale MS)

The ceremonial aspect of the fire is introduced in a passage of prose describing an Indian ceremony dedicated to "the Spirit of Fire, He-Who-Lies-With-His-Eyes-Bulging-In-The-Smoke-Hole." The source is Nelson's history, where the ceremony illustrates the religious beliefs of the Indians of the area

---

[20] In this version these lines were followed by the locust tree passage, now placed at the outset of section 1 (95).

(the Leni Lenape), and touches on the doctrine of earth as universal mother, and the veneration of fire and light.[21] This native religious ceremony involving fire keeps in play Williams's celebration of the "related" culture destroyed by the invading white man, and suggests the poet's attempt to relate to his locale, as the Indians did to theirs. The ceremony is something that Paterson reads about in the Library, a ritual not actually available to him, but suggestive of possibilities. (Among Williams's notes in the Yale collection is an indication of how he planned to use the Indian ceremony: "Book III Begins with the tobacco spell—[the religious spell]".)

Paterson reading in the Library, then, resembles an Indian participating in the ritual. A short passage of verse identifies the ceremonial hut with the Library, and Paterson breathes "the books in," as the Indians breathed in the "acrid fumes" in the hut. Paterson is pictured as attempting "to break/ through the skull of custom/ to a place hidden from/ affection, women and offspring—an affection/ for the burning" (115). The primitive religious isolation from one's family becomes here a symbol for the "cost" implied by the poet's difficult quest. There is something unnatural about it; the poet must acquire a love for the action of fire.

The "hush" of the Library is malignant, and the books cannot penetrate this malignity. Why malignant? Because the Library imposes silence on the books, prevents them from acting; they remain "men in hell,/ their reign over the living ended" (115). The men who are entombed within the books would like to act but cannot; they are unable to act against the Library.

The poet would like to have a message from the books, but he hears them saying "clearly" only one thing: that it is difficult to

[21] The ultimate source of this account is a Latin dissertation presented at the University of Upsala by a "learned (Swedish) American" named Tobias E. Biörck, *Dissertatio Gradualis: De Plantatione Ecclesiae Svecanae in America* (Upsaliae, 1731), p. 28. In Nelson the account appears on pp. 35–38; Nelson translated some of Biörck's Latin, quoted some of the Latin. Williams obviously liked the effect of this mixture of English and Latin in which some Indian exclamations also appear. One manuscript version of the passage included a fuller quotation of the ceremony, beginning: "It is certain that they held in veneration fire and light, and their common source, the sun; and by a natural deduction, the sun's place of rising—the east" (Yale MS).

distinguish a book from the man who wrote it, and to decide which is to be valued the most, the man or his book. Since there is no clear answer to the question, the books can give no clear advice as to how much the poet should be willing to "pay" for the beauty he is seeking.

As he establishes the Indian ceremony, Williams begins to describe the actual Paterson fire. According to Zabriskie, the fire started on the night of February 8 and burned on into the next day, until a shifting wind allowed firefighting companies (including reinforcements called in from neighboring towns) to bring it under control. Insurance companies paid out more than four million dollars in claims; but—Zabriskie adds—many of the older companies never went back into business, and "many of those who reopened were crippled by their losses for the rest of their corporate existence."[22] Williams gives a straightforward prose account of how the fire started in the city ("in the car barns of the street railway company, in the paint shop," where "the men had been working all day refinishing old cars . . .") (139); and this account is taken up a page later—"When discovered it was a small blaze . . . ," but the wind spread it.[23]

The fire, then, is the actual Paterson fire of 1902; it is the Indian ceremony; and it is Paterson reading in the Library.

Paterson's reading, as his imagination takes up the materials, becomes a ceremonial conflagration, a huge fire spreading through the city at night, to end at dawn.

> Breathless and in haste
> the various night (of books) awakes! awakes
> and begins (a second time) its song, pending the
> obloquy of dawn   .
>   It will not last forever
> against the long sea, the long, long
> sea, swept by winds, the "wine-dark sea"   .   (115)

The reference to the sea is sudden and unexpected: a quick ominous warning that death will come to "quench" the poet's

---

[22] Zabriskie, pp. 214–215.

[23] The prose on 115 seems to be paraphrased from Nelson and Shriner, II, 505–507.

fire. This vivid night in which the books seem to live again will end abruptly—when the cock crows.

The city now is "doomed." As the fire spreads, the flames tower and take many forms, ("like a mouse, like/ a red slipper," and so on); they become an image for thought:

> thought, thought
> that is a leaf, a
> pebble, an old man
> out of a story by
>
> Pushkin   .   (116)

Here the subject is the *action* of mind on reality.

The fire of Paterson's mind feeds on the books of the Library. There is both enlightenment and destruction—a hint of the "cost" paid by the poet. We are nourished by the flames—

> . . . grubbing the page
>   (the burning page)
> like a worm—for enlightenment   (117)

But the flames that supply this illumination end by destroying us "(as we feed)." The flames have requirements of their own: "a belly of their/ own that destroys . . ." (117).

As he begins to list things touched by the fire, Williams again intones the chorus "So be it." Actual writings are burned or made illegible, "the ink burned, metal white. So be it." The poet calls for the advent of "overall beauty"—or "tatterdemalion futility."

> Come overall beauty. Come soon. So be it.
> A dust between the fingers. So be it.
> Come tatterdemalion futility. Win through.
> So be it.   So be it.   (117)

This is the poet accepting the cost, "winning through," celebrating the action of his imagination on a world given over to it. He accepts the fire: swallows it, chortles "at flames/ sucked in . . . ," calls it good.

The fire is hot enough to reshape completely a preexistent object—thus (as Williams puts it) to reclaim "the undefined."

An old bottle, mauled by the fire
gets a new glaze, the glass warped
to a new distinction, reclaiming the
undefined.   (118)

The bottle can represent both the world of objects and the heritage of the past (it was created once, had a function, but now
must be remade by the fire).[24] The bottle also represents the con-
version of a utilitarian object into a work of formal beauty—the
poet turns history into a poem.

As the glass cools, it is "splotched with concentric rainbows/
of cold fire . . ." (118). Now there is a "second flame," the trans-
forming power of the poem itself. The action of the "second
flame" on the actual flame is described in sexual terms—"de-
flowered, reflowered"—which provide a punning elaboration of
Williams's argument that a new "flower" (beauty) emerges from
the assault of the fire. The central notion of a man like a city and
a woman like a flower reappears; the poet's male force attacks
and transfigures the female.

The "second flame" explains the challenge issued by the poet:
"Hell's fire. Fire. Sit your horny ass/ down. What's your game?
Beat you/ at your own game, Fire. Outlast you. . . ." Williams
cites the bottle as proof of what he can do. The bottle, then,
participates in two orders of events. Literally it is a real bottle
mauled and remade by the fire, but the description of its metamorphosis becomes an instance of what the imagination can do.

As the fire approaches the Library itself, the idea of the Library
burning suggests to Williams the poems that have been burned
deliberately because "beauty is/ a defiance of authority"—Sappho's poems, for instance, "(or are they still hid/ in the Vatican
crypts?)" Williams plays with the subject of how Sappho's poems
have come down to us: "flying papers/ from old conflagrations"
used in mummy-wrappings to preserve the dead in Egyptian
sarcophagi. The "old conflagrations" are Sappho's passions when

[24] A very interesting analogue to Williams's notion appears in Brassaï's
book *Conversations avec Picasso*, (Paris, 1964), pp. 91–92. In 1943 Picasso
showed Brassaï a collection of wine glasses that had been transformed—
"created"—by the eruption of Mount Pelée in 1902. "Tous ces verres refon-
dus par la chaleur de la terre, c'est aussi beau qu'une oeuvre d'art, ne
trouvez-vous pas?"

she was alive, as well as the actual fires that burned the poems. The dead paradoxically "revived" the Greek Anthology, since its pages had served as mummy wrappings, to be discovered centuries later.

The poet addresses "Beautiful thing"—"you who understand nothing/ of this." Her beauty, the beauty of the present, though "vulgar," surpasses all "their perfections"—that is, presumably, the perfections of works now dead and stored on the library shelves. Dürer's *Melancholy* (gears "lying disrelated to the mathematics of the/ machine") illustrates the deadness and uselessness of past perfections. In contrast:

> Vulgarity surpasses all perfections
> —it leaps from a varnish pot and we see
> it pass—in flames!   (120)

The leaping flame, quickly moving on, represents the elusiveness of beauty; we perceive it (barely) and it escapes. This elusive beauty is not the world itself, but—Williams continues—"An identity/ surmounting the world, its core. . . ." Unless a poet comes along to capture it in language, the beauty of the present will be lost:

> Poet.
>   Are you there?   (120)

Searching for an image to make this argument clear, Williams thinks of a soldier heroically driving a bulldozer through a barrage (and back) on Iwo Jima—the action is lost (in a sense) because no fitting language exists.

> No twist of the flame
> in his own image: he goes nameless
> until a Niké shall live in his honor—   (120)

There is a subject, the soldier's heroic action, but "invention" and "the words" are lacking. This is essentially the same point that Williams had made in prose: "Until your artists have conceived you in your unique and supreme form you can never conceive yourselves, *and, have not, in fact, existed.*"[25]

Only the artist can provide that record or celebration of existence. The act of heroism is a fact, an instance of the flame that leaps out then moves on; but a poet must bring it into "existence."

Williams pictures the fire momentarily as a "waterfall of the/ flames, a cataract reversed. . . ." The comment "what difference does it make?" seems to mean that for the poet the fiery cataract going upward is just as much a challenge as the waterfall. The *force* is similar.

Williams's subject now is the *effect* of beauty—an astonishment, a foolishness. The poet "makes a fool of himself" for "Beautiful thing," and fire in this case is the passion of love, something spontaneous and violent, valuable yet feared. It is for the beauty of the present that the poet mourns the inadequacies of language:

> mourning its losses,
> for you
>
> Scarred, fire swept
> (by a nameless fire, that is unknown even
> to yourself) nameless,
>
> drunk. (121)

The joy we experience calls for a "roar, an outcry," but we can't afford it (another reference to cost); so we keep "a secret joy in the flame which we dare/ not acknowledge."

To illustrate the violence of beauty, Williams picks out a recorded instance of the action of fire: "a tin roof (1880) entire, half a block long, lifted like a/ skirt, held by the fire. . . ." This is another of the poem's wonders, an "awesome sight." The roof rises and floats, "riding the air"

> . . . clearing the railroad tracks to fall
> upon the roofs beyond, red hot
> darkening the rooms
> (but not our minds). (122)

[25] "An Approach to the Poem," p. 60. Followed in an earlier version of this lecture (Buffalo MS) by: "You have to be created, all of us, you have to be proved by your artists before living."

And "we" are astonished at the sight, saying "My God, did/ you ever see anything like that?" The reaction to beauty is summarized:

> The person submerged
> in wonder, the fire become the person   .   (122)

The *silence* of the Library has represented the hidden authorities, the social and economic interests that in every age have something to lose from the emergence of beauty. Now the Library's silence dooms it. It stands in the path of the flames, which now punish it for having contained nothing of "Beautiful thing":

> They spit on you,
> literally, but without you, nothing. The
> library is muffled and dead.   (122)

She is the living embodiment of that beauty which the poets, now dead, dreamed when still alive: "the dream/ of dead men." Her absence explains the silence and death of the Library. "Nameless"—she eludes conceptual language. Any attempt to explain her would fail without her aid:

> Let them explain you and you will be
> the heart of the explanation. . . .   (123)

As the Library begins to burn, the dead writers entombed in the books beg to be warmed by the fire, cry out "wanting to be chaffed/ and cherished." Once they were "white-hot" men—alive, and caught up in the passion aroused by living beauty. But their books are not flames "but the ruin left/ by the conflagration." The living poet sitting in the Library now senses the import of their death. The book is only a surface, "a nothing surrounded by/ a surface. . . ." A pathetic hollowness takes the place of the once living man.

A half-literate letter from a Negro girl presents a paradox: the books have a language, but when we read them we discover "nothing," their authors dead; yet here is a human being, very much alive, but with no language worth anything—"unable." The homemade language, "Tut," is a pitiful attempt to do what the poet must do.[26]

Dr. P. remembers going to visit a Negro girl, lying on a dirty sheet in a basement apartment. There he was "overcome/ by amazement, shaken" by her beauty (124–125). The girl showed him where her legs had been scarred by the whip when she was a child. Still in the Library, he tries to bring his mind back to what he is reading:

> Read. Bring the mind back (attendant upon
> the page) to the day's heat. The page also is
> the same beauty : a dry beauty of the page—
> beaten by whips.   (126)

The beauty of the page, like that of the girl, includes the record of having been whipped. The beauty is "dry" because on the page: dead and stable.

Williams connects the whipped beauty of the girl and the page with the beauty of a unicorn at bay, attacked by hounds—a tapestry scene, presumably here an illustration from a book in the Library.[27] The scene shows a white hound "with his thread teeth drawing crimson from/ the throat of the unicorn." The unicorn appears as a "docile queen," indifferent and queenly, (like the girl)

> in bad luck, the luck of the stars, the black stars.

The poet's work, and the price that he pays, are for the sake of this embodiment of distressed beauty—the girl, the unicorn, the page—"you, my dove, my/ changeling."

"Beautiful thing" appears as a girl at a dance, afterward caught up in a gang war and socked across the nose "for good luck and emphasis."[28] Like the bottle in the fire, she gains a "distinction"

---

[26] Compare "Tituba's Children," in *Many Loves and Other Plays*, pp. 247–248: "Senator Yokell: What kind of language are those colored kids talking to each other? Fred: Some sorority lingo of their own, I guess. Tut, I think they call it."

[27] Presumably a scene from the unicorn tapestries in the Cloisters, which become a main subject in Book Five.

[28] From "Patterson: Episode 17."

by being mauled. The section ends with a half-joking address to
the fire (and the girl) in the words of Billy Sunday's theme song:

BRIGHTen
                          the cor
                                        ner
    where   you   are!
                                        —a flame,
               black plush, a dark flame.   (128)

The joke is that the fire really does brighten a corner. (The revival hymn appears again in Book Four.)

The argument of section 2 has touched on the cost to the poet
of his love for beauty and his attempt to embody it in a poem.
Instinctively fearful, like the others, his impulse is to "extin-
guish" the flame and to suppress the violence of his own recognition. He has to overcome his own fear. In celebrating the
elusive "flagrant" beauty of the present, the poet sponsors a force
that inevitably attacks that Library which, earlier, he had attempted to use as a refuge.

SECTION 3

In the third section the poet recognizes the danger of being
drowned by the flood of words from the past, halts his search,
and leaves the Library. The flood that ravaged Paterson in 1902
provides the vehicle for an account of the poet's attempt to im-
merse himself in the past. The flood also represents death, carrying human achievements (cultures, works of art) "towards Acheron." There is, then a correspondence between the action of
death on human works and the action of the "dead" books on a
man's mind. A flood creates a "soil," in this case not a good one
but a field of infertile muck. This detritus represents the state
of a man's mind after he has given himself over to the study of
the past; it also describes the present cultural "soil" of America.
Old institutions and traditions are "fossils." If the poet stays in
the Library, he's done for; so he makes his escape.

Williams's distrust and fear of literary "tradition" are well
known. Eliot's "classicism" seemed an apostasy: "Eliot had turned

his back on the possibility of reviving my world. And being an accomplished craftsman, better skilled in some ways than I could ever hope to be, I had to watch him carry my world off with him, the fool, to the enemy" (*Autobiography*, p. 174). The "enemy" is of course English poetry. For Williams, the American poet's language is not English, though derived from it. Whitman, with all his faults, had chosen the right course in attempting to arrive at a language for poetry based on the language (languages) actually spoken in this country. The best thing for an American poet is to follow Whitman's lead, hoping to go on to discover "A NEW MEASURE CONSONANT WITH OUR DAY." This is the gist of Williams's essay, "An Approach to the Poem," which can serve as a partial gloss on this section. The poet must "invent," reconstruct, build anew. Though in a sense he competes with the poets who have already written, he can do so only on his own terms, and in a new form. Whitman's work had been the first step "in our formal regeneration." Though Whitman himself did not achieve a "measure," he pointed the way for those to follow.

Given the choice between staying within the rules of English prosody or "breaking out" as Whitman did, the American poet must take the second course. And so it is not really possible for the American poet to attach himself to the great "tradition" of English literature. But what about the past of his own locality? The answer to this is not quite the same, since the poet must know his own region in order to write about it. But Williams held that the poet can use the past only if he acts upon it instead of letting it act upon him. He can select elements from the past, but he has to supply a new shape for what he finds there. Paterson, studying the history of his own region, is struck by the fact that these men now dead lacked a language; they obviously will not be any help to him in that respect. In the *Autobiography*, discussing a small stone cottage Charles Sheeler had used as the basis for his home, making it "a seed of intelligent and feeling security," Williams wrote: "It is ourselves we organize in this way not against the past or for the future or even for survival but for integrity of understanding to insure persistence, to give the mind its stay." Sheeler's act provides an analogue for what the poet must do: "The house that they have set up (I continue to refer to the construction, the reconstitution of the poem as my major theme) is the present-day necessity" (p. 333).

A bit further on he applied the same principle to the contemporary use of Shaker furniture: "That is a feat of the intelligence, to transfer an understanding from an aristocratic past and from another context of thoughts to this context, the context of Shaker pieces, a New York Modern Museum, bad as it can be at times. To transfer values into a new context, to make a poem again" (p. 334).

"Again" is a key word in this section of *Paterson*. Williams's point was that the intelligence does not simply continue or repeat the work of the past, but must do something *new* in order to do "again" what had been done in the past.

We may regret, for instance, the passing of the Indian cultures or the early Dutch settlements of New Jersey, and admire the records they left behind; but for us they are not vital. Death's flood has carried the old cultures away. Given the deadness of the past, what can the poet do? He can't wait for an authentic living culture to form, though he may work indirectly to bring it about. The process will take time, and he doesn't have time; he is not working "for" the future. And so he must simply go to work, taking what aid he can enlist, but without kidding himself about support from the past. If he fails to act, he will continue to be the "dazed sleeper," puzzled and victimized by the roar of the present.

The Library, of course, has offered real temptations, and without those temptations Book Three would have no plot. Paterson had entered the Library with high hopes that it would provide a "respite" from the roar of the present, and even help him to solve the "riddle" of the Falls. But these hopes will not be fulfilled. The "winds" from the books were derivative, echoes of actual winds formerly present, owing their existence to the power of Paterson's imagination that evoked them. The books of the Library are burned-out shells, records of fires long extinct: the "real" fire of creation acts against the static order of books on the shelves of a Library. Now the flood exhibits in a third way the encounter of the poet with the past. The vision of the flood as death makes it impossible for him to stay in the Library. He has spent too much time with the books—with records of his own region, with "words" spoken by dead men. The attraction of the Library is understandable; but it is a dangerous place. When Paterson clearly recognizes the danger, the "real" rhetoric of the shout "Let me out!" brings Book Three to a close.

Williams once thought of entitling this section "The serious sermon—of Noah."[29] "Noah," of course, is Paterson's middle name (15) referring to the fact that he does survive the flood of texts to which he now exposes himself, and to the possible survival of his work by virtue of its freshness. The section begins with a dialogue on the best way to write:

It is dangerous to leave written that which is badly written. A chance word, upon paper, may destroy the world. Watch carefully and erase, while the power is still yours, I say to myself, for all that is put down, once it escapes, may rot its way into a thousand minds, the corn become a black smut, and all libraries, of necessity, be burned to the ground as a consequence.

Only one answer: write carelessly so that nothing that is not green will survive. (129)

The advice to "write carelessly" is the gist of the argument. "Greenness" is more important than care. The poet's awareness of consequences must not tempt him to play it safe.

The dreamlike underwater scene that follows locates us in the past, or perhaps in time, attempting to capture the past. An early version (Yale MS) locates the action "among the words." We are out of our element, deprived of the ordinary uses of our senses:

The ears are water. The feet
listen. . . . (129)

"Boney fish bearing lights" endanger our eyes, "which float about,/ indifferent," undirected by living passion. Then a puzzling metaphor, possibly referring to the odds against survival:

[29] In that earlier version (Yale MS), this section would have concluded the poem. See n. 33, below.

> . . . A taste of iodine
> stagnates upon the law of percent-
> ages: thick boards bored through
> by worms whose calcined husks
> cut our fingers, which bleed   .   (129)

The image of "calcined husks" prepares for the skeletons that will represent what we inherit from the past, the "fossil shell" of 142–143. Our movement through time is a walk "from certainty to the unascertained." We catch a glimpse of the past, as of the tail of a fish swimming away.

And now the flood begins. The Paterson flood, on which Williams's account is based, occurred about a month after the fire; it is described by Zabriskie: "On March 2, barely a month after the fire, the Passaic River, which, like most postglacial rivers, has an inadequate channel and valley for its maximum demands, became swollen from melting ice and heavy rains in the uplands. The lower city became a swirling lake, as the roaring water over the Falls nearly filled the Valley of The Rocks. The flood was one of the most disastrous the city had known. In the poem, it figures as antithesis to the fire, but at the same time, its identity is deliberately merged with the many later, less serious floods which have plagued the entire river valley."[30]

In *Paterson* the flood begins its work by quenching the "creative" fire of the second section; there is a "sour stench of embers."

The passage that follows describes the formation of the floodwaters as rain falls in "the river's upper reaches," and uses the gathering force of the waters to show what happens to Paterson's mind as he continues to read. The waters draw together, search, move things that are unattached. Among the things attacked by the flood are particulars that have already acquired symbolic meaning in the poem: the white crane that flies away, the lilies that "tug/ as fish at a line," then are pulled under, "drowned in the muddy flux." Here the lilies are a manifestation of the woman or flower, Paterson's wife. The mud drowning the flower is equivalent, then, to the "sour stench of embers": a destruction of living beauty by an accumulation of words and texts. The "well that gave sweet water," defiled by the flood, no doubt refers to what

[30] Zabriskie, p. 215.

happens to the poet's language as books accumulate. The second
part of the passage interprets the flood allegory: there is "a counterpart, of reading . . . ," the mind overwhelmed by a flood of
texts. As the lilies are "anchored" by their stems, so Paterson
reading in the Library is "anchored" to his chair. The stream
"within" Paterson—the river of his life—becomes "leaden" as it
is touched by the flood of dead texts.

> The stream
> grows leaden within him, his lilies drag. So
> be it. Texts mount and complicate them-
> selves, lead to further texts and those
> to synopses, digests and emendations. So be it.   (130)

Just as some things are moved by the actual flood and others remain, so "the words break loose or—sadly/ hold, unshaken."

In the meantime, men gather on the bridge and "look down"
at the scene. These are presumably the same onlookers who
gather to watch Sam Patch leap to his death.

The "So be it" chorus, repeated here, has Paterson accepting
the action of the flood, welcoming its destructive force. Later
Williams marks the flood's acceleration with a kind of chant, "to
the teeth,/ to the very eyes," "a sort of praise, a/ peace that comes
of destruction" (132). Paterson is following through, resigning
himself to the consequences of entering the Library. The chant
of praise has a different reference: the poet endorses and cel-
brates the action of death, finding "peace" in a recognition of
death's finality.

Among the objects that the flood carries "towards Acheron"
as it gathers power is one of the poem's dogs—literally, a dog that
Dr. P. had reported after it bit him three times. The owner, a
man named Henry, claims that the dog had never hurt anybody.
Possibly Henry's dog stands for recent American culture, dangerous to the poet—a "dog" he had to put away for his own good.

> A dog, head dropped back, under water, legs
> sticking up :
>   a skin
> tense with the wine of death
>
>   downstream
>   on the swift current   :   (131)

The action of the flood is interrupted and illustrated by two prose passages referring to earlier cultures, now dead and gone. First, the local Indians and their culture, represented by Pogatticut and his dog, buried with great ceremony. Pogatticut, described as a "man of gigantic stature," appears here as a figure for the giant Paterson, one of the forms in which Paterson had lived. The details touch on the Indians' reverence for the "local," for a place made sacred by its association with the dead leader.[31]

Also dead and gone is the old Dutch colonial settlement, with its customs and beliefs—among them superstitious variants of Protestant themes, of which the "curious" story of Merselis Van Giesen and his wife (133–134) can be an instance.[32] The wife had been sick, and during her illness she would see a black cat staring at her through the window. In order to kill the cat and put an end to the spell exercised upon his wife, Van Giesen loaded his gun with silver sleeve buttons (and so the dead dog is joined by a dead cat.) The story concludes with Van Giesen's assessment in 1807 "for 62 acres of unimproved land, two horses and five cattle," to which Williams adds the comment: "(that cures the fantasy)." The enumeration of possessions corrects the "fantasy" about witchcraft; these people may have engaged in superstitious practices, but their faith is clear enough; they believed in property. So the juxtaposition of witchcraft and real estate symbolizes (half-comically) the "Protestantism" of the Dutch settlers.

Nelson's large volume of local history, from which the story is taken, becomes *The Book of Lead*, its pages heavy with death: "he cannot turn the pages."

> (Why do I bother with this
> rubbish?)   (134)

The "rubbish" comprises stories like this one, in which Paterson

---

[31] The prose describing Pogatticut's burial is Williams's, based apparently on several sources (Yale MS). The "giant stature" and the dog seem to have been added by Williams. Two of Williams's sources appear to have been Gabriel Furman, *Antiquities of Long Island* (New York, 1875), p. 60; and Ralph G. Duvall, *The History of Shelter Island*, (Shelter Island Heights, N. Y., 1932), p. 14. This material may have been collected along with other information concerning rituals and traditions of the Indians of New York and New Jersey—note the reference to the Kinte Kaye here and on 102.

[32] Nelson, p. 269.

had hoped to find meaning and assistance; instead he finds himself making sardonic comments in the margins.

The floodwaters appear as "Heavy plaits/ tumbling massive, yellow into the cleft,/ bellowing": the insistent roar of the Falls, exaggerated by the flood. "Plaits" picks up the image of the Falls as hair to be "combed" by the poet into straight lines.

And the physical force of the floodwaters is translated into a "recognition" of what the flood metaphor signifies:

> —giving way to the spread
> of the flood as it lifts to recognition in a
> rachitic brain. (135)

The floods have coursed violently through the city of Paterson; books and commentaries have run through Paterson's brain. And now the condition of his mind, exposed to the onslaught of the metaphorical flood, resembles the condition of the land after an actual flood. His thoughts have been knocked down, dragged along, soiled by the action of the waters:

> (the water two feet now on the turnpike
> and still rising).

What can he do?

> But somehow a man must lift himself
> again—
>   again is the magic word   .
>   turning the in out   :
> Speed against the inundation. (135)

The subject is *recovery* from the flood. At one point in the planning of *Paterson* this "again" was the "magic" word that closed the poem, solving the riddle:

> —"again" is the magic word, for it can never recur.[33]

---

[33] Yale MS. The concluding passage went like this:

The final passage:

> the act
> that links future with the past
> joins and envoices

He will do "again" what earlier poets had done for their own people.

Here again the implied argument parallels that of "An Approach to the Poem," where Williams had pointed out that the "form of an age" will not spontaneously appear: an artist must invent it.[34] In *Paterson* the rough progress of the flood forces the poet to hurry: he must do his work before the flood of texts, of death, overwhelms him (and his people). A passage of dialogue dramatizes the poet's desire to rescue the people of his world:

> He feels he ought to *do* more. He had
> a young girl there. Her mother told her,
> Go jump off the falls, who cares?—
> She was only fifteen. He feels so frustrated.
> I tell him, What do you expect, you
> have only two hands   .   ?   (135)

This is the poet in the role of minister (maybe), or social worker, or simply as Dr. P., dismayed because he is unable to "save" the people who need his help. The indifferent mother telling the girl to "jump off the falls" restates the motif of girls who "go to the Coast without gain," (die before a poet can express the meaning of their lives). That the man only has "two hands" echoes Williams's claim for the poem: "a reply to Greek and Latin with the bare hands."

The "speed" motif appears once more in the speakeasy rem-

> The riddle solved he walks into the night
>
> the river lies sleeping
>
>   (once more
> within its bounds)
>
> Solved!
>   —his mind at ease, the roar that links
> the old and new.   It is
>
> The present that links the future and
> the past
>
> —joins, (unites) and gives voice (to them
> Gives voice and) links them to the living
>
> —"again" is the magic word, for it can never recur.

[34] "An Approach to the Poem," pp. 60–61.

iniscences and anecdote on 135–136: an orchestra leader making
his getaway before the police arrive. (And the flood theme continues, as the man flees "into the mud along the river bank.")[35]

This is one more bit of the past that dies and is carried toward
Acheron, a fragment of someone's "good old days." So also the
reminiscences on 136: Williams's mother, perhaps, remembering
Santo Domingo.

Instances of the action of the flood at this stage:

> —the water at this stage no lullaby but a piston,
> cohabitous, scouring the stones   .

>   the rock
> floating on the water (as at Mt Katmai
> the pumice-covered sea was white as milk).   (136)

The current is so strong that one can imagine the fish "at full
speed/ stationary/ in the leaping stream." A progress report:
"it's undermining the railroad embankment."

The flood is a cataclysmic force, like a volcano. The sea covered
with pumice appears in Williams's story "In Northern Waters."[36]

The water and rock "cohabitous": a reference to the marriage
of rock and river, brought about here by the violent action of the
flood.

An equivalent to the rocks jarred loose and driven by the floodwaters is the jumble of phrases on 137, representing words
knocked loose by the action of the flood of texts as Paterson reads.
The phrase "All manner of particularizations/ to stay the pocky
moon" restates part of Williams's own program. Particulars "anchor" the beauty of the moon; and the word "pocky" is such an
anchor, its force of specification holding the beauty in place. The
slanting of words on the page imitates the disarray in the poet's
mind as the flood of words does its work. These are references to
time: today's date (January 11, 1949), "10,000,000 times plus
April," and "a red-butted reversible minute-glass." Death and
marriage appear together in a flower shop advertisement for

---

[35] In a typescript at Yale, the White Shutters passage is typed out
with penciled revisions: presumably Williams's prose based on someone's
recollections.

[36] *The Farmers' Daughters*, p. 258.

funeral designs and wedding bouquets. Williams jokes that "plants" does not in this case refer to interment. And the florist's advertisement keeps in play the "flower" who is Paterson's wife.

Another analogue for the flood appears on the next page in some reading advice from Ezra Pound. The letter, headed "S. Liz," complains that Williams has mistaken an allusion to someone's play for a recommendation to read it, and goes on to list some of the books Williams *needs* to read: the Greek tragedies, Frobenius, the economist Gesell, Brooks Adams. . . . Pound appears here as a spokesman for a brand of cosmopolitan culture, full of good advice to Williams whom he likes to treat as an uneducated provincial. The heading identifies the letter as Pound's, and also hints, "Well, the guy is a bit crazy." (Maybe he read too much.)

The drilling record on 139, quoted from Nelson's *History of Paterson*, answers Pound and marks the end of Paterson's "drilling" into the past.[37] The attempt to drill into the past has failed; there's no point in going any further. The drillers, looking for water, had found mainly sandstone and shale, all the way down, and at 2,100 feet had abandoned "the attempt to bore through the red sandstone . . . , the water being altogether unfit for ordinary use." The report goes on to speculate that rock salt may be present here, as it is in England in rocks of the same age. The equiv-

---

[37] Nelson, p. 11. The title "SUBSTRATUM" is the only thing apparently added by Williams. Martz (p. 152) interprets the drilling record to mean that the poet can find what he's looking for in this country. Martz's reading places heavy emphasis on the last sentence quoted, which speculates about the possible presence of "rock salt" here as in similar parts of England: "For Williams, it may and it will be found here, as he proves by giving in the final section of Book IV a recovery of the source: the pastoral Paterson of early days at peace with the Falls." This argument, according to Martz, also explains Williams's quoting of Pound's reply on 183: ". . . just because they ain't no water fit to drink in that spot (or you ain't found none) don't mean there ain't no fresh water to be had NOWHERE . . ." My impression is that Williams is not affirming the American past, but giving a critique of "tradition" as part of an examination of what death does to all things, including literary works. Martz's interpretation seems to assume that the drillers were looking for rock salt, and that Paterson has been searching for the equivalent of rock salt. But they were after "wholesome water," a metaphor for the living inspiration (or language) Paterson sought in order to answer the riddle of the Falls. The descriptions of colonial New Jersey in Book Four have a different bearing on the past, which will be discussed later.

alent of the water for which they had been drilling is the language
for which Paterson has been searching in order to reply to the
"roar" of the present. Like the drillers, the poet has gone as far
down as he can reasonably be expected to go. The drilling stops.

A typescript in the Yale collection reproduces the same drilling record from Nelson, with this comment at the bottom of the
page:

> Dublin spring ###!
>
> | | repeat this |
> | & the | unexplained |
> | *eels* | several times.[38] |

This rejected comment may have been intended to suggest that
the people would not have had to drill for water if they had paid
proper attention to the source already available. (On 198 Williams alludes to the water of Dublin Spring: "The/ finest water
he ever tasted, said Lafayette.") The poetic or cultural analogue
would be an attempt to drill into the past for what can only be
found in the present, or the attempt to go "back" to Europe for
what this country offered.

The drilling stops; and so does the flood:

> FULL STOP. (140)

Now the aftermath. The flood has left behind a deposit of "scum."
If it were fertile, this deposit would fill the role customarily assigned to cultural traditions. It would be the "soil" out of which
new poems would grow. But Williams doubts its fertility.

> —fertile (?) mud.

> If it were only fertile. Rather a sort of muck, a detritus,
> in this case—a pustular sum, a decay, a choking
> lifelessness— (140)

The stench "fouls the mind": so much for the flood of words from
the past.

[38] "Dublin spring # # # !" is typed, the other comments in pencil.

The poet, disorganized by his quest, looks around for a course of action. The mud left by the flood defines the condition of Paterson's mind and the condition of the language available to him. Old forms have been destroyed, but no new form has appeared.

> How to begin to find a shape—to begin to begin again,
> turning the inside out: to find one phrase that will
> lie married beside another for delight . ?
> —seems beyond attainment   .   (140)

It seems "beyond attainment" because of the present condition of the language. The destructive work has been done, but what presently exists does not provide a "soil" for poetry.

The use of "soil" to stand for the conditions necessary for poetry continues in the next passage, where Williams argues that there is nothing to do but "Give/ it over to the woman . . . ." The "woman," or nature, can create a soil in her customary slow way—a long process of "digestion," by which the fallen leaves "that were varnished/ with sediment, fallen . . ." are slowly transformed by the action of insects and decay (140–141).

Now an instance of fertility in a soil analogous to the land befouled by the flood: a white hop clover with cordy roots blossoming "massively" where "the dredge dumped the fill." This tough plant can grow in such a place: it represents the kind of poetry possible under present conditions. The hop clover is again the "flower" of the poem, as is the abused woman in the story Williams connects with the place, a farmer's wife whose husband had broken her cancerous jaw because she was too weak "to/ work in the field for him as he/ thought she should." (Another "practical" American, destroying what is of no use to him.) The short poem that Williams dedicates to the wife, "to entertain her/ in her reading," presumably corresponds to the clover with "cordy roots."

> The birds in winter
> and in summer the flowers
> those are her two joys
> —to cover her secret sorrow.[39]   (141)

---

[39] The short passage beginning "The birds in winter . . ." was published in *Gale* (Arroyo Hondo, N.M.), I, 2 (May 1949), 15, according to Wallace [C 428]. Its title: "Song, From Patterson [*sic*] III."

Now "—the edema subsides." Is there anything to salvage? What follows is an express rejection of the program of "saving" the past (or being saved by it). Williams refers sarcastically to the April-rebirth theme of *The Waste Land*: "Who is it spoke of April? Some/ insane engineer. There is no recurrence./ The past is dead." "Women are legalists" and think that they can save the old structures and adapt them to their own purposes:

> . . . they want to rescue
> a framework of laws, a skeleton of
> practices, a calcined reticulum
> of the past which, bees, they will
> fill with honey   .
>
> It is not to be done.   (142)

The work of the flood is conclusive: "The seepage has/ rotted out the curtain. . . ." The old cultural structures, the old poetic forms, are finished—and Williams advises himself and his contemporaries to "build no more/ bridges," perhaps an allusion to Hart Crane's poem. Instead of ambitious works of reconstruction, "Let the words/ fall any way at all—that they may/ hit love aslant." (This echoes the advice to "write carelessly so that nothing that is not green will survive.")

The "women" who attempt to save too much from the past are traditionalists like Eliot.

Accepting the destruction caused by the flood, the poet picks up a fossil conch and examines it.

> Here's a fossil conch (a paper weight
> of sufficient quaintness) mud
> and shells baked by a near eternity
> into a melange, hard as stone, full of
> tiny shells
> —baked by endless desiccations into
> a shelly rime—turned up
> in an old pasture whose history—
> even whose partial history, is
> death itself.   (143)

This passage elaborates an image used in the "Without invention" passage in Book Two. The *word* used to live in the line, but is "crumbled now to chalk." Williams's fossil conch is a noble relic, but the life is dried out of it, and it can represent death. (The "old pasture" may be England—and the "shelly rime" a pun on the name of the English poet.)

Here again the argument parallels "An Approach to the Poem," where, after giving past work its due, Williams compared old poems to fossil shells, the life gone out of them. True, the "monumental poems of the past" represent "the record of certain accumulations of human achievements; summations of all that is distinguished in men, the most distinguished, as far as we know, that those various ages produced. But those times came to an end leaving those works of art, those poems in their perfections, like complex shells upon a shore. Men lived in those poems as surely as fish lived in the shells we find among the fossils of the past. But they are not there now."[40]

Set off against the "women" who attempt to save old forms is "Vercingetorix, the only/ hero"—that is, a man willing to hold out for place and people against the forces of "Rome," a culture mastering and undermining the local (170). In the *Autobiography* Williams spelled out this meaning: "If there will ever come a prince to wake us from our modern utilitarian sleep, he may be from under a gray stone roof of Dijon, smelling of the grapes of the Côte d'Or where lived Vercingetorix, the last of the Gauls to hold out against Caesar. He was betrayed by his own tribesmates, as we all are in the end."[41] Williams's present line of argument, then, can be summarized roughly in this way: unless we recognize the deadness of the past, we will continue to be victimized by the forces of empire. In the *Autobiography* passage, Caesar represents those forces which are indifferent to the local (and, by extension, to the needs of particular *times*). The poet must be a Vercingetorix, defending the local (and his own time) even against great odds.

"Does the pulp need further maceration?" The question presumably refers to women chewing pulp for a ceremonial beverage—and here, metaphorically, to the formation of a language for poetry. Further destruction may be necessary before the dead matter of the past can form soil.

[40] "An Approach to the Poem," p. 55.
[41] *Autobiography*, p. 210; noted by Thirlwall, p. 274.

take down the walls, invite
the trespass. After all, the slums
unless they are (living)
wiped out they cannot be re-
constituted .   (143)

A slum is counterpart for a decayed language:

The words will have to be rebricked up, the
—what? What am I coming to .
                              pouring down?   (143)

That is: what am I doing planning for the language of the future? The roar of the Falls ("pouring down") still persists with
its challenge.

To develop a living cultural tradition—or a language capable
of supporting great poetry—will take a long time:

—in a hundred years, perhaps—
the syllables
            (with genius)
                        or perhaps
two lifetimes

Sometimes it takes longer .   (144)

Obviously, the poet does not plan to wait that long to get on with
his own work.

Into this argument, in which skeletons and fossil shells stand
for dead works and traditions, and soil represents the conditions
for a living language, Williams introduces two passages of prose,
obliquely thematic. The long account of Ibibio tribal beliefs and
ceremonies seems to mean that the past must be properly buried
or we will remain sterile.[42] Literally, the prose describes the
proper conduct of rites for burying warriors slain in battle:
"Were the rites once disclosed—few or no babies would be born,
barns and herds would yield but scanty increase, while the arms

[42] The Ibibios are a Nigerian tribe, whose customs are described in several
books by P. Amaury Talbot, and in D. Amaury Talbot's *Woman's Mysteries
of a Primitive People* (London, 1915), pp. 205–208, from which Williams apparently derived his information about Ibibio funeral customs, as well as
some of the language of this prose passage.

of future generations of fighting men would lose their strength and hearts their courage." The Ibibios' confidence in the efficacy of ritual contrasts with the present situation of the poet, looking around at the wreckage left by the flood, doubting his own resources. The ritual, associating death and burial with the principle of fertility and strength, suggests an alternative to the clogging effects of a dead tradition.

The second stretch of prose (144), a letter mentioning the murder of a woman, gives one more in the series of women mauled or raped or killed. The murderer will be out of prison soon. Another man, Clifford, who used to "follow her around," has been sick and is unable to leave the house any more: "He wrote to us to send him some dirty jokes because he can't get out to hear them himself. And we can't either of us think of one new one to send him." The anecdote parodies the "without invention" theme. The women in the poem who are beaten and murdered usually represent the American continent (the "ravaged park"); here the murdered woman is also the language—that language which might have "emerged" in America if someone had not killed the promise of it. In an early prose work Williams had personified language as a woman as he attacked the "idea vendors": "Language, which is the hope of man, is by this enslaved, forced, raped, made a whore by the idea vendors. It has always angered me that other classes of men write their books in words which they betray. How can a philosopher, who is not an artist, write philosophy in words? All he writes is a lie."[43]

The poet's speech to the "sweet woman" (144) must also have something to do with language. An earlier version of the passage (Yale MS) went like this:

> The cherimoya of Peru
> > The object of caresses is not by stealth
> > to overpower her but that she so enjoy
> > that she will turn about and ask again
> > sweetheart How like you this?[44]

"Three will seek a language to make them vocal." There is no

---

[43] "The Simplicity of Disorder," *Selected Essays*, p. 96.

[44] The "sweetheart How like you this?"—presumably an echo of Wyatt—was scribbled in pencil; it's not clear from the typescript whether this passage was originally intended for its present location.

sign that the search has been a success. The poet can't wait a hundred years for the muck and debris to be transformed into a fertile soil. Still, he has no choice: he must improvise a language to serve as counterpart and answer to the "roar of the present." He tried going upstream to the past; that did not work, and downstream is death.

> The past above, the future below
> and the present pouring down: the roar,
> the roar of the present, a speech—
> is, of necessity, my sole concern .   (144)

The roar, "unrelenting," witnesses neither past nor future. Other people, (e.g., Patch and Mrs. Cumming) had "plunged," deliberately or not, "to make an end." The poet does not want to follow their example. But it's not enough to stare at the Falls, "amnesic." He is like a sinner who must make a "replica" of the Falls in order to have his sins forgiven and his "disease cured."

> No meaning. And yet, unless I find a place
>
> apart from it, I am its slave,
> its sleeper, bewildered—dazzled
> by distance . I cannot stay here
> to spend my life looking into the past:
>
> the future's no answer. I must
> find my meaning and lay it, white,
> beside the sliding water: myself—
> comb out the language—or succumb
>
> —whatever the complexion. Let
> me out! (Well, go!) this rhetoric
> is real!   (172–173)

During all of Book Three Paterson has been sitting in the Library, and the three large-scale metaphors (cyclone, fire, and flood) have presented three ways of conceiving the poet's relation to material inherited from the past: to the dead men's souls, imprisoned in books. The flood—both as a symbol for death (Acheron) and as a flood of (dead) printed matter—has threatened him and forced him again to see the danger of his own situation. He must find the meaning in his own place, time, people: or else he will succumb. The last event of Book Three is an *escape* from the Library. He had entered the Library in search of a language, but what he found was that the past could provide no answer—with this realization, and the urge to get out of the Library, comes the "real" rhetoric of the shout: "Let me out!"

Book Four

THE RUN TO THE SEA

The fourth book describes symbolically the completion of the poem and the poet's "death." For this, Williams continues the allegory of a "river of life," following the river to the sea. And the course of the river also supports a historical allegory, in which life in America is polluted by the city. The first section tells the story of a young nurse from the provinces who becomes involved with a wealthy Lesbian in New York; the story restates obliquely Williams's theories about the inadequacy of culture and language in America. Behind the failure of language is that economic and social "stasis" which Williams held responsible for the poet's difficulties. And the subject of section 2 is the opposition between forces defending the "stasis" (e.g., Billy Sunday) and the power of "invention," represented by Madame Curie. Williams associates scientific discovery with the poet's act of formal invention and with pregnancy and childbirth—and the third section treats the completion of the poem as a "birth of Venus" from the sea.

George Zabriskie gives an excellent account of the geographical facts employed by Williams, and summarizes the main lines of his argument:

Book IV, "The River Below the Falls," deals with a river which has lost its identity in the poet's eyes. To quote the autobiography: "Flossie is always astonished when she realizes that we live on a river, that we are a river town" (Rutherford). From Dundee Dam the river flows past Clifton, Passaic, and Williams' home town of Rutherford. Prior to the 1920's when the Passaic Valley trunk sewer was constructed, the lower river was, in Williams' words, "one of the greatest swillholes in creation." Not only industrial wastes, but raw sewage from Paterson and every town below it, fouled its waters. Today, pollution of the upper river and industrial wastes darken its waters, heavy with oilslick. Here and there, among the marshes, the

ruins of an occasional paddlewheel steamer sink deeper
into the muck. After Newark, the river enters Newark
Bay, and merges with salt water. For the river, the jour-
ney to the sea is ended, without reaching that open sea the
poet desires.

Instead, we are transported to an unnamed part of the
Jersey coast, where the open sea

> —the sea that sucks in all rivers,

provides a background for the close of the poem, and with
the mind's return to the hanging of John Johnson on
Garrett Mountain brings us to

> This is the blast
> the eternal close
> the spiral
> the final somersault
>   the end.[1]

When *Paterson III* was published, Williams summarized the
argument and went on to describe how Book Four would continue the theme of the poet's search for a "redeeming language."

Paterson is a man (since I am a man) who dives from cliffs
and the edges of waterfalls to his death—finally. But for
all that he is a woman (since I am not a woman) who is the
the cliff and the waterfall. . . . The brunt of the four
books is a search for the redeeming language by which a
man's premature death . . . might have been prevented.
Book IV shows the perverse confusions that come of a
failure to untangle the language and make it our own as
both man and woman are carried helplessly toward the
sea (of blood) which, by their failure of speech, awaits
them. The poet alone in this world holds the key to their
final rescue.[2]

This argument includes both a defeat and a rescue. Man and
woman are headed for a "sea of blood"—by which Williams
means, roughly, a meaningless death. Only the poet can save
them, by discovering the language capable of expressing the
"secret" of their lives.

---

[1] Zabriskie, pp. 215–216.
[2] Dust jacket of *Paterson III*, as quoted by Thirlwall, p. 254.

Before proceeding to the action of Book Four, it will be useful to quote from some of Williams's notes to himself. One sketch in the Yale collection is entitled "OVERALL PLOT AND STRUCTURAL SCHEME: hint for the nature of a poem." Some of the themes from this early "scheme" appear in *Paterson IV*.

OVERALL PLOT AND STRUCTURAL SCHEME:
hint for the nature of a poem

There are two interchanging themes through whatever else, alternating, interrupted as may be desired, in sequences but always returning: The finish is a resumé in new terms—in the figure of the river below the falls: loveliness, the thoughtful man: the imagination and dreams take over the action, in the form of a serpent.
  1. The rejection of the religious, and
  2. The positive acceptance and use of knowledge
Asinine calculators who believe that one rich man and one poor man make two. Never. They remain forever unreconcilable [*sic*].

Over all the imagination, the dream. I accept implicitly that the subconscious is the whole substance of poetry, that the revelation is its purpose, lucidity, the penetrating introspection which releases the unconscious—is all loveliness. The extraordinary, the unsuspected: final result the miracle. Unless a poem be beyond thought new, full of amazing juxtapositions, a new pace a new and unsuspected order—it is not worthy.

Another page of typed notes gives a plan for Book Four fairly close to that followed in the published version.

    Flossie   *the* woman
Book IV   —   The River   (as it courses to the sea)

—the river also of blood (which is the actual of that
      symbol (?)

(Love) — the singular outcome of the language.

    Statement of the — confession, the peculiarity
        that is the personal: the individual: Beatrice—
        the humiliating (intrinsic) truth.

    The flow of factual history—alongside

The consolation of the river (below the falls)

The letters concluded.

Praise of the river: short appearances of it
    through the other texts.

What of Paterson himself, that solitary man—?

The river of blood (escape or attempted escape
    to N.Y. his return "home"

The river as a WOMAN.

Murder and blood. The crowd gathered to
    witness.

In the left margin near the top of the page Williams wrote in
ink: "The Old House." In the same margin, toward the bottom
of the page, he wrote: "Repeat the 'encounter' 3 times: variants."[3]

There is a page headed "Buffalo decisions re. Paterson IV"
that reads as follows:

Part 1   The young girl (Pat) and old woman (MAN)
          incident. Pat's letters to her Dad to be in
          small type (?) The PASTORAL to be incor-
          porated here. Trip to Anticosti etc.

Part 2   The "gist" (Curie) incident to "my son". etc.

Part 3   A sea (the sea) "of blood"—Begin with the
          first murder and end with the spectators on
          the Park cliff watching the hanging. To in-
          corporate the last M.N. letter.

(The M.N. letters are the letters signed "Cress" in Book Two.
Williams apparently did not include any such letter in Book
Four.)

A brief note touches on the river motif:

The River
(Begin with the long summary of the city's history—
rambling, to the *fall*, catastrophic, then—the lower river,
now.)

[3] All these notes are in the Yale collection.

The "long summary of the city's history"—or part of it—is used in section three. (This note may refer to a plan for the poem as a whole, not only for Book Four.)

And another page gives this account of the opening of Book Four and the use of the river:

A calm lies over the whole of this book—

an effete calm at the beginning
but revived by a "transfusion" at the end . The river
the foulest [gutter] in the world , next to the Severn

but a river, a to and fro river.[4]

SECTION 1

The first section introduces the subject of "bringing forth" negatively in a story of two unproductive liaisons. It is "An Idyl," using motifs from Theocritus ironically. There are three characters: (1) Dr. P.; (2) a wealthy New York Lesbian who takes the name of Corydon; and (3) a young woman from the back country of New Jersey, "Phyllis," whom Williams evidently considered a "female Paterson."[5] Dr. P. wants to make love to Phyllis; they talk, and there is a bit of love play, but this "marriage" is not consummated. Corydon, who has hired Phyllis to give massages, finally persuades the girl to accompany her on a fishing trip to Anticosti. In the meantime, Corydon reads to Phyllis a poem about the course of the river into the city, the river's pollution signifying the "defilement" of love by modern urban civilization.

Thirlwall commented on the course of the river: ". . . but the River has gotten so far off course as to wander through Sutton Place in New York City, far from Newark Bay, where the Passaic River empties. . . . The crystal clear River has been contaminated by the refuse of capitalist activity. It wearily empties into the Jersey Meadows, 'vilest swillhole in christendom.' "[6]

In letters, Williams pointed out that Corydon represents "the 'great world' against the more or less primitive world of the

---

[4] On the same page appeared the passage beginning "If I am virtuous/condemn me . . ." (160).

[5] Letter to Robert Lowell, *Selected Letters*, pp. 301–302.

[6] Thirlwall, p. 304.

provincial city." She is "informed, no sluggard, uses her talents
as she can. There has to be that world against which the other
tests itself." He had begun writing of the "old gal" in a satirical
mood, "but she won me quite over."[7] An embodiment of the
city, Corydon exhibits the traits Williams associated with the
American city: "retrograde," looking toward Europe, out of
touch with the local setting.

Phyllis, the "more or less primitive world of the provincial
city," is a feminine version of Paterson. She comes from the
Ramapos—the area used early in the poem by Williams to illustrate the absence of significant local culture in the United States
(12–13). She is one of the girls who, lacking a language, dies "incommunicado."

> —girls from
> families that have decayed and
> taken to the hills: no words.
> They may look at the torrent in
> their minds
> and it is foreign to them. .   (11–12)

The inadequacy of the two cultural strains appears in the
language: Corydon's strained attempts at the high-poetic alternating with embarrassed self-critical irony; Phyllis's rum-and-
coke offhandedness. Corydon's language is "cosmopolitan," eclec-
tic and derivative; she has taken over the "poetic" language of,
say, early Yeats, but has no real confidence in it. Her words are
inappropriate to her "audience" (Phyllis).

> —and its silver
> shall be our crest and guerdon (what's a guerdon?)
> drawn struggling .   (167)

Not dishonest, she writes in a "false" language. Phyllis's language, on the other hand, is provincial and undernourished.

The subject of "failure of speech," implicit in the main narrative, appears explicitly in the passage in which the "poet" addresses Paterson:

[7] Letter to Marianne Moore, *Selected Letters*, p. 304; letter to Robert
Lowell, p. 302.

Oh Paterson! Oh married man!
He is the city of cheap hotels and private
entrances . of taxis at the door, the car
standing in the rain hour after hour by
the roadhouse entrance .

Good-bye, dear. I had a wonderful time.
Wait, there's something . but I've forgotten
what it was . something I wanted
to tell you. Completely gone! Completely.
Well, good-bye .[8]   (154)

This dialogue is another instance of someone looking at the "torrent" in her mind and finding it foreign, because there are no
words. (Throughout the section Williams interjects phrases like
"what, I didn't hear you?")

The problem of language appears again later in the section, as
Phyllis describes to her father the trip to Anticosti:

It's wild, they say, but we have a marvellous guide, an
Indian I think but it's not sure (maybe I'll marry him
and stay up there for the rest of my life). Anyway he
speaks french and the Missis talks to him in that language. I don't know what they're saying (and I don't care,
I can talk my own language).   (168)

Corydon's invitation had been issued in an embarrassed half-
imitation of Yeats. Phyllis does have her "own" language, not
French, not an Indian language, not English; but it's not much
of a language and won't be until a "poet has come." That Phyllis
does not know what the other people are saying illustrates the
need for a language appropriate to American experience, without which individuals are isolated and mute, "incommunicado."

(Phyllis's whim about marrying the guide is no doubt a playful reference to the "marriage" between the American and his
place. A "marriage" between the country girl from the Ramapos
and an aboriginal who speaks French restates a theme from the
"Jackson Whites" passage in Book One: the heterogeneity of
American backgrounds.)

As representatives of the two strains in American culture,

[8] The passage seems to come from an earlier poem entitled "Paterson/
or/ A Slave of Passion" (Yale MS).

Phyllis and Corydon confront the elemental—or what's left of it. Talking to Phyllis, Corydon looks south of Blackwell's Island at the "three rocks tapering off into the water ./ all that's left of the elemental, the primitive/ in this environment" (180). The rocks are the primitive and permanent: both the native landscape and (indirectly) the elemental human faculties and needs. Neither woman commands a language appropriate to the subject. Corydon, continuing her efforts at pastoral, calls the rocks her "sheep" and asks Phyllis to be their shepherdess; to which Phyllis skeptically replies, "sheep, huh?" and comments in a letter to her father:

Today she was telling me about some rocks in the river
here she calls her three sheep. If they're sheep I'm the
Queen of England. They're white all right but it's from
the gulls that crap them up all day long.   (152)

A sardonic comment on "pastoral": what suits or used to suit the "Queen of England" will not do for us. The gulls are Williams's "mass," indifferent to the elemental—like the Sunday crowd in the Park.

The "elemental" also finds itself embodied by Phyllis's father, a drunk, to whom she writes letters about her activities, punctuated from time to time by complaints about his drinking and by admonitions to reform. Williams seems to identify the father half-seriously with the giant Paterson as "elemental character" of a place now generally deteriorated (150): "Maybe your family did once own the whole valley. Who owns it now?"

The plot illustrates a failure of love—a "marriage" that does not take place, as Phyllis refuses Paterson.[9] The story ends with

---

[9] There is a typed early version in the Yale collection, heavily revised in pencil, in which the Paterson-Phyllis encounters are rendered more fully and "realistically." In that version Williams emphasized Phyllis's *refusal*: e.g., in this scratched-out passage:

I desire you. I desire your consent. You have it in your
power to grant me the one

most exquisite pleasure one person can give another.
You love me?

Yes, darling, but—I don't know what it is. I don't do
that any more

—not with anyone.

the fishing trip to Anticosti—a kind of "marriage" of the big city Lesbian and the girl from the backcountry, and at the same time a "run" to the sea (Williams's title suggests the fish returning to the sea after spawning). In terms of the symbolism, the section ends "after the little girl gets herself mixed up at last in the pathetic sophisticate of the great city, no less defeated and understandable, even lovable, than she is herself. . . ."[10] The cosmopolitan principle of the big city wins out, dominating and perverting the local. Phyllis's inexperienced self-assurance makes her vulnerable. In a sense, then, America is headed "downstream," out to sea, and the poet recognizes this, at the same time that he attempts to "rescue" the people represented in this section by the two women. The degradation of contemporary America is described bitterly in the poem that Corydon reads aloud.

Corydon's poem about the city begins on 151 ("That is the East River . . .") and continues through 166, interrupted by dialogue and by Phyllis's letters to her father.[11] On 161 Corydon gives the poem a title:

. . . But here goes! Here it is. This is what I've been leading up to. It's called, *Corydon, a Pastoral.* We'll skip the first part, about the rocks and sheep, begin with the helicopter. You remember that?

On 167 the poem shades over into Corydon's invitation to Phyllis to accompany her on a fishing trip to Anticosti.

In Corydon's poem, the river entering the city becomes a symbol for human love defiled by the modern setting. The pollution of the river suggests that urban civilization has "polluted" the stream of life (and the course of American history), a pollution that Williams describes in metaphors of sexual mutilation.

---

[10] Williams's summary, quoted by Thirlwall, p. 264.

[11] Corydon's poem is based on a long unpublished poem, "A Pastoral," which starts out: "The 3 rocks south of Welfare—that is/ Blackwell's Island— across from/ *Durtle*—that is Turtle Bay and the eminence/ (East 51st St.) . . ." (Buffalo MS). Most of the important metaphors Williams uses in this section are to be found in "A Pastoral," which does not, however, seem to have been intended originally for inclusion in *Paterson*.

A helicopter goes by, searching the river for a corpse (161). The helicopter, a "whirring pterodactyl/ of a contrivance," stands for the imagination (or the poem—a contrivance), attempting a rescue of identity:

> lest the gulls feed on it
> and its identity and its sex, *as* it hopes, and its
> despairs and its moles and its marks and
> its teeth and its nails be no longer decipherable
> and so lost   .   (161)

The gulls, here as elsewhere in Williams, represent the indifferent mass: that from which the individual with his distinguishing "moles" and "marks" must be saved. The gulls "raven," tear the identifying flesh from the body; they scatter and survive.

The elemental persists, providing the energy that drives the helicopter. Though there are no more "woods and fields," or rather *therefore*, the elemental is "present, forever present." It is the three rocks, a focus on which the gulls "close again," having scattered before the oncoming helicopter.

In this argument, Corydon speaks for Williams, her poem an attempt to convey the "truth" about the city without deceit or ornament. When Phyllis comments that the poem "stinks," Corydon replies that "jaws would open" if it were in rhyme: but such "embellishment" would get in the way of "the measure of it." The mind must be kept lean, "fit for action ./ such action as I plan." Her action is a "brooding" wait to receive the deaths of the many—an expectancy defined in the image of a hand held up for rain:

> —to turn my hand up and hold
>   it open, to the rain
>   of their deaths
>   that I brood   .   and find none ready
>   but my own   .   (162)

Her "own" death—the death of the poet, and perhaps that of the city. "Rain" here reintroduces the water cycle mentioned at the outset of the poem: the waters, divided as the dew, form the river, which moves toward the sea.

When Corydon's poem takes up again on 164, "At the entrance to the 45th Street tunnel," placards designating houses "Unfit for habitation" recall the sign Dante had read at the entrance of the Inferno:

> *Voi ch'entrate*
> revisited! Under ground, under rock, under river
> under gulls . under the insane .   (164)

The underground entrance to the city: traffic entering the tunnel to emerge "never."

And the poem's "voice" cries out—this time a newspaper boy calling out "in the hubbub" the news that "love is begrimed, befouled ." The news, not to be evaded, cannot be disguised ("covered") by rhyme.

This "news" continues at the top of the next page, where the river (as love) enters the city and suffers a "sea-change," losing its identity, like the body preyed on by gulls.[12]

> shorn of its eyes and its hair
> its teeth kicked out . a bitter submersion
> in darkness .   (165)

It becomes a "gelding, not to be/ listed ."

The river, mutilated and deprived of its character as it enters the city, suggests the fate of the people heading into the tunnel. The mutilation renders them "fit to/ serve. . . ." (In the river, "vermin trout" look up through the "dazzle," searching for salmon eggs: an anticipation of "predatory minds" of the next passage.)

Now, in a parody of sex, the skyscraper elevators become symbols for the act of making money: huge impersonal phalluses, "sliding" up and down in the tall buildings where the "money's made," a mechanized act of generation. "Unmoved," the people in the elevators are paradoxically in violent motion, as the elevators move rapidly up and down like "directed missiles."

---

[12] No doubt an echo of the "sea-change" in the song from *The Tempest*: "Those are pearls that were his eyes. . . ."

> While in the tall
> buildings (sliding up and down) is where
> the money's made
> up and down
> directed missiles
> in the greased shafts of the tall buildings .
> They stand torpid in cages, in violent motion
> unmoved
> but alert!
> predatory minds, un-
> affected
> UNINCONVENIENCED
> unsexed, up
> and down (without wing motion) This is how
> the money's made   .   using such plugs.   (165)

"Unmoved" and "unaffected": deprived of their affections, yet "alert," as they must be to do their job.

They lack even sexual identity: "packed woman to/ woman (or man to woman, what's the difference?)." Their faces lack a "recognizable/ outline," the flesh gone to "fat or gristle," each face fixed in a "mould/ for all faces (canned fish)." Eating sandwiches and reading the paper they talk excitedly of the corpse that resembles them in its lack of distinguishing features:

> the flesh a
> flesh of tears and fighting gulls   .   (166)

Corydon exclaims:

> Oh I could cry!
> cry upon your young shoulder for what I know.
> I feel so alone .   (166)

What she "knows" is the mutilation of the individual, the indifference of the mass, her own solitude.

The rest of section 1 completes the two "love" stories. Phyllis refuses Paterson and agrees to accompany Corydon on the trip to Anticosti. Corydon asks Phyllis about her men:

> Have any of these man
> you speak of . ?
> —and has he?
> No.   (169–170)

No "marriage" has taken place. What does take place, perhaps, is a perverse "marriage" between Phyllis and Corydon: allegorically, the absorption of the provincial town by the modern city.

SECTION 2

The second section presents several analogues for what the poet does when he "invents."

The chief analogue is the discovery of radium by the Curies, an instance of scientific discovery that Williams uses to represent all discovery. As he begins to tell about Madame Curie's investigations, he feeds in prose material illustrating exploration, research, discovery—a letter from Allen Ginsberg, for instance, in which the younger poet describes his exploration of the city of Paterson and tells about his work in progress. A passage clipped from a medical journal illustrates the study of disease. And Williams quotes Columbus's journal entry for Friday, October 12, recording the discovery of America. In addition to these instances of investigation and discovery, there are several metaphorical elaborations. The process of discovery is an application of "love," the "sledge that smashes the atom" (177). Discovery can therefore be described in sexual terms, and Williams works out an analogy between sexual generation and the gestation and "birth" of an idea. And modern chemistry gives Williams a good instance of mind's predictive power: the atomic tables of Mendeleev, "the elements laid/ out by molecular weight, identity/ predicted before found!"

Williams seems to have had three main discoveries in mind as he worked out the plan for Book Four:

> The lecture on uranium (Curie), the splitting of the atom (first time explained to *me*) has a literary meaning . . . in the splitting of the foot . . . (sprung meter of Hopkins) and consequently is connected thereby to human life or death. . . .
> Three discoveries here: 1. radium. 2. poet's discovery of modern idiom. 3. political scientist's discovery of a cure for economic ills.[13]

[13] Thirlwall, p. 273.

He treats the discovery of radium at length in the account of Madame Curie's work; the "discovery of a cure for economic ills" appears in the full-page advertisement printed on 181. As far as I can see there is no reference to Hopkins, but Ginsberg's letter bears on the "discovery of modern idiom," and the topic is implicit throughout the section.

The act of discovery is set off against death and the loss of identity. The forces responsible for present conditions are summed up and symbolized by "money," to which Williams opposes the concept of "credit," an expression in economic terms of " 'the radiant gist' against all that/ scants our lives" (186). Money is the "cancer" eating at society. Credit is that which must be liberated. Like radium, it can "cure" us.

The section begins with Williams's account of taking his son to a lecture on atomic fission, in the hope of discovering an "interest" on the boy's part. "Interest" in quotation marks: he wanted to find out whether the boy was "interested," and also to establish a fund of knowledge that would "draw interest." Later Williams argues that dissonance leads to discovery "if you are interested."

The lecture that Williams is remembering took place in the hospital Solarium, and for Williams the hospital serves to locate the struggle between the human mind and death. In his notes Williams observed that the typical disease in the hospital was cancer, of which his father had died: "I think we'll get it in the next 25 years."[14]

Noting that the boy's mother misses the "pure poem" of the earlier sections, Williams quickly gives the lecture something of a "poetic" setting, and introduces the figure of Artemis, the midwife.[15]

---

[14] Scribbled notes for Book Four in the Yale collection:

Cancer : the typical disease
in the same hospital   —
                                          my father
                                          died of it

    I think we'll get it in
the next 25 years

[15] Davenport, p. 189.

> The moon was in its first quarter.
> As we approached the hospital
> the air above it, having taken up
> the glow through the glass roof
> seemed ablaze, rivalling night's queen.   (171)

The light from the hospital "rivals" the light of the moon; and
the illumined air above the glass roof stands for intellectual "enlightenment." The scene associates light with paternity and discovery: a propitious setting for a birth, and here the "birth" is
the discovery of radium, as Williams begins to tell the story of
Madame Curie's career.

Williams interrupts the opening scene with a passage compar-
ing the poet's act to that of the scientist who "smashes" the atom.
The "world" appears as a "fetid womb, a sump": that is, roughly,
the modern scene described in the first section.

In an earlier version of the opening passage Williams treated
the Curies' work as a renewal of the alchemists' attempt to trans-
mute metals:

> The night he took his elder son
> to the lighted solarium above the hospital
> to hear the talk on Curie and Radium
> —the preliminaries interest him most the
> transmutation of metals: alchemy
> redeivivus—and the unforseen modern
> physico-chemical status: a bastard word.[16]   (Yale MS)

A "bastard word": a reminder of the limitations of the categories
available to us, and of the poet's responsibility to renew the
language.

Williams first has Madame Curie appear as a public figure—a
"movie queen," receiving international acclaim, "a drug" (as
experience is a "drug"). And he sketches a comic scene in which
the evangelist Billy Sunday summons the scientist to the stage:
"Come up Sister and be/ saved. . . ."

The point, of course, is the contrast between the actual process
of discovery and the public celebration of it, a celebration in

---

[16] This passage appears in a file of material for Book Three. There are
other versions of the argument of Book Four, section 2, including one with
a fuller and somewhat clearer account of the Curies' life and work.

which there is an element of incomprehension and bad faith. The Curies carried out their work without much public support, and at great "cost" to themselves. Once the discovery has been publicized, a "crowd" gathers, as it does for Patch's leap.

In this argument, Billy Sunday represents the forces opposed to discovery, though in the imaginary scene pretending to honor it. The behavior attributed to him in the labor struggles of the early part of the century fits him for this role. He held a large revival in Paterson in 1915, following the big strike. According to Upton Sinclair and others, the purpose of the revival had been to undermine "the radical union movement," and Williams evidently accepted this judgment, along with the rumor that Sunday was paid by the owners to break strikes:

> . to "break" the strike
> and put those S. O. B.'s in their places, be
> Geezus, by calling them to God![17]   (173)

Paid to hamper the union movement, Sunday can illustrate the way in which the profit motive works in this society to prevent adaptive change—like Williams's "scholars," he is a mask for the special interests. In the name of religion and harmony, he works to maintain the divisions and privileges of the "stasis."

Williams has a couple of jokes at Sunday's expense, describes him standing on the table to sing, and offers a parallel between strike-breaking and splitting the atom. Sunday is a "split personality"—that is, he split the "atom of bitterness" (the strike), split "the plate" (as baseball player), and also split the take, allegedly receiving $27,000 for his efforts on behalf of the factory owners.

"Brighten/ . . the corner where you/are!" was one of the

---

[17] One of Sunday's assistants explained how the message affected labor relations: "The great gospel of Jesus Christ finding its way into the hearts of men makes man love man, makes capital appreciate labor and labor appreciate capital. Labor agitation disappears in some places because of the meetings in the plants and factories. That is its moral and economic value. In some places strike agitation has been eliminated altogether." A critic, Rabbi Stephen S. Wise, called Sunday "the greatest theological strike breaker in history" (McLoughlin, *Billy Sunday Was His Real Name* [Chicago, 1955], pp. 236–237). Sinclair's accusation appeared in *The Profits of Religion* (Pasadena, 1918), p. 210.

songs used by Sunday at the great revival meetings, a kind of theme song; Williams had used it earlier to conclude the celebration of "Beautiful thing" (128). Here the song is both a trademark for Sunday and a move back to the subject of Madame Curie's work, which is an instance of the flamelike "Beautiful thing."

Williams's account of Madame Curie (172, 175–179) emphasizes her poverty and the determination with which she prepared herself for scientific work despite the poverty. "For years a nurse-girl" (172): before she came to Paris, she had worked in Poland as a governess and tutor in a wealthy family to enable her sister to complete her medical training in Paris, part of an arrangement in which her sister was later to help her. Williams picks out a few details of her life as a student in Paris.

The hardships undergone by Madame Curie illustrate the "cost" of discovery, a "cost" inherent in the work of any discoverer, but exaggerated by society's indifference to the point that good work may be nearly impossible. The conditions under which the Curies carried out their investigations could have been more favorable if the French authorities had shown more interest, and Williams touches on these conditions briefly as he describes the work that led to the discovery of radium:

> .   in the old shed used
> by the medical students for dissections.
> Winter. Snow through the cracks.   (177)

(At that point Williams quickly links Madame Curie with another "pauvre étudiant," Villon—both discoverers, both leaving a "legacy" [178].)

One theme, then, in Williams's retelling of the discovery of radium, is the public neglect of those capable of doing original work, a neglect that to Williams seemed a form of conspiracy.[18]

[18] In this connection it is worth quoting from Williams's statement at the end of *A Novelette and Other Prose, 1921–1931*: "Living in a backward country, as all which are products of the scientific and philosophic centuries must be, I am satisfied, since I prefer not to starve, to live by the practice of medicine, which combines the best features of both science and philosophy with that imponderable and enlightening element, disease, unknown in its normality to either. But, like Pasteur, when he was young, or anyone else who has something to do, I wish I had more money for my literary experiments" (*Imaginations*, pp. 362–363).

The social and economic basis for this neglect will be the subject
of the concluding passage of this section.

A second main theme is the analogy between discovery and
"love," or discovery as a form of love. Williams describes Madame Curie's mind, for instance, as she prepares for her life's
work:

> —a furnace, a cavity aching
> toward fission; a hollow,
> a woman waiting to be filled.   (176)

Her "idea" is a pregnancy, and Williams plays with the notion of
a heavenly visitation:

> But she is pregnant!
>   Poor Joseph,
>
> the Italians say.   (176)

(Madame Curie was in fact pregnant as she continued the work
that was to lead to the discovery of radium: as Williams has it,
"—with ponderous belly, full/ of thought!" [177].)

Toward the beginning of the account Williams lists some of
the miscellaneous elements that had prepared for the discovery:

> —a luminosity of elements, the
> current leaping!
> Pitchblende from Austria, the
> valence of Uranium, inexplicably
> increased. Curie, the man, gave up
> his work to buttress her.   (176)

Pitchblende, of course, was the "ore" from which extremely small
quantities of radium were finally extracted. The actual discovery
is described a couple of pages later: the months of hard work, the
apparent failure, the "stain at the bottom of the retort,"

> ... And then, returning in the
> night, to find it   .
>   LUMINOUS!   (178)

There follows a metaphorical elaboration of the concept of "discovery," using the Curies' work as the point of departure. The central analogy is sexual.

> not half asleep
> waiting for the sun to part the labia
> of shabby clouds   .   but a man (or
> a woman) achieved
> > flagrant!
> adept at thought, playing the words
> following a table which is the synthesis
> of thought, a symbol that is to him,
> sun up! a Mendelief, the elements laid
> out by molecular weight, identity
> predicted before found![19]   (179)

Discovery is prepared for, Williams argues, by the perception of a "dissonance" (176) and a recognition of what the dissonance means. The recognition that old forms do not explain all the facts forces us to devise a new form. And this is what Mendeleev, for instance, had done (179), in working out the periodic law, which was an intellectual breakthrough, a new form, even capable of predicting successfully what would be found later.

The point is that discovery cannot be simply a matter of waiting and gathering evidence, though that is part of it. Discovery or invention requires a "flagrance," an act of intellectual love. An order like that supplied by Mendeleev does more than summarize what is already known; it supplies an instrument for making further discoveries.

By extension this applies to what the poet does, restating in a new context the argument of the "Without invention . . ." passage in Book Two. The poet's material does not supply him with a form. The poet invents the form, which the material then fits if the form works properly.

The principle of order may become in turn the basis of what Williams calls "empire."

[19] In an earlier version the passage "not half asleep," appears as part of a much longer passage, beginning: "And love? Bitterly contesting, waiting/ that the mind shall declare itself, not/ in dreams, not half asleep waiting for the sun/ to part the labia of shabby clouds—but. . . ." For the significance of Mendeleev, see *Selected Letters*, p. 243.

> Ah Madame!
> this is order, perfect and controlled
> on which empires, alas, are built.   (179)

"Alas," because a principle of order, once fixed, may die and impose itself by the weight of tradition.

In this scheme, then, Madame Curie appears as a great innova-
tor and renewer—not indifferent to the work of the past, but alert
to what could not be fitted into the inherited molds.

If the old schemes continued to work, no discovery would be
necessary or possible; but new facts appear, to undermine the
existing "empire":

> But there may issue, a contaminant,
> some other metal radioactive
> a dissonance, unless the table lie,
> may cure the cancer   .   must
> lie in that ash   .   Helium plus, plus
> what? Never mind, but plus . . a
> woman, a small Polish baby-nurse
> unable   .   (179)

The mind itself is the last necessary cause or ingredient. "Unless
the table lie"—that is, if the order predicts accurately, we'll discover precisely that new element which is needed to "cure the
cancer." The "ash" is the ore, pitchblende, from which radium
will be drawn (176: helium the "pregnant ash," of which hy-
drogen is "the flame").

The mind is the source of strength— but paradoxically "unable," since it cannot affect directly the course of the world. Still,
it is the "most powerful connective,"

> a bead linking
> continents, brow and toe.   (179)

Williams speaks of the uranium atom as a "city in itself," and
then reverses the analogy, so that the city appears as the complex
atom uranium, breaking down ultimately to lead (178). In this
way, the decay of a uranium atom parallels the "course" of the
city, its final stage a condition of inertness and death. (Compare
the leaden flood and *The Book of Lead*" in Book Three.) But
uranium also gives off an element (radium) that will reveal itself

"to an exposed plate." And so, the analogy suggests, the decaying city may give off something "luminous" which the poet can register, and which (by a twist in the analogy) can perhaps be used to cure our "city."

The three passages of prose interrupting this account all touch obliquely on the subject of discovery.

(*a*) The two-and-a-half page letter from a young poet presents the poet's "descendant," who has "got the gist" of what the poet has been saying (173–175). The poet, Allen Ginsberg, introduces himself and discusses his projects: he is "gestating." Ginsberg's program for himself includes "a renewal of human objectivity which I take to be ultimately identical with no ideas but in things." He speaks of inheriting Williams's experience "in his struggle to love and know his own world-city." (In a letter written in 1952 Williams said that Ginsberg was "coming to personify the place for me.")[20]

(*b*) An example of discovery in medicine, or rather the process of search, appears in the report of a case (177)—a nurse tested and found to carry "salmonella montivideo"—evidently clipped out of a medical journal (Yale MS). Williams includes a sentence on the method used in investigations like this one to eliminate the fear of economic loss: a detail possibly not too important in the original report, but here emphasizing the connection between economics and discovery.

(*c*) Immediately after "LUMINOUS!"—the moment at which Madame Curie knows that she has something, Williams presents the discovery of America, quoting from his own version of Columbus's account: "On Friday, the twelfth of October . . ." (178).[21]

[20] *Selected Letters*, p. 312. Williams encouraged Ginsberg and a number of the other "beat" poets, writing introductions to two of Ginsberg's volumes, for instance; later he expressed some reservations about their work, specifically about their handling of the line, in an interview with Walter Sutton (*Minnesota Review*, I [Spring 1961], 309–324).

[21] From *In the American Grain*, pp. 25–26. Joseph Slate points out that Williams's prose account was a careful reworking of Markham's translation of Columbus's Spanish Journal ("William Carlos Williams' Image of America" [unpublished dissertation, University of Wisconsin, 1957], pp. 299–300.)

The mind is "neutral"—neither a man nor a woman, but "at best" a conciliatory power, "replacing murder."

Sappho vs Elektra!   (180)

Sappho, the ordering force of the poem, is placed in opposition to the vengefulness of Elektra.

The word "replacing" suggests, possibly, a kind of progress. But the two forces are old, permanent. (In a sense it makes no difference that they are figured here by two women; but the entire section uses women to represent mind and its potentialities.)

In this symbolism, the moon or Artemis appears as the virgin sponsor of childbirth and "invention," the birth of the poem. Here she is set off against Carry Nation:

As Carrie [*sic*] Nation
          to Artemis
                    so is our life today   .   (180)

Artemis: the beauty of the moon, virginity, yet a principle of creation and order, the goddess presiding over Madame Curie's great discoveries. Carry Nation was twice divorced; she "smashed" saloons.

The annulled marriage (180) is another instance of the American "divorce" story—though this time there is a baby with which the woman can shock the "girls."

In contrast, a painting of the funeral of the Abbess Hildegard, showing the women singing, peasants kneeling, illustrates the "order" characteristic of another age.[22]

The "shock" of the American girls, for whom virginity is a moral convention, is contrasted with the beauty of a scene from a period when virginity was a positive ideal. The ideal may not be something we can recover, but the painting is another challenge to the poet, who must do for his own world what the medieval painter did for his: "as you may see."

The argument now turns to economics, as Williams reprints a cranky-looking advertisement proposing a new way to finance

---

[22] The Abbess Hildegard is described in Butler's *Lives of the Saints* as the first of the "great German mystics." She died on September 17, 1179.

government purchases (181). The suggested "National Credit Certificates" connect this advertisement with the "Social Credit" movement, or some post–World War II offshoot from that movement.[23]

Having described throughout *Paterson* a "stasis" attributable in part to economic causes, Williams now wants to offer at least the hope for a breakthrough. This hope is the concept of "credit." Implicit in the first part of section two, this concept now makes its overt appearance in the advertisement, set off against the quiet medieval scene of the preceding page. "Credit" will be the subject of Williams's fragmentary and metaphorical discussion on the next few pages, where he attacks (once again) the existing order, and develops an analogy between credit and radium. (In this argument both are "discoveries," both cataclysmic forces.) Credit is the power latent in money—

> "the radiant gist" against all that
> scants our lives. (186)

The reader may ask how seriously Williams means him to take the method of financing proposed on 181. The answer, I think, is pretty seriously. A general reform of economic policy, along the lines suggested by the advertisement, would prepare the way for reform in other areas. "Credit" would provide for the rebuilding of cities, for instance. In a general way, Williams's description of the blight of present conditions, and his insistence on the need for a radical remedy, are persuasive. Except for printing the advertisement, Williams does little to "argue" these policies. His verse on the subject of credit is a celebration rather than an argument.

Augustus Edward Baker provides a brief general account of "social credit" doctrine which may be of some use in following

[23] The specific source of the material on 181 is a newspaper clipping, originally carrying the heading: "DO YOU FAVOR LENIN OR UNCLE SAM?" (Yale MS). The sentence at the top of the page, and the slogan "ENFORCE THE CONSTITUTION ON MONEY" can be explained, I believe, by reference to Eustace Mullins's attack on the Federal Reserve System, in which he argued that the system ran counter to Article 1, Section 8, Paragraph 5 of the Constitution: "Congress shall have the power to coin money and regulate the value thereof; and of foreign coin (*The Federal Reserve Conspiracy* [Union, N.J., 1954], p. 11).

Williams's argument.[24] "Social credit" is the name given to certain doctrines expounded by a Scottish engineer, Major C. H. Douglas, in a work entitled *Economic Democracy* (1919) and in later works. Douglas held that there was "a permanent deficiency in consumers' aggregate incomes compared with the aggregate price of productive output. . . . The money distributed to workers, managers, shareholders, etc. in the course of producing goods is always less than the total cost of the goods as reflected in their final price. The goods, therefore, can never be entirely sold unless incomes are supplemented by money distributed in some other way than as a reward for productive services." To correct for this, Douglas proposed either a periodic payment to consumers as citizens, or the sale of all goods at a fraction of cost, "producers being recompensed for their losses by payments out of the national credit."

A version of "social credit" was introduced into one Canadian province (Alberta) in the thirties, where it met with mixed success. Orthodox economists have never accepted Douglas's theories, but Baker points out that many who doubted the validity of Douglas's analysis "or professed not to understand it, were attracted by his advocacy and development of ideas which he did not claim to originate."

Whatever the merits of Douglas's theory, Williams accepted a version of it as the basis for his critique of the present system.

Williams insists on a distinction between what he calls "money" and what he calls "credit." "Money," evidently, implies all the inefficiencies and inequities of the current financial system. "Credit" is the productive power latent within money—now concealed or imprisoned there. As the poet attempts to locate and release the meaning imprisoned in the modern city, so, here, the economist attempts the release of credit from the prison of money.

Money is a "joke," or worse than a joke.[25] To maintain the

[24] This summary is based on Augustus Edward Baker's article "Social Credit" in *Chambers's Encyclopedia*, XII, 630–631. Williams's interest in Douglas's theories may have derived largely from Pound; Davenport glosses this section by reference to Pound's writings on economics.

[25] A version of this passage appeared in *Poetry New York*, no. 3 (1950), 24–25 (Wallace, C 438).

present system is a crime, given the urgency of our circumstances:

> —do you joke when a man is dying
> of a brain tumor?   (182)

Several pages later (185), Williams uses the fact of devaluation
(gold and the pound) to demonstrate that financial conventions
are arbitrary:

> . . . joke
> to be wiped out sooner or later at stroke
> of pen   .   (183)

Since money is a contrivance, we ought to be able to replace it
with a better contrivance when one is discovered.

Set off against the convention of money are the "facts"—people
needing medical attention, for instance. Under the present system, patients are charged excessive rates, in part to support the
treatment of the poor. But what poor? At "$8.50 a day, ward
rate" (182). The present system requires adjustments whenever
real social needs are encountered. But the adjustments are at
best half-measures. Until the system itself is radically changed,
we can hope only for a series of half-measures, unsatisfactory to
everyone concerned.

Williams now attacks one of the specific consequences of the
money system, with the warning:

> And not enrich the widow either
> long past fertility.   (182)

The "widow" presumably stands for the entire *rentier* class;
"past fertility" is a punning reference to the subject of marriage
and childbirth. Madame Curie has been the key instance of fertility—and therefore someone who should be given "credit." Her
opposite is the aging woman collecting dividends.

In this argument, "usury" (183) refers to the entire system
based on lending money for profit. If society could grant "credit"
for important work, "usury" would disappear.

Credit is compared to radium; money is like uranium: it's
"bound to be lead." Williams shouts:

> while the leak drips
> Let out the fire, let the wind go!
> Release the Gamma rays that cure the cancer
> . the cancer, usury. . . .   (182–183)

"Credit," then, takes its place as one of the poem's cataclysmic forces; the "leak," presumably, is the flood of death.

Credit should go to the people who can do constructive work. The absence of "credit" explains, for instance, the old shed in which the Curies carried on their research. In this respect, "credit" is practically synonymous with intelligent patronage. A page later Williams argues that credit is "the Parthenon," while money is the gold Phideas managed to steal:

> You can't steal credit : the Parthenon.   (184)

That is, credit supports the work without enriching the individual.

An intelligent state as patron would "give credit" (pun) to Tolson and to Allen Tate (183). M. B. Tolson's *Libretto for the Republic of Liberia* appeared in 1953, with a preface by Tate. Williams may also have in mind Tate's "Ode to the Confederate Dead," and goes on to offer credit "to the South generally."

Civil War: a reminder of the divisive forces that Williams sets off against the reconciling power of credit (and of the poem). (The American Civil War is implicit in the reference to Tate and the South; the Spanish Civil War is presumably the subject in the middle of 184.) If we don't offer "credit," we may have internal war instead.

Obviously influenced by Pound's views on usury, Williams may be amused to find himself arguing like Pound: "Here follows a list of the mayors of/ 120 American cities in the years following/ the Civil War . . . ." The passage reads like a parody— of Williams himself, echoing Pound.

The statement on local purchasing power (185) is directly quoted from Pound, as is the prose on 183 ("just because . . ."), evidently Pound's answer to the implications of the drilling record of Book Three.[26]

[26] Yale MS. The Pound quotation on 185–186 starts with "In/ venshun" and goes through "renaissance cities." It's apparently a comment on *Paterson II*.

The notion of local purchasing power touches, by implication, on Williams's general view of American history as developed earlier in the poem: Americans as invaders from Europe, bringing with them alien habits and institutions. Among the alien traditions is that of European industrialism, supported by finance capitalism ("usury" and the rest of it). Hamilton's program, described in Book Two, had failed to take into account the peculiar genius of the New World. It is "imperial" rather than local, destroying the natural promise of the region around Paterson by converting it to industrial use. The Hamiltonian system exploits the wealth of the land, but fails to distribute it.

All of which has been argued previously, chiefly in Book Two. Here it is implicit.

The concept of credit offers a way to break through the conceptual prison in which, according to Williams, we are trapped; it will release the power latent in the New World, and in each locality. The section ends with another reference to the "radiant gist": credit as radium, the "gist" of the ore (pitchblende), the latent power, destructive of the old categories, creating the new.

SECTION 3

Book Four concludes with Paterson's emergence from the sea—that is, with a resurrection by means of the poem. This emergence is followed by a brief coda, announcing that this is the "final somersault" and "the end." Evidently Williams means to have it both ways. Something has ended; but something will survive. To paraphrase roughly: though the man dies, the work lives on.

Section 3 of Book Four was to have been the conclusion of the poem; and, since *Paterson* is the poet's lifework, its termination is an equivalent to death. Also, if the poem fails, it will be a "fall," and therefore a death like that of Sam Patch. Patch's fatal leap has come to represent both termination and failure; the "somersault" that closes Book Four may be a glimpse of Patch as he falls awkwardly to his death. (It may also be the baby's "somersault" before emerging from the womb.) Death also appears in several references to murder; Paterson's emergence from the sea is paired off with a symbolic hanging. The concluding section of the poem also presents the birth of the poem, a birth of "beauty," hence of Venus, goddess born of the sea. (The newly washed Collie bitch of Book Two was a version of Venus; and so, presumably, is the dog who accompanies *Paterson* as he comes out of the sea.) And the theme of birth is illustrated by passages of historical reminiscences—early days of the Dutch settlement near the Falls, and scenes from nineteenth-century Paterson. As he brings the poem to a close, the poet reflects on the nature of accomplishment, using the motto on an ashtray—"Virtue is all in the effort"—to indicate what he thinks of his own "virtue."

The conclusion of the poem is also for Williams an awakening. As he put it in a note to himself, Paterson "wakens from a dream (this dream—of the *whole poem*)."[27] This gives another twist to the notion of Paterson as sleeping giant.

In devising this conclusion for the poem, Williams evidently relied heavily on material written quite early (apparently as early as 1941). A version of the passage on 191–192 (from "All the professions" to "not one to escape. Not one.") appears typed on yellow sheets, numbered "79" and "80," with the date 1941 penciled across the first page (Yale MS). The same early typescript seems to have supplied the long passage of historical reminiscences (193–198): nine typed yellow pages in the Yale collection.[28]

The passage of historical reminiscences would seem to have been part of a long verse introduction to *Paterson* as planned earlier. One of Williams's late notes to himself about Book Four indicates that the "old city part" was to be an insert: "Remniscent [*sic*]: the old city part—as it stands (incomplete)."[29]

Two other fairly late notes can be quoted here: one is from a notebook in the Buffalo collection:

> The "sea" of Book IV is a sea of objectively (Chaucer) indifferent *men*: bring it back finally to *that*.
>
> *Not* the actual ocean—

[27] Yale MS. The note is incorporated into *Paterson*, 200.
[28] For a few details, see below, n. 36.
[29] It may be that Williams had this early version of *Paterson* in mind when, later, he described Paterson's trip to the Library in Book Two. The early version appears to have been an attempt to find meaning in the local past.

> *Note*—Book IV—In speaking of the sea as the river's end
> the old original end must not be forgot—all right about
> "the sea"—but it is necessary & true—April.—the 2nd
> murder—crowds gathered to watch the hanging—the sea
> is a sea of indifferent men.[30]   (Buffalo MS)

(The "old original end" is the murder and the "sea of blood.")

The other note reads as follows:

> Part 3
>
> To the sea!
> (The two murders, between two murders)
>   —a sea of blood.
>
> (the last M. N. letter—with permission!)
>   —via.[31]   (Yale MS)

The discussion of "credit" has just concluded, and a voice reminds the poet of his "virgin purpose,/ the language." The answer:

> What language? "The past is for those who
> lived in the past," is all she told me.   (187)

This answer presumably refers back to the outcome of Book
Three. Paterson's search in the Library had convinced him sim-
ply that the terms of the past were unusable. ("She" is apparently
Williams's English grandmother, who is quoted again in Book
Five, 239.)[32]

The sleeping "old man," Paterson, is about to awaken; the
poet is about to complete his work, to "give birth" to the poem.
But who ever heard of a "sixty year/ woman with child"? Death
approaches:

> the ocean yawns!   (187)

---

[30] A typed version of this note (in the Yale collection) is somewhat different. "Objectively" appears as "objectivity." Thirlwall seems to quote from
the typed version.

[31] The "M. N." letter would be another letter from "Cress" of Book Two.

[32] See *Autobiography*, pp. 4–5, and "The Last Words of My English
Grandmother," *Collected Earlier Poems*, pp. 443–444. She is probably the
"stout old bird" celebrated a few pages later (*Paterson*, 190).

(Yawns as the old man sleeps; yawns to engulf him.) The "someone" coming up the path turns out to be a party of Tories come
to murder the old man.

Death for Williams is a "sea of blood," and in the prose that
follows (187–188), a man is savagely stabbed with bayonets until
a pool of blood forms in his bed (the "dark bed" mentioned in
Book Three).

> After the murderers were gone, his wife and a neighbor
> took the blood out of the bed in double handfuls. . . .   (188)

The murder is first of all simply an instance of death, used here
to stand for the approaching death of Paterson. (Murder in bed
also corroborates one of the poem's allegorical motifs: the "river
of life" ending in the "sea of blood" or death.) The incident is
also an action of the "many" against an individual (and so the
individual stands for the poet, isolated and defeated). And it is
a representative event from the American past: the "stuff" of
civil discord, as a group of men takes the occasion of the Revolutionary War to exact personal vengeance. And, like so much of
the prose material in the poem, the account has the quality of
local history: a vivid amateur narrative, based presumably on
the "facts," claiming little except to be interesting to later inhabitants of the region.[33]

An earlier version of the poem's conclusion had used this murder scene to present the "sea of blood" toward which the poem
had been moving:

> [Andries], this
> is an old grudge! as they bayoneted
> him lying there. His wife scooped
> up the blood from the bed-top in double
>
> handfuls.   (Yale MS)

"*Finis*" was written at the bottom of the page.[34]

---

[33] The prose is taken from a footnote in Nelson, pp. 345–346.

[34] The passage was preceded by typed yellow pages on the river, not used
in the final version of *Paterson*. Williams (or his typist) had "Adrience" for
"Andries" of the prose account. (This is the man speaking to one of his
attackers.)

Paired off with the murder is an anecdote told to Williams by a friend who had been in the hotel business.[35] The key to this juxtaposition is presumably the "bed"; a "marriage," set off against the death (and "divorce") of the historical incident. In the story, the sleeping man and woman "wakened later, simultaneously, much refreshed" (an instance of virtue as "complex reward").

The short stretch of verse between the two prose passages expresses impatience: now is the time to finish the thing. But take it easy:

> . . . Virtue,
> my kitten, is a complex reward in all
> languages, achieved slowly.   (188)

As one friend gave the poet a usable anecdote, so another had given him an ashtray with a usable motto: "La Vertue / est toute dans l'effort," which now provides the aging poet with "a quieting thought."

> Virtue is wholly
> in the effort to be virtuous .   (189)

Williams has in mind what it has required to persevere and write the poem, but "virtue" is also in a sense what excuses the poem. What counts is the effort, not the quality of the finished work. The effort itself requires time and "connivance" and "convoluted forms."

To these qualities Williams adds another, as he thinks about a woman now dead, who had her own ideas on the subject:

> Virtue, she would say   .
>   (her version of it)
>   is a stout old bird,
>   unpredictable.   (190)

A sketch for a definition of "virtue," as it applies to the poet: patience, intricacy, toughness, unpredictableness.

---

[35] Nathaniel West. Yale version has: "That reminds me. Pep West told me once. . . ."

In the meantime, the old porcelain ashtray has been metamorphosed into the shell in which Venus emerges from the sea: a "sea-shell," a "glazed Venerian scallop."

The passage that follows is incorporated with a few revisions from an early version of *Paterson*.[36] It is a complex account of Paterson's attempt to "bring himself in," while attacked by "all the professions, all the arts," as a crow is sometimes attacked by small birds. (Williams had described such an attack briefly in "Sunday in the Park" [46]; and he had used the detail symbolically in "The Wanderer.")

For the poet to bring all that he knows together is to "bring himself in," and, in terms of the poem's mythical marriage, to

> hold together wives in one wife and
> at the same time scatter it,
> the one in all of them   .   (191)

As in the "Preface," the poet both unifies and disperses ("scatters"). He brings together as well as he can the particulars of his world, and he broadcasts their essential meaning ("the one in all of them").

This act of unification and radiation is the poet's "mastery," but in fact the brain is weak and "fails mastery," which remains an ideal, "never a fact" (191).

> Weakness,
> weakness dogs him, fulfillment only
> a dream or in a dream. No one mind
> can do it all, runs smooth
> in the effort: *toute dans l'effort*.   (191)

The job is too much for one man to perform; but the poet can reassure himself that "virtue" resides solely in the effort.

---

[36] Typescript on yellow sheets in the Yale collection. "1941" is penciled across the top of the first yellow sheet, but one of his "sources," Longwell's book on the Falls, was published in 1942. The passage incorporated runs from "All the professions," to "not one to escape. Not one." "You remember" (192) is added; there are some other changes. The pages are numbered "79" and "80," as though they originally belonged in another section; or, more probably, they belonged to a very early version of the entire poem, a version from which the historical reminiscences a few pages later were also taken.

Williams's glimpse of the president of Haiti occurred during his trip by air to a conference at the University of Rio Piedras, Puerto Rico. When the plane landed at Port au Prince, Haiti, Williams and his party "were allowed to alight upon a narrow boardwalk which had a high fence at the end, beyond which we were not permitted to go. The pavilion, or covered dock space at our left was crowded by natives of the better class, the political class, in holiday dress, come to cheer their white-haired president on his way by special plane to Washington with his retinue to negotiate a loan. After he had zoomed out of the harbor we were permitted to follow" (*Autobiography*, pp. 313–314). Earlier in the poem (26) Williams had used the plane's landing on water to illustrate the symbolic encounter of the elements air and water, and to touch on his family's origins. Here the president of Haiti with his blonde secretary appears as a stray detail, as Paterson reminisces, attempting to give a pattern to what he remembers.

(And the president of Haiti may serve here as another symbol for the poet—like Sam Patch, taking a "plunge" into another element, as, after appropriate ceremonies, the plane takes off "over the blue water." The crowd gathered to send him on his way is perhaps the same crowd that gathers to watch Patch jump, or to watch the hanging that concludes the poem.)

Now:

> Scattered, the fierceness
> of knowledge comes flocking down again— (191)

Knowledge is "fierce"; the multiplicity of all that he has known challenges the poet, comes "flocking down" now in the form of girls he remembers (a version of the "snows of yesteryear" theme): Margaret, Lucille, Alma; and "the cold Nancy, with the small/ firm breasts. . . . There were/ others": pitiable,

> staring
> out of dirty windows, hopeless, indifferent,
> come too late and a few, too drunk
> with it—or anything—to be awake to
> receive it. (192)

"Dirty windows," of course, suggests the isolation of the individual, something the poet ("pity for all of them") attempts to remedy. (In the first book the poet spoke of perceiving his own "source" as through clear ice, and in this section the river is said to stare through "thin ice" [193].)

These are Paterson's wives, the particulars with which the mind must deal, inarticulate and isolated, to be given definition and a "voice" by the poet who calls them to mind. All of them are now brought together as one, "caught"

> —shining, struggling flies
> caught in the meshes of Her hair, of whom
> there can be no complaint, fast in
> the invisible net—from the back country,
> half awakened—all desiring.   (192)

Imperfect individuals, brought to perfection in the "one" mythic wife of Paterson. They are "from the back country": like Phyllis, from the Ramapos; "half awakened" and "desiring," they resemble the women in the Park. The poet's job is to "fulfill" them.

None escape the act of synthesis:

>   Not one
> to escape, not one   . a fragrance
> of mown hay, facing the rapacious,
> the "great"   .   (192)

"A fragrance/ of mown hay": the smell of flowers cut down, by the poet who "gathers" them, but also by death, the grim reaper.

A page of notes in the Yale collection gives this hint of the significance of "the rapacious,/ the great": "Paterson & [something illegible]/ that instance/ (the big city) it/ becomes a woman/ (the sea)/ the rapacious/ the great." So, perhaps, the phrase refers to the sea: the final metamorphosis of the poem's woman.

The idea of women as flowers to be "cut down" had been illustrated in an earlier version by a page giving the names of flowers, arranged in special patterns.[37] The comments on the significance of colors (193) seem to connect with that notion.

---

[37] Williams had a page headed "Paterson: A Bouquet," starting with the key passage "A man like a city and a woman like a flower" (7), and continuing with a list of flowers (Marsh marigold, and so on). Penciled near "Marsh marigold" was "Part 3," presumably indicating Williams's decision

Purple signifies "wind over water": and so, in Williams's scheme, the mind's play over its material.

A prose passage (193) tells about the discovery of Peter the Dwarf's grave in 1885 by the undertaker, moving bodies from the cellar of the old church to make room for a new furnace.[38] Presumably this reminder of Peter's death is intended to support the symbol of the approaching death of Paterson.

In an earlier version, a passage on Walt Whitman followed at this point:

> Walt Whitman stood looking to sea
> from the New Jersey sands
> and the waves called to him and
> he answered, drilling his voice to
> their roar, with courage,
> and abandon—driving his words
> above the returnin [*sic*] clatter—
> word upon word . .[39]   (Yale MS)

Williams seems to have intended a partial identification of Whitman and his giant Paterson; and this identification is still implicit in the conclusion of Book Four, where Paterson emerges from the sea and heads inland.

---

to break up the original passage and distribute it within the poem: to Book One, and to what was to have been "Part 3," that is, to the section that concludes Book Four.

[38] Note in Yale collection: "Exhuming the skeleton of the *dwarf* in Passaic. See Kitty's note."

[39] Evidently at one time Williams intended to feature Walt Whitman in this section; and some of Williams's comments on the poem indicate that Whitman was still much on his mind as he completed Book Four of *Paterson*, though the explicit celebration is omitted. In one of the drafts Williams refers to Whitman as "my own man," and as someone who terminated an era. Another version (Yale MS) reads in part: "The greatest moment in the history/ of the american poem was when/ Walt Whitman stood looking to sea/ from the shelving sands/ and the waves/ called to him and/ he answered drilling his voice to/ their advance/ driving the words above/ the returning clatter of stone./ with courage, labor and abandon/ the word, the word, the word." In "An Essay on *Leaves of Grass*" (p. 26), Williams wrote: "There is a very moving picture of Whitman facing the breakers coming in on the New Jersey shore, when he heard the onomatopoeic waves talk to him direct in a Shakespearean language which might have been Lear himself talking to the storm. But it was not what it seemed; it was a new language, an unnamed language which Whitman could not identify or control."

Williams now praises the poem's symbolic river, which is "un-spoiled by mind," yet percipient:

> observer of pigeons, rememberer of
> cataracts, voluptuary of gulls! Knower
> of tides, counter of hours, wanings and
> waxings, enumerator of snowflakes, starer
> through thin ice, whose corpuscles are
> minnows, whose drink, sand   .   (193)

It is that principle by means of which the poet himself knows what he knows; it acts upon (observes and remembers) the key terms of the poem (cataracts, gulls, tides). It is an equivalent, in a way, to the poet's imagination; it also provides an image for the course of life. (In Book Five Williams mentions it again: "the river has returned to its beginnings," and the serpent has its tail in its mouth [233], a traditional emblem for time.)

Williams addresses the river (or serpent) because he is about to take a final glimpse into the past before bringing the poem to a close. The river can represent that operation by which the poet is able to "return" in this way—his "lucid retrospect."

A short lyric celebration of birth appears on 193: Williams "looking to the birth of his next grandchild."[40] Here, of course, it is also the birth of the settlement around the Falls—of Paterson. And it is the birth of the poem itself.

Williams's "Author's Note" had promised that ". . . Four, the river below the falls, will be reminiscent of episodes . . ." He now (193–198) offers an account of earlier days around the Falls as part of a final gathering and synthesis. The tone is appreciative nostalgia; the purpose is not to celebrate the past, but to give a sense of the continuity of life in the area, a historical "view" of the city, including notes from a younger poet about ramblings in present-day Paterson.

The historical reminiscences beginning "In a deep-set valley between hills" are from earlier material—evidently from the same early draft that supplied the passage beginning "All the

---

[40] The lyric appears in a draft for Book Four, with this scribbled: "William Carlos Williams 8/ 5 / 50/—looking to the birth of his next grandchild—." Typed on the next page: "August 5 (Suzie's birthday), 1950" (Yale MS). See *Selected Letters*, p. 316.

professions . . ." (223–225). In that version, the historical material appeared very early, with an introduction that begins:

> A little story of Paterson: as told by an old man—
> The city of Paterson owes much of its importance
> to its historical associations . . .
>
>   . . .
>   the birth and life of a city
> is like the birth, infancy
> growth and development of a human being.

Much of what now appears (193–198) is incorporated from the earlier version, with a few changes.[41]

The style of this historical passage, then, belongs to an earlier period than that of most of *Paterson*. This is an interesting style: quiet and matter-of-fact, with long lines and a heavy reliance on runovers. An old man is talking. In the earlier version his talk would have introduced the reader to the place, more or less as the descriptions and prose interruptions do in the first book.

One major omission is worth noting. The earlier version had included a verse account of Sam Patch, which is omitted presumably because Patch has now been treated in Book One. When Williams was working on Book One, he returned either to the earlier material, or to some of his notes, for details about Patch. Longwell's book on the Falls supplied some of the details used in the historical reminiscences, as well as most of the details for the account of Patch in Book One.[42]

The poem's "birth" corresponds to the beginnings of Paterson in the seventeenth century Dutch settlement near the Falls: a beautiful valley, still pretty wild, inhabited by Dutch landowners "with a toughness to stick and/ hold fast, although not fast in making improvements"; simple lives. Williams's attitude seems to be that despite the injustices to the Indians (Book Three), this

---

[41] The historical material (193–198) corresponds closely to nine typed yellow pages in the Yale collection. Williams penciled some changes on the earlier typescript presumably when he returned to this material to use it in Book Four. There are some reorderings, adjustments, and insertions; but basically the published version resembles the typescript.

[42] The story of the farmer and the produce (195) is taken from Longwell, p. 57; the comments on Sandby and Pownall (194) reproduce some of Longwell's phrasing (p. 15). Williams's use of Longwell for the material on Sam Patch has already been noted.

was not such a bad beginning—in its way, perhaps, the promise of a "related" culture.[43] And for a time the small manufacturing town of Paterson that grew up later, as a result of Hamilton's project, kept some of the beauty of its situation.

Zabriskie describes the change from agriculture to an economy based on manufacturing:

The idyllic section III of Book IV is built around the factory neighborhood of Paterson below the Falls, and the mills which were powered by the old Race. We first see it in its rustic aspect: then there is a sudden transition to the early days of the industrial revolution. Hamilton and L'Enfant's grandiose plans for an aqueduct to Newark, mentioned earlier in the poem, had vanished, leaving a small town depending on its manufactures, but still tied to the land. Already the mills were drawing a polyglot group of immigrants, but the Dutch farmers still had control of the countryside and stubbornly refused to speak English.[44]

The "quiet of those colonial days" is broken by one of Ginsberg's letters, describing his explorations in Paterson: the bars around Mill and River Streets, "negroes, gypsies, an incoherent bartender in a taproom overhanging the river, filled with gas, ready to explode . . ." (194–195). The younger man tries to bring Williams up to date, introducing him to the present form of his city ("Do you know?" repeated a couple of times). The letter is an attempt to communicate to the older man what it's like to be there, at these places, in the present: just as the historical account attempts to convey what "it was like," in earlier days. Ginsberg carries along some of the themes of the city's story: the mixed population, the symbolic "incoherence" of the bartender.

A page later the reminiscences are again interrupted: a newspaper account of a man's murder of his infant daughter (196). (Again, of course, thematic: another brutally abused female; and the murder is set off against Williams's celebration of the birth of

---

[43] But it also seems possible that Williams's attitude toward the Dutch settlement had changed since he wrote this passage, and that Book Three can be thought of as an account of that change—as he discovers that the past was not so "quiet."

[44] Zabriskie, p. 210.

his granddaughter.) The murderer buried the child on Garret Mountain—the "Park" of Book Two.

When the historical account resumes (196), we are in the nineteenth century, and the "old man" speaking describes what he himself had experienced: "I remember going down to the old cotton/mill one morning when the thermometer was/ down to 13 degrees below on the old bell/ post. . . ." In the 1860s, Zabriskie points out:

> the town was still one of tree-lined streets. The Old Town Clock, of which Williams writes, dominated the scene. Its spire was a kind of New England Doric: the building from which it rose had two unadorned wings containing stores, and an arched center entrance which was what? The Godwin Tavern, later the Passaic Hotel, was the kind of architecture which passed for "Dutch," like many other old structures. Certainly the heavy courses of brownstone, from Little Falls, or more likely, from Nutley or Belleville on the lower river, were of Holland inspiration. Quite often, however, the roofs betrayed an English touch. The modern city, seen from Garret Mountain, spreads past its political boundaries: the old town centered about the Falls, the Race, the Morris Canal, and what is now Broadway was a kind of limit. The Erie Railroad, now in the center of the city, ran through open country before it reached the Passaic River.[45]

Paterson in those days was a mill town, with bells calling the men to work, and a "breathing spot," a square

> > Well shaded
> by trees with a common in the center where
> the country circus pitched its tents.   (197)

Describing the old circus Williams hints at his own "show," the poem, devoting twelve lines to the "giant candles" used to illuminate the performance:

> The candles lasted during the performance
> presenting a weird but dazzling spectacle
> in contrast with the showy performers—   (197)

[45] Zabriskie, p. 213.

Since those days, the city has changed quite a bit: "Many of the old names and some of the/ places are not remembered now . . . ." He lists some. One section of the town, settled by Irish immigrants, was called "Dublin"; and if you lived "in the old town you'd/ drink of the water of Dublin Spring. The/ finest water he ever tasted, said Lafayette." The reference to the fine water is another reminder of the natural promise of the place.[46]

The visit to an earlier Paterson at length brings Williams back to the Falls. Stairs led "to a cliff on the opposite side of the river."

> At the top was Fyfield's tavern—watching
> the birds flutter and bathe in the little
> pools in the rocks formed by the falling
> mist—of the Falls . .   (198)

A quick move, deft and not obtrusive, by which the image of mist forming "pools in the rocks" illustrates the metamorphosis of water, and, by implication, the poet's act of "division and re-gathering."

The thematic connection of death and birth is confirmed (198–199) by two passages from Nelson: an account of the murder of John S. Van Winkle and his wife by a man named John Johnson, and a Dutch lullaby ("Trip a trap o'troontjes") which Nelson had used to illustrate early days in Paterson "From the Cradle to the Grave."[47]

Book Four ends with the hanging of Johnson for this murder (204). The lullaby is translated (in Nelson):

> pigs in the beans,
> cows in the clover
> horses in the oats
> ducks in the water puddle—

Something for which the Van Winkles can be symbols has been killed/destroyed.[48] The death is both a termination and a point of departure: it can be a new beginning.

Throughout this section Williams indicates that the poem will end with a death—the death of the man in bed, the hanging of the

[46] See above, p. 159.
[47] Nelson, pp. 103–104, 395.
[48] For Williams's use of the Van Winkles, see above, p. 37.

murderer, the symbolic death of Paterson. Foreshadowings of this
final death have appeared from time to time, and now Williams
admits the arbitrariness of tragic death, a device "to move the
mind."

>   a convincing strewing of corpses
>   —to move the mind.   (199)

Death in a poem or play exhibits a "poverty of resource"; and
war (the Korean War, for instance), demonstrates mankind's
"poverty of resource."

The crowd (*Paterson*'s readers) has gathered to see a man
killed: "as if it were a conclusion . . ."

>   as tho' the mind
>   can be moved, the mind, I said
>   by an array of hacked corpses:
>
>   War!
>   a poverty of resource . .   (199)

Williams is willing to use death as a showman might. Sam Patch
himself had gathered a crowd by risking death, and in the end
people came to watch him fall to his death. But can death "move
the mind"? The resort to the tragic scheme is a makeshift.

The irony is uneasy. Death is the subject (why else all the
literal accounts of murders?) but literal death is not what interests the poet. There are claims of another kind.

What follows is a complicated warning (to the poet himself, to
his people) to "turn back" from the sea, in a stretch of dialogue
in which two voices debate the question of whether the sea is
"our home."

>   Turn back I warn you
>   (October 10, 1950)
>   from the shark, that snaps
>   at his own trailing guts, makes a sunset
>   of the green water .
>
>   But lullaby, they say, the time sea is
>   no more than sleep is . afloat
>   with weeds, bearing seeds .
>
>   Ah!
>
>   float wrack, float words, snaring the
>   seeds .   (200)

The "wrack" of a man's life (here, no doubt, *Paterson* itself)
floats toward shore, "snaring" seeds, which bear the promise of a
future birth. It is the "word" that rescues man from death (from
man's own sharklike bloodlust). And in Williams's terms this is
true even if the individual dies.

Some of this is spelled out in a letter Williams wrote at about
this time to José García Villa:

A cold east wind, today, that seems to blow from the
other side of the world—seems at the same time to be
blowing all poetry out of life. A man wonders why he
bothers to continue to write. And yet it is precisely then
that to write is most imperative for us. That, if I can do
it, will be the end of *Paterson*, Book IV. The ocean of
savage lusts in which the wounded shark gnashes at his
own tail is not our home.

It is the seed that floats to shore, one word, one tiny,
even microscopic word, is that which can alone save us.[49]

In the dialogue (200–202) Williams is playing with one of the
central metaphors of the poem: the sea as the receptacle of all
rivers, and hence, death as a receptacle of all life. The river
"runs" to the sea; it is a "hungry sea" (201). Obviously, by this
logic the sea is the "home" of all rivers:

> The sea *is* our home whither all rivers
> (wither) run   .   (201)

But even if it "is" our home, Williams warns us against accepting
it. It extinguishes the individual:

> . draws us in to drown, of losses
> and regrets   .   (201)

Associated with the "hungry sea" is a form of historical nostalgia: a strong wish that the old Greek institutions, and "the
great theatre of Dionysius" could still speak to us. . . . But, even
in this sense,

> The sea is not our home   .

---

[49] *Selected Letters*, pp. 291–292.

We cannot live in the past, no matter how much we regret the death of old cultures.[50]

Several classical themes are implicit. The poet is warned to "Put wax rather in your/ ears against the hungry sea . . . ," an echo of the Odysseus story, with the sea as a siren, tempting the sailors. And the poet (or his poem) is addressed as "Seed of Venus."

The passage closes with a striking picture of

> the blood dark sea!
> nicked by the light alone, diamonded
> by the light . from which the sun
> alone lifts undamped his wings
> of fire! (202)

(Only the sun can survive immersion in the sea. The *light* and *fire* of the sun survive; and so, the poem. . . .)

Someone, looking out at the sea, perceives an object moving in the water and tries to identify it ("a duck, a hell-diver?"). The object is "Flotsam of some sort," Paterson himself, swimming to shore, where he is joined by "a large, compact bitch," who had been waiting for him, "lying/ under the bank." He gets dressed (work clothes, "the/ sleeves were still rolled up"), climbs the bank, tastes a beach plum, and heads inland. (A detail, girls playing ball on the beach, alludes to the Nausicaä episode in the *Odyssey*.)

In this way the poem ends; or almost. Four lines of prose report the hanging of "John Johnson," who had murdered John S. Van Winkle and his wife.[51] Then the concluding verse:

[50] Martz (pp. 153–154) suggests that the sea symbolizes "something more than simple death, national or personal annihilation. . . . The sea appears to represent the pull of longing toward a lost culture, a pull outward from the source, as he goes on to indicate by the overwrought cry that seems to parody the longing of a Pound or an Eliot:

Oh that the rocks of the Areopagus had
kept their sounds. . . ."

Martz also notes the similarity between the heading inland at the end of *Paterson* and the closing pages of *In the American Grain* (Poe . . . "faced inland, to originality").

[51] Paraphrased from Nelson, p. 104.

> This is the blast
> the eternal close
> the spiral
> the final somersault
> the end.   (204)

A number of themes are present here, but perhaps uppermost in Williams's mind was the question of "identity." The sea stands for death but it is also a sea of "indifferent men"; it is that in which the living river loses its identity. In swimming to shore, Paterson does not escape death, but he does save his own identity; he will die later.

It is this question of personal (and local) identity that explains Williams's tacit association of his hero with Walt Whitman, and his notion that in heading inland Paterson is choosing America, as Whitman had done. Williams himself may have felt that the symbolism is clear; still, he went out of his way to explain it, and three of his explanatory comments are especially illuminating:

Paterson IV ends with the protagonist breaking through the bushes, identifying himself with the land, with America. He finally will die but it can't be categorically stated that death ends *anything*.[52]

Again, in the *Autobiography*:

In the end the man rises from the sea where the river appears to have lost its identity and accompanied by his faithful bitch, obviously a Chesapeake Bay retriever, turns inland toward Camden where Walt Whitman, much traduced, lived the latter years of his life and died. He always said that his poems, which had broken the dominance of the iambic pentameter in English prosody, had only begun his theme. I agree. It is up to us, in the new dialect, to continue it by a new construction upon the syllables.[53]

And, in a publisher's release:

[52] *I Wanted To Write a Poem*, p. 22.
[53] *Autobiography*, p. 392.

And I had to think hard as to how I was going to end the poem. It wouldn't do to have a grand and soul-satisfying conclusion, because I didn't see any in my subject. Nor was I going to be confused or depressed or evangelical about it. It didn't belong to my subject. It would have been easy to make a great smash up with a "beautiful" sunset at sea, or a flight of pigeons, love's end and the welter of man's fate. Instead, after the little girl gets herself mixed up at last in the pathetic sophisticate of the great city, no less defeated and understandable, even lovable, than she is herself, we come to the sea at last. Odysseus swims in as man must always do, he doesn't drown, he is too able, but, accompanied by his dog, strikes inland again (toward Camden) to begin again.[54]

Several things are worth noting in these explanatory remarks. First, that the concluding passage is a deliberate avoidance of "grand" effects and a "soul-satisfying conclusion." Second, that Paterson, like Odysseus, is "too able" to drown. Third, that in the symbolism of the conclusion, Williams had specifically in mind the job of continuing Whitman's attack on "the dominance of the iambic pentameter in English prosody," and of constructing something "in the new dialect."

All three things bear on the poet's mastery, and on the question of style. In the canceled passage celebrating Whitman, Williams had described him as listening to the ocean; and in the concluding passage of Book Four Williams had the emerging Paterson turn "to look back to the waves," then knock at his ears to clear them. After dressing, he turns once more to listen to "the water's steady roar, as of a distant / waterfall   ." In this way Williams touches lightly on the challenge of the poem's beginning: "What common language to unravel?"

The implied reference to Whitman would perhaps not appear to a reader who had not seen the earlier version or Williams's later comments.

The conclusion of Book Four is intended to indicate both death and a continuation. The hero is dead (the river has entered the sea, where it loses its identity); his death is attributable to a

[54] Quoted by Thirlwall, pp. 263–264.

failure of language. Or is he dead? He "swims in" and strikes inland. (". . not our home! It is NOT/ our home.") And in striking inland he is "answering" the challenge of the Falls, as reiterated by the sea.

A NOTE ON BOOK FIVE

When the fourth book of *Paterson* appeared, Williams had completed the poem as projected in the "Author's Note." But he continued to work on *Paterson*, and a fifth book was published in 1958; later he worked on plans for still another book, and the publisher includes "four pages of notes and drafts for Book 6" as an Appendix to the standard edition of *Paterson*.[1]

Williams's early plan had given *Paterson* clear boundaries and an arbitrary symmetry; and within that plan he had worked out a symbolic vocabulary with its own special precision and resonance. With the addition of a fifth book, the character of the poem changes. The boundaries have been eliminated, and the symbolic vocabulary has shifted. In a sense, then, the fifth book is a separate poem—a commentary on the original poem rather than a continuation of it. But Williams offered it as a continuation, and it is appropriate at this point to suggest his main reasons for doing so and to give a short summary of the action.

A principal reason for the addition of a fifth book was the symbolic identification of the poet's life with *Paterson*, his lifework. The poem is now completed; but the poet is still alive, and he has ideas about the significance of what he has done. Why not develop these ideas in a new installment of the big poem? After all, as Williams noted, "there can be no end to such a story I have envisioned with the terms I had laid down for myself" (letter to the publisher, quoted with "Author's Note"). The poet's work will end only with his death; and the *Paterson* format, with its provision for letters, reminiscences, odds and ends, gives him a place for those things which interest him as he attempts to keep going.

What especially interested Williams at this time was the question of continuity and survival; the old poet offers his work as

---

[1] For bibliographical information on Book V, see Wallace, A 44; also B 75, C 505, C 535, C 547, C 552, C 553, and C 558.

something to be used by people who are just getting started; he thinks of imagination as the "hole in the bag" through which death can be eluded. Williams commented on these subjects in a conversation with Edith Heal: "*Paterson V* must be written, is being written, and the gulls appear at the beginning. Why must it be written? *Paterson IV* ends with the protagonist breaking through the bushes, identifying himself with the land, with America. He finally will die but it can't be categorically stated that death ends *anything*. When you're through with sex, with ambition, what can an old man create? Art, of course, a piece of art that will go beyond him into the lives of young people, the people who haven't had time to create. The old man meets the young people and lives on."[2] The poem survives; and the poet's "influence" enters the lives of younger writers.

Book V is dedicated to "The Memory/ of/ Henri Toulouse Lautrec,/ *Painter*," and Williams's comment on this dedication underlines another theme. Walter Sutton had asked him whether Toulouse-Lautrec interested him "because he is the artist of the whore house, as you call him, or because of the nature of his work?" Williams replied, "Well, I was attracted to Toulouse-Lautrec by his social position, which I sympathized with. A whore is just as much a human being as a saint, and I wanted to emphasize that. He is a man that respected the truth of design. For God's sake, what the hell difference is it to him that she's a whore? He was indifferent to it, and the poet is also indifferent to it. . . ."[3] This attitude toward the artist and his subject matter comes out most clearly perhaps in Williams's shrewd and respectful account of the Brueghel nativity (section 3); the implicit *claim* is that Williams himself has done something comparable.

SECTION 1

The first section describes the poet's recovery after an illness and the land's rebirth in spring. The old man's memories are stirred by "the angle of a forehead/ or far less" (207); a fox sparrow sings, and the "world/ of Paterson" reawakens, though frail, after the

---

[2] *I Wanted To Write a Poem*, p. 22.

[3] "A Visit with William Carlos Williams," *Minnesota Review*, I (Spring 1961), 322. See also Thirlwall, pp. 288–289; this is quoted by Wallace, A 44.

winter sleep. It is early spring, and "the bare rocks/ speak!" In terms of the argument of the first four books, it is a victory—for the poet, and for the world that now returns to life with spring. But as Paterson looks out the window at "the birds still there" (Williams is still alive, the external world still exists), he advises himself "Not prophecy! NOT prophecy! / but the thing it-self!" And his mind turns to the "moral" that he draws from a play by Lorca.[4] Flying over Paterson in an airplane, the poet looks down at the present scene and back at the past, revisiting "the old scenes/ to witness/ What has happened/ since Soupault gave him the novel/ the Dadaist novel/ to translate—" (209).[5] This passage alludes to Williams's connection with the world-wide experimental movement of the period between the wars; no matter what may have happened to the period slogans, "A WORLD OF ART" has in fact survived. (And the museum has become real: *The Cloisters*, where are located the unicorn tapestries celebrated in *Paterson V*.) On 210 Williams asserts an identity (though "disguised") between "whore" and "virgin"; and this identification introduces the symbolic unicorn of the poet's quest— a unicorn glimpsed by Audubon, it seems, as he scouted the interior of America, following "a trail through the woods/ across three states/ northward of Kentucky . ."(210). A mythic embodiment of "Beautiful thing," the unicorn is associated here with the living beauty of the new country. The poet's search for the unicorn connects with the thought of death. The unicorn (211) has no peer; nor does the artist; nor does death. Flowers rot and die (212): the artist dies, and so do the individuals he celebrates. Still, there is a "hole" in the bag through which we escape, by virtue of the imagination; and in that sense the artist wins out:

> Through this hole
> at the bottom of the cavern
> of death, the imagination
> escapes intact.   (212)

[4] "The Love of Don Perlimplín and Belisa in the Garden" (1931).
[5] Philippe Soupault's *Last Nights of Paris* was published in 1928; Williams's translation in 1929. See *I Wanted To Write a Poem*, pp. 47–48, and Wallace, A 11.

(A friend suggests that Williams may be remembering the last chapter of Tolstoi's "The Death of Ivan Ilyich.")

The four passages of prose incorporated in the first section give a sense of the old man thinking and corresponding; he keeps up old friendships and receives reports from young poets. There is a letter from a friend whose place Williams and his wife have visited (209–210) thanking him for his "memories of the place" ("Country Rain"?); a letter from Ginsberg (212–213) includes an irreverent variant of Williams's search for local beauty: "In any case Beauty is where I hang my hat."[6] The prose on 214–215, describing whores in a border city, is from a sketch by Gilbert Sorrentino; the fourth passage, an anecdote about "G.B.," who later "turned whore and got syphilis," leads into Williams's verse comment, concluding the section, on the relation of mind and body.

> 'n cha cha cha
> you'd think the brain
> 'd be grafted
> on a better root.   (216)

SECTION 2

Section 2 opens with Williams's version of a poem by Sappho (fragment 31): an instance of the violence of love and the "flagrance" of beauty, but in a poem written for "a clear gentle tinkling voice" by a poet who "avoided all roughness." The poet's mind is possessed by the thought of beauty—by the "dream" that urges him to write. (The Sappho poem is followed by a letter from Ezra Pound, one of the men with whom the poet set out; what's he up to? Still concerned with economics and politics; and so is Williams, after his fashion.) Now appears a fine restatement of the theme of "Beautiful thing": a woman "in our town," whose "face would attract no/ adolescent." Williams has seen her, but never spoken to her; she disappears into the crowd before he knows her name, but by singling her out the poet gives her an identity. If he sees her again he will ask whether she has

---

[6] Williams had written to Ginsberg: "You shall be the *center* of my new poem—of which I shall tell you: the extension of *Paterson*" (quoted by Wallace, A 44).

"read anything that I have written?/ It is all for you" (220). And so, he dedicates his work to the nameless woman; or it is for "the birds" or—in a quick transition—for Mezz Mezzrow, whose account of playing in a Negro jazz band now illustrates the search for living beauty: "To be with those guys made me know that any white man if he thought straight and studied hard, could sing and dance and play with the Negro."[7] Whereupon Williams reintroduces a theme from the second book: the connection of ribaldry and the "satyric" with the "devout." Art is a "satyric" dance; as the satyrs dance, their "deformities take wing" (221). All artists are pursued by "the dream," and Williams's reflections on this pursuit lead him to instances of what specific painters have tried to do, and to a letter he has recently received from a friend, saying that for three nights he had been able to sleep like a baby "without/ liquor or dope of any sort!" (223). Other subjects haunt him: for instance the Jew in the pit comforting his friends as they are sprayed by machine-gun fire. Such dreams "possess" the poet—and he is possessed by the dance of his thoughts, "involving animals/ the blameless beasts" (224).

The section ends with the transcript of a portion of Mike Wallace's interview with Williams, including Williams's characteristic statement that "Anything is good material for poetry" (225). The interview is another reference to the poet's isolation, as Williams attempts with some difficulty to justify his own experimental work to the public, represented by the interviewer.

SECTION 3

As the second section began with the great classical love theme of Sappho's poem, the third begins with a religious motif, a Brueghel nativity (*The Adoration of Kings*, 1564, in the National Gallery, London). The logic and design here are reminiscent of Book Two, where Williams had exhibited the two impulses producing art, sex and the religious instinct. Williams comments on details in the painting: the armed men, the baby in an *authentic* pose (Williams, like Brueghel, has *seen* poor people with babies), the three men, come "to propitiate their gods." Brueghel

---

[7] From Milton "Mezz" Mezzrow and Bernard Wolfe, *Really the Blues* (New York, 1946), p. 53.

painted the "bustle" of the scene; he saw the subject "from the two sides," not a partisan but a painter; the imagination must "be served," and "he served/ dispassionately." In the prose comment that follows (228) Williams attacks the poor workmanship characteristic of the present age, "the age of the shoddy." Our shoddiness is set off against the kind of poverty represented in the painting: better to be poor than to be one of "this featureless tribe that has the money now. . . ." (The concern with economics is carried along in a letter Williams prints from a friend describing conditions in some of the countries of postwar Europe [229–230].)[8] Paterson, grown older, takes care of his yard and tries "to get the young/ to foreshorten/ their errors in the use of the words/ which he had found so difficult, the errors/ he had made in the use of the/ poetic line" (231). He accepts the role of elder statesman, attempting to advise poets like Ginsberg. The presence of a flight of birds "calms him," and he is led to "think/ of bus schedules" (in order to go take another look at the unicorn tapestries). Starting on 231 he describes the "living fiction" of those tapestries— which (as Martz has pointed out) provide him with an analogue for the pattern of his own work.[9] Williams deals affectionately with the particular flowers that "fill in" the tapestries, and he calls attention to nonvisual details in the scene implied by the tapestries: the stench of the horses, yelping of the dogs, the woods *cold* though in summer. It is a hunt that leads to a "marriage." "Anywhere is everywhere": if you start with a given place, you can give it a distinction; one place is as good as another. These tapestries from a royal and aristocratic past are as "local" as *Paterson*.

This section includes two references to Williams's family: Godwin (232–233) is his crazy uncle; the old woman celebrated

[8] Edward Dahlberg. See *Epitaphs for Our Times: The Letters of Edward Dahlberg* (New York, 1967), pp. 182–185.

[9] Williams's symbolic unicorn hunt is based on a series of fifteenth-century tapestries in the Cloisters at the Metropolitan Museum of Art. There are six tapestries and fragments of another; five of the tapestries were probably made for Anne of Brittany in celebration of her marriage to Louis XII (Jan. 8, 1499). For a discussion of Williams's use of the tapestries, see Martz, pp. 154–161. Martz points out that Williams made use of a work by E. J. Alexander and Carol H. Woodward, *The Flora of the Unicorn Tapestries* (New York, 1947).

on 238–239 is his English Grandmother (*Autobiography,* pp. 4–5).

On 233 Williams uses the "serpent" as an emblem; like the river it represents his own "time," the course of his life. Now, in his old age, "the river has returned to its beginnings," and after this doubling back it "tortures itself within me/ until time has been washed finally under." That will be the end of personal identity. The symbolism echoes Book Four and the "Preface" to Book One. This late retrospect is an attempt at whatever "synthesis" is possible. And the poem ends with a statement of what is possible: "a choice among the measures . ." We *do* know something; what we know is

> the dance, to dance to a measure
> contrapuntally,
> > Satyrically, the tragic foot.   (239)

CONCLUSION

Forced by his medical practice to do most of his writing in spare time, including short intervals between patients, Williams had long projected a large-scale work to affirm and give coherence to the concerns of a lifetime. *Paterson* is what he chose to write when he finally found the time. The poem is an important personal document, touching on the life and the mature convictions of one of the best writers of the century. Like the short stories, it provides an untidy record of small things Williams noticed as he went about his business. It deals convincingly with the day-to-day geography of a region. Williams knew his area and its people and had watched them for years; his eye had been trained by years of describing his impressions in verse and prose. *Paterson* extends Williams's work as close observer of the life of an American city, as "realist" and descriptive writer, and as one of the best.

But there was another side to Williams's temperament. Williams's early novel, *A Voyage to Pagany* (1928), hints at how precarious the whole enterprise must have been. Williams had his reasons for being a physician, but he never loved the work as he loved writing; and what he loved about writing was not devising plots or figuring out the interrelationships among characters, but inventing metaphors and rhythms, working for new arrangements of the sentence. With all his willingness to work among ordinary people and to pay attention to "a nondescript world," Williams was at the same time very much an "artist" in his basic commitments. He wanted to write. And he was so impressed by the demands involved in writing well that the problem of writing engrossed him; sometimes the act of writing supplied his subject matter. Williams was introspective—impatiently introspective. The character Doctor Evans in *A Voyage to Pagany* appears to be a reasonably close self-portrait of Williams in the twenties;

and for Evans an intensity of perception, and of writing about what he notices, serves as an escape from a blank and agitated self. The man writing is attentive, notices unexpected things; but his mood is tense, overwrought, even desperate. He is "lyrical."

Evans, traveling in Europe, at length chooses to return to America; and the novel shows clearly what the return to America meant to Williams. Though he understood the claims and temptations that were embodied for his generation by the idea of "Europe," he has his hero come back to this country; there was no way for him to come to terms with the forms and subject matter of the Old World.

There is something else. A part of the novel deals with Evans's enrollment in medical courses in Vienna. (Williams himself had attended courses there for about a month.) Evans admires the professors, greatly impressed by their love of medicine as a science. He finds an austere intellectual beauty in their approach to the study of disease, an approach inconceivable at that time in the United States. He is struck by the special conditions under which they carry out their investigations, the large public institutions offering many more cases of a given disease than an American doctor could expect to see (p. 143): "Toward this veritable city of the sick—rich in the knowledge of its chief men as it is overflowing with clinical material, Evans went after lunch. . . ." The other side of the coin appears at the beginning of chapter 29: "He talked to Rosa [the maid]. . . . She was feeling quite ill. Go to the Clinic? Never, she said. I never went there but once. Treat you like a 'Tier'—An animal. . . ." The Viennese professors exhibiting a diseased patient are strikingly lucid in their analysis, but indifferent to the patient's feelings. Evans notes this opposition between the intellect and "humanity," and is troubled by it.

Paterson was written a long time after Williams's commitment to America had been made and confirmed. But the idea of a conflict between the intellect and its materials continued to obsess him. He loved order for its own sake; he both admired and feared the order that he attributed to Europe. To Williams Europe was old and class ridden, a museum or cemetery. It would have been a good thing, no doubt, to be able to find in

Europe a set of forms ready to master and apply; but Williams did not believe that the old forms *could* apply to the world he knew. America is unformed, but requires new forms; Williams knew that in choosing to return he was giving himself a difficult job; but he had no choice. When he came to write *Paterson* he insisted on the difference between his own line of action and what an Eliot or Pound had chosen. The poem was to be "a reply to Greek and Latin with the bare hands." *Paterson* is an attempt to tell the story of Williams's search (in the past, in his own mind) for the new form by which to master the materials of specifically American experience.

To tell his story, Williams makes use of a set of doctrines and prejudices, many of which he had expounded in prose works; these have been summarized earlier and traced through the poem. How sound are the ideas at stake in *Paterson*? And how much difference does it make whether they are sound or not? A tentative answer can be offered.

Williams's views on such matters as American history, as they appear in his prose and in *Paterson*, are for the most part simplifications of ideas that were "in the air" in the twenties and the thirties. Some of his views are no better than personal hobbyhorses. His views on the writing of poetry, and on the poet's relation to his subject matter, are personal reworkings of old philosophical themes—notions with a long history, but thought through again by Williams in the light of his own experience. What he has to say about the city is a mixture of theory and personal judgments on what he had seen for himself. Even when he wrote in prose, Williams was never especially concerned with giving these views and impressions an intellectual coherence. Indeed, he had a violent distrust of systematic thinking, and he never attempted to give his own notions the kind of order that a philosopher would trust.

To an unsympathetic reader of Williams's prose, then, and even to a sympathetic reader in certain moods, Williams will often appear as something of a wild man, an irresponsible rhetorician, assertive and self-indulgent, quick to risk purple prose when the opportunity arises. The ideas form a miscellaneous as-

sortment, a collection of scraps: some Platonism, some ideas
skimmed from the thought of John Dewey, some notions about
history and anthropology; and so on. They are expressed vigor-
ously, and with formidable powers of invention and illustration,
but are not argued carefully or made coherent. The collection
gains momentum and order from the persistence of Williams's
faith that there is an order emerging from it. Perhaps what Williams distrusted most about philosophy was the attempt to use
words as fixed counters with assigned meanings. Since an exact
and permanent assignment of meaning is impossible, why try
to use language "logically"? The life of a language seemed to
depend on each writer's willingness to push a word out past the
limits of its customary meaning, and to make statements and
develop arguments without regard to rules of denotation or consequence. But the reader who takes Williams's statements seriously will want to know what they mean and how they hang
together; and this exercise in interpretation brings the critical
intellect into play. The reader makes distinctions among Williams's usages, notes inconsistencies, and performs various oper-
ations which Williams must have hoped to discourage by not
using language "philosophically."

Any reservations a reader may have about the ideas argued in
Williams's prose will apply equally to the argument of *Paterson*.
No doubt many of the ideas are true enough, provided not too
much weight is placed upon them. Did Williams ever clearly understand the Indian cultures or the Protestantism of the early settlers? Yes and no. He saw certain facts very clearly, and ignored
others. Taken together the views form a "myth," if you wish.
How much weight does Williams mean to place upon this
"myth"?

The answer, presumably, is quite a bit. The poem is not a
treatise, but it does have "intellectual content," and Williams
evidently meant the reader to take this content seriously. He himself took these ideas seriously. True or false, connected or not, the
ideas "apply" to the country as Williams saw it, to the world of
"Paterson." They "apply," roughly as the views of Lewis Mumford or Waldo Frank apply. Though polemical and onesided,
they offer a version of American culture and the artist's place in

it; they offer a critique of the past and guarded hope for the future. They even offer a course of action; and all of this with a strange persuasiveness.

In a sense, of course, the subject of *Paterson* is not the American past or the modern city, but simply the poet's attempt to do his own work. Williams's theories describe more or less accurately the world in which he had fought to do his work. They supply the background, or what he saw as the background, for that work; and for that he must be the authority. Williams is convinced that there are general implications to be developed from his own case. The representativeness, and the urgency, which he attributed to his own case, supply the steam that keeps the argument going; they do not necessarily win the reader's assent.

The reader will sometimes be put off by the tone in which Williams offers his reactions to the world. A certain shrillness and desperation run through the poem. The argument is obsessive, self-conscious: few long poems are as self-conscious as *Paterson*. Williams chose to treat the subject of the poet's relation to his material, and the subject is interesting; but the poem threatens at times to become a discourse on poetry, or on the psychology of the writer. Even the "things" appearing in the poem, particular events and objects described sharply and persuasively, are sometimes infected by the poet's self-concern. Williams may have meant *Paterson* to compete in its way with the work of Homer and Villon, but he is too obsessed with his own role to approach his subject matter as naïvely or as confidently as those poets had done.

In *Paterson* there is always some tension between Williams's governing scheme and the material used to carry it out. The overall design makes allowance for improvisation, and attempts to guide it. But there is often a discrepancy between Williams's present concern, when he comes to write a given section, and the plan intended to give particulars in the poem their place and significance. This tension between detail and the general argument is one source of the poem's interest, and Williams knew this. It is part of the plan, and up to a point it was something Williams understood and controlled. But not entirely. It is sometimes a source of difficulty to the reader, and this difficulty suggests that Williams himself was often unsure about the conduct of his argument.

Williams's method of handling detail works best for him when he can make a given detail do two or three jobs, suggesting the overall relevance of descriptive material without sacrificing the literal. The early description of the movement of waters (7–8) is a good example. It is a fine account of the action of the waters, detailed, persuasive in its detail, and at the same time capable of sustaining Williams's argument that the waters are Paterson's thoughts. Williams can generate excitement simply by his evident feeling that he himself is watching a meaning emerge from the particular occasion. The method does not always work. At times the description is impressive, but its meaning unclear. At times Williams must insist on what it means. In some of the "Beautiful thing" passages he is obviously straining, as when he mentions "the scabrous/ dirt of the holy sheets" (125). This is a pretty inexpensive rhetoric. Sometimes Williams editorializes, as with the comment on 51: "among/ the working classes SOME sort/ of breakdown/ has occurred." The commentary seems an attempt to make up for the opacity of the material.

The trouble is that the plot or symbolic structure of the poem does not suffice to take care of the movement from one event to the next. It is not, like medieval allegory, say, a vehicle with its own logic. The method of *Paterson* is, I think, a form of allegory; but Williams wants to improvise the rules for giving significance to his material. In fact, he is working fairly close to the conventions of Gray's "Elegy," in which the poet describes a scene and makes generalized moral comments on it. No matter how neutral a description may be, Williams's attention (and "bias") gives it a shape and a role in the argument. Or, rather, Williams attempts to give it such a role, sometimes with great success, but not always. The motto "No ideas but in things" does not prevent a certain insecurity and arbitrariness in drawing out "ideas" (tenor) from "things" (their vehicle).

Williams seems to have allowed his original ingenuity and enthusiasm to prepare difficulties that he had no way of solving. The early part of the poem, with its descriptions of the Falls and the landscape, and its tantalizing prose fragments, sets up a system of promises to the reader, not all of which are fulfilled. Williams in a sense "promises" to deliberate on the topics introduced and to give them as the poem moves on a fullness of meaning, an emotional resonance, that they do not have at the outset. For a time the reader is carried along by the skill and assurance Williams displays in getting the poem under way. And his expectations are fulfilled, in large part. But the principles ordering the poem lack the power available within a traditional "plot" to gather up meanings and associations, to "cash in" on detail, to achieve a conclusion. The conclusion of Book Four is an impressive stretch of writing; but it fails to satisfy all the expectations aroused by the excitement and promise of the earlier parts. The fact that Williams later chose to add a fifth book shows that something seemed to be missing; the fifth book attempts to supply it, but its allegorical vocabulary is so different from that of the earlier books that Williams loses much of what he might have gained by sustaining an argument for so long. Book Four could not do the work that Williams had left himself to do; nor could Book Five.

Williams of course intended even the failures of the poem to be part of its meaning, hence a part of its success; and this is a tempting notion. The poem had to be written as it was to be written at all; and no doubt all of the poem's elements gain something from inclusion in the large scheme. It would be a mistake to claim too much for that scheme; *Paterson*, nonetheless, is one of the great modern "experimental" poems, like *The Bridge* or *The Cantos*, and readers will approach it to see what a modern poet can do. It is a "success," perhaps, as any impressive experiment is a success.

BIBLIOGRAPHY

Book One of *Paterson* was published in 1946. The other books appeared as follows: Book Two, 1948; Book Three, 1949; Book Four, 1951; and Book Five, 1958. The first "complete" *Paterson* (Books One to Four) appeared in 1951; the complete collected edition of Books One to Five appeared in 1963, the year of Williams's death, in a volume that included notes for a projected Book Six. So far there have been two hardbound printings of *Paterson* from the original letterpress plates, and five paperbound printings, the fifth of which (June 1969) is printed from new offset plates. As noted in my Preface, the pagination in the fifth printing differs from that of earlier printings. New Directions informs me that *Paterson* is now going into a sixth printing.

Emily Wallace's bibliography of Williams's writings (1968) is indispensable. Most of the work on the present study was completed before her bibliography appeared, but I have made some use of it, specifically in checking references to earlier poems incorporated into *Paterson*. Linda Wagner's bibliographical essay, "A Decade of Discovery," provides a good list of essays and books about Williams. Mrs. Wagner's book on Williams's poetry also contains a good bibliography, as does James Guimond's *The Art of William Carlos Williams*. J. Hillis Miller's anthology of critical essays includes a Selected Bibliography.

The Wallace bibliography reprints some of Williams's remarks on *Paterson* (A 24, A 25, A 30, A 34, A 44, A 49). Williams discussed *Paterson* in *I Wanted To Write a Poem* and in chapter 58 of his *Autobiography*; some of the letters printed in *Selected Letters* deal with *Paterson*. John C. Thirlwall quotes some important comments in his essay on *Paterson*.

Unpublished material is collected at the Lockwood Memorial Library of the State University of New York at Buffalo, and at Yale's Beinecke Library. Together the two libraries possess a valuable collection of notes and manuscripts for *Paterson*; for the material at Buffalo I have worked from microfilm copies. There is no clear-cut division between the material deposited at Buffalo and that at Yale, but in general the Buffalo collection is most useful for Books One and Two, the Yale collection for Books Three, Four, and Five. I have quoted from the notes and earlier versions of the poem chiefly when I thought this information clarified Williams's intentions. In a few cases I have called attention to variants that seemed interesting as a matter of style. Sometimes I have silently corrected minor errors of spelling in order to avoid overusing *sic*. I have not attempted a careful history of Williams's revisions, though in a few cases I have tried to indicate what seemed to be the order of composition.

The main sources for material on local history in *Paterson* are Nelson's *History of the City of Paterson and the County of Passaic, New Jersey* and the *Historical Collections of the State of New Jersey* of Barber and Howe. Another important source was a short-lived weekly newspaper, *The Prospector*, which published many items on local history. Professor Thirlwall informs me that Williams owned a bound file of *The Prospector* for 1935–1936. Other sources include Charles P. Longwell's book on the Falls, and two books on New Jersey by the Federal Writers' Project.

Williams used these "sources" in various ways, sometimes quoting directly, sometimes paraphrasing, sometimes adding his own inventions to a factual account.

I have done my own hunting for Williams's sources, but some of his borrowings have been noted by other readers. Sister Bernetta, for instance, made use of Nelson and of Barber and Howe; Joseph Slate refers to Williams's use of Longwell.

Of the many essays and books about Williams and *Paterson*, I have found George Zabriskie's essay most useful for my purposes, and I have quoted from it extensively. Zabriskie's essay appeared in a special issue of *Perspective* (Autumn-Winter 1953), which also included important studies by Ralph Nash and Guy Davenport. The best short account of the poem's symbolism is perhaps Sister Bernetta's essay in *The Metamorphic Tradition*. There are several other important essays, including those by Glauco Cambon, Louis Martz, and Joel O. Conarroe.

Walter Peterson's book on *Paterson* appeared after most of my own work had been done; but I have learned some things from his interpretation and tried to incorporate what I learned.

A. WORKS OF WILLIAM CARLOS WILLIAMS

This list is intended mainly to identify works by Williams actually referred to in the text. A few additional works of special relevance are included.

Williams, William Carlos. *Al Que Quiere!* Boston, 1917.

—————. "The American Background." In *America and Alfred Stieglitz.* Ed. Waldo Frank, Lewis Mumford, Dorothy Norman, Paul Rosenfeld, and Harold Rugg. New York, 1934. Pp. 9–32.

—————. "The American Language—Again," *Pound Newsletter,* no. 8 (Oct. 1955), 2–7.

—————. "An Approach to the Poem." In *English Institute Essays, 1947.* New York, 1948. Pp. 50–75.

—————. *The Autobiography of William Carlos Williams.* New York, 1951.

—————. *The Broken Span.* Norfolk, Conn., 1941.

—————. *The Collected Earlier Poems.* Norfolk, Conn., 1951.

—————. *The Collected Later Poems.* Norfolk, Conn., 1950.

—————. "An Essay on *Leaves of Grass.*" In Milton Hindus, ed., *Leaves of Grass: One Hundred Years After.* Stanford, 1955. Pp. 22–31.

—————. *The Farmers' Daughters: The Collected Stories of William Carlos Williams.* Norfolk, Conn., 1961.

—————. "The Fatal Blunder," *Quarterly Review of Literature,* II, 2 (1945), 125–126.

—————. *The Great American Novel.* Paris, 1923.

—————. "Howl for Carl Solomon." Introduction to Allen Ginsberg, *Howl and Other Poems.* San Francisco, 1956.

—————. *Imaginations.* Edited and with an introduction by Webster Schott. New York, 1970. Contains *Kora in Hell, Spring and All, The Great American Novel, The Descent of Winter,* and *A Novelette and Other Prose.*

—————. *In the American Grain.* Introduction by Horace Gregory. New York, 1956. Originally published in 1925.

—————. *I Wanted To Write a Poem.* Reported and edited by Edith Heal. Boston, 1958.

—————. *Kora in Hell: Improvisations.* San Francisco, 1957. Originally published in 1920.

—————. Translation of Phillippe Soupault's *Last Nights of Paris.* New York, 1929.

—————. "Letter to an Australian Editor," *Briarcliff Quarterly,* III (Oct. 1946), 205–208.

—————. *Many Loves and Other Plays.* Norfolk, Conn., 1961.

—————. *A Novelette and Other Prose, 1921–31.* Toulon, 1932.

—————. *Paterson.* New York, 1963.

—————. *Paterson (Book One).* Norfolk, Conn., 1946.

—————. *Paterson (Book Two).* Norfolk, Conn., 1948.

————. *Paterson (Book Three).* Norfolk, Conn., 1949. "A Note on *Paterson*: Book III" appears on the dust jacket.

————. *Paterson (Book Four).* Norfolk, Conn., 1951.

————. *Paterson (Book Five).* Norfolk, Conn., 1958.

————. "Patterson [*sic*]: Episode 17," *New Directions* 2 (1937).

————. *Selected Essays of William Carlos Williams.* New York, 1954.

————. *The Selected Letters of William Carlos Williams.* Ed. John C. Thirlwall. New York, 1957.

————. Unpublished manuscripts and notes. Lockwood Memorial Library Poetry Collection. State University of New York at Buffalo. Buffalo, New York.

————. *A Voyage to Pagany.* New York, 1928.

————. *The Wedge.* [Cummington, Mass.], 1944.

————. Manuscripts, notes, and letters. Collection of American Literature. Yale University Library. New Haven, Conn.

————. *Yes, Mrs. Williams.* New York, 1959.

Williams, William Carlos, and Robert McAlmon, eds. *Contact.* Vols. I–IV. 1920–1923.

B. SOURCES

This list comprises works that Williams seems to have consulted in writing *Paterson*, including the obvious "sources" (and some *possible* sources) for the prose.

Alexander, E. J., and Carol H. Woodward. *The Flora of the Unicorn Tapestries.* New York Botanical Garden, 1947.

Barber, John W., and Henry Howe. *Historical Collections of the State of New Jersey.* Newark, 1853.

Biörck, Tobias E. *Dissertatio Gradualis: De Plantatione Ecclesiae Svecanae in America.* Upsaliae, 1731.

Cuffee, Nathan J., and Lydia A. Jocelyn [Smith]. *Lords of the Soil: A Romance of Indian Life among the Early Settlers.* Boston, 1905.

Duvall, Ralph G. *The History of Shelter Island, from its Settlement in 1652 to the Present Time, 1932.* Shelter Island Heights, N.Y., 1932.

Federal Writers' Project of the Works Progress Administration for the State of New Jersey. *New Jersey: A Guide to Its Present and Past.* New York, 1939.

————. *Stories of New Jersey.* New York, 1938.

Furman, Gabriel. *Antiquities of Long Island.* New York, 1875.

Graf, Edward M. *Short Sketches on Passaic County History*. Paterson, 1935.

Longwell, Charles P. *Historic Totowa Falls and Vicinity*. [Paterson], 1942.

MacCall, Seamus. *Thomas Moore*. London, 1935.

Mezzrow, Milton "Mezz," and Bernard Wolfe. *Really the Blues*. New York, 1946.

Nelson, William. *History of the City of Paterson and the County of Passaic, New Jersey*. Paterson, 1901.

Nelson, William, and Charles A. Shriner. *History of Paterson and Its Environs: The Silk City*. 3 vols. New York and Chicago, 1920.

The Prospector: Weekly Newspaper for Northern New Jersey Devoted to Historical Interests. Prospect Park, N.J., 1935–36.

Santayana, George. *The Last Puritan: A Memoir in the Form of a Novel*. New York, 1936.

Shriner, Charles A. *Four Chapters of Paterson History*. Paterson, 1919.

Storms, John C. *Origin of the Jackson-Whites of the Ramapo Mountains*. Park Ridge, N.J., 1936.

Talbot, D. Amaury. *Woman's Mysteries of a Primitive People: The Ibibios of Southern Nigeria*. London, 1915.

Talbot, P. Amaury. *Life in Southern Nigeria: The Magic, Beliefs and Customs of the Ibibio Tribe*. London, 1923.

———. *Tribes of the Niger Delta: Their Religions and Customs*. London, 1932.

Tate, Allen. *The Vigil of Venus*. Pervigilium Veneris. The Latin text with an introduction and English translation by Allen Tate. [Cummington, Mass., 1943.]

Van Derhoven, O. *Visitors' Guide to Passaic Falls*. Paterson, 1859.

C. ESSAYS AND STUDIES OF WILLIAMS AND PATERSON

This list is selective, but I have attempted to give a fairly full list of essays dealing directly with *Paterson*, including a few of the important reviews. It identifies all articles and books actually cited in the text.

Bennett, Joseph. "The Lyre and the Sledgehammer," *Hudson Review*, V (Summer 1952), 295–307.

Brinnin, John M. *William Carlos Williams*. University of Minnesota American Writers Series, no. 24. Minneapolis, 1963.

Cambon, Glauco. *The Inclusive Flame: Studies in American Poetry.* Bloomington, 1963.

Carruth, Hayden. "Dr. Williams' 'Paterson'," *Nation*, CLXX (April 8, 1950), 331–332. Review of *Paterson III*.

————. "The Run to the Sea," *Nation*, CLXXIII (Aug. 25, 1951), 155–156. Review of *Paterson IV*.

Conarroe, Joel O. " 'You Can't Steal Credit': The Economic Motif in *Paterson*," *Journal of American Studies*, II (April 1968), 105–115.

Davenport, Guy. "The Nuclear Venus: Dr. Williams' Attack on Usura," *Perspective*, VI (Autumn 1953), 183–190.

Dupeyron-Marchessou, Hélène. *William Carlos Williams et le renouveau du lyrisme.* Paris, 1967.

Ellmann, Richard. "From Renishaw to Paterson," *The Yale Review*, XXXIX (Spring 1950), 543–545. Review of *Paterson III*.

Fiedler, Leslie. "Some Uses and Failures of Feeling," *Partisan Review*, XV (Aug. 1948), 924–931. Includes a review of *Paterson II*.

Grigsby, Gordon K. "The Genesis of *Paterson*," *College English*, XXIII (Jan. 1962), 277–281.

Guimond, James. *The Art of William Carlos Williams: A Discovery and Possession of America.* Urbana, 1968.

Gunn, Thom. "Poetry As Written," *The Yale Review*, XLVIII (Winter 1959), 297–305. Review of *Paterson V*.

Gustafson, Richard. "William Carlos Williams' *Paterson*: A Map and Opinion," *College English*, XXVI (April 1965), 532–539.

Honig, Edward. "City of Man," *Poetry*, LXIX (Feb. 1947), 277–284. Review of *Paterson I*.

Kenner, Hugh. "To Measure Is All We Know," *Poetry*, XCIV (May 1959), 127–132. Reviews of *Paterson V* and *I Wanted To Write A Poem*.

————. "With the Bare Hands," *Poetry*, LXXX (Aug. 1952), 276–290. Review of *Paterson I–IV*.

Koch, Vivienne. *William Carlos Williams.* Norfolk, Conn., 1950.

Koehler, Stanley. "The Art of Poetry VI: William Carlos Williams," *Paris Review*, VIII (Summer–Fall 1964), 110–151.

Lawrence, D. H. Review of *In the American Grain.* In *Phoenix: The Posthumous Papers of D. H. Lawrence.* Edited and with an introduction by Edward D. McDonald. New York, 1936. Pp. 334–336.

Litz, A. Walton. "William Carlos Williams." In *The Literary Heritage of New Jersey.* New Jersey Historical series, vol. 20. Princeton, 1964. Pp. 83–130.

Lowell, Robert. "Paterson II," *Nation*, CLXVI (June 19, 1948), 692–694. Review.

Martz, Louis L. *The Poem of the Mind.* New York, 1966.

———. "The Unicorn in *Paterson*," *Thought,* XXXV (Winter 1960), 537–554.

———. "William Carlos Williams: On the Road to *Paterson*," *Poetry New York,* no. 4 (1951), 18–32.

Massie, Lillian. "Narrative and Symbol in *Paterson*." Unpublished dissertation. University of Arkansas, 1955.

Miller, Joseph Hillis. *William Carlos Williams: A Collection of Critical Essays.* Englewood Cliffs, N.J., 1966.

Mottram, Eric. "The Making of *Paterson*," *Stand,* VII, 3 (1965), 17–34.

Nash, Ralph. "The Use of Prose in 'Paterson,'" *Perspective,* VI (Autumn 1953), 191–199.

Nussendorfer, Sister Macaria. "William Carlos Williams' Idea of a City," *Thought,* XL (Summer 1965), 242–274.

Ostrom, Alan B. *The Poetic World of William Carlos Williams.* Preface by Harry T. Moore. Carbondale, Ill., 1966.

Paul, Sherman. *The Music of Survival: A Biography of a Poem by William Carlos Williams.* Urbana, 1968.

Peterson, Walter Scott. *An Approach to Paterson.* New Haven, 1967.

Quinn, Sister M. Bernetta. *The Metamorphic Tradition in Modern Poetry.* New Brunswick, 1955.

Racey, Edgar F. "Pound and Williams: The Poet As Renewer," *Bucknell Review,* XI (March 1963), 21–30.

Seamon, Roger. "The Bottle in the Fire: Resistance As Creation in William Carlos Williams's *Paterson*," *Twentieth Century Literature,* XI (April 1965), 16–24.

Slate, Joseph Evans. "William Carlos Williams, Hart Crane, and 'The Virtue of History,'" *Texas Studies in Literature and Language,* VI (Winter 1965), 486–511.

———. "William Carlos Williams' Image of America." Unpublished dissertation. University of Wisconsin, 1957.

Spencer, Benjamin T. "Doctor Williams' American Grain," *Tennessee Studies in Literature,* VIII (1963), 1–16.

Stephens, Alan. "Dr. Williams and Tradition," *Poetry,* CI (Feb. 1963), 360–362. Review of *Pictures from Brueghel and Other Poems.*

Sutton, Walter. "A Visit with William Carlos Williams," *Minnesota Review,* I (Spring 1961), 309–324.

———. "Dr. Williams's *Paterson* and the Quest for Form," *Criticism,* II (Summer 1960), 242–259.

Thirlwall, John C. "William Carlos Williams' 'Paterson': The Search

for the Redeeming Language—A Personal Epic in Five Parts,"
  New Directions 17 (1961), 252–310.
Thompson, Frank. "The Symbolic Structure of *Paterson,*" *Western
  Review,* XIX (Summer 1955), 285–293.
Wagner, Linda Welshimer. "A Decade of Discovery, 1953–1963:
  Checklist of Criticism, William Carlos Williams's Poetry," *Twen-
  tieth Century Literature,* X (Jan. 1965), 166–169.
————. *The Poems of William Carlos Williams: A Critical Study.*
  Middletown, Conn., 1964.
Wallace, Emily Mitchell. *A Bibliography of William Carlos Williams.*
  Middletown, Conn., 1968.
Weimer, David R. *The City As Metaphor.* New York, 1966.
Zabriskie, George. "The Geography of 'Paterson,' " *Perspective,* VI
  (Autumn 1953), 201–216.

D. OTHER REFERENCES

Adams, Brooks. *The Law of Civilization and Decay: An Essay on
  History.* With an introduction by Charles A. Beard. New York,
  1943.
B[aker], A[ugustus] E[dward]. "Social Credit." In *Chambers's En-
  cyclopedia.* Oxford and N.Y., 1966. Vol. XII, pp. 630–631.
Belshaw, H. *The Douglas Fallacy.* Auckland, New Zealand, 1933.
Berry, Brewton. *Almost White.* New York, 1963.
Brassaï [pseudonym for Gyula Halasz]. *Conversations avec Picasso.*
  Paris, 1964.
Clune, Henry W. *The Genesee.* New York, 1963.
Coughlin, Charles E. *Money! Questions and Answers.* Royal Oak,
  Mich., 1936.
Dahlberg, Edward. *Epitaphs of Our Times: The Letters of Edward
  Dahlberg.* New York, 1967.
Davis, Earle. *Vision Fugitive: Ezra Pound and Economics.* Lawrence,
  Kansas, 1968.
Douglas, C[lifford] H[ugh]. *The Big Idea.* Liverpool, [1942].
————. *Economic Democracy.* London, [1920].
————. *The Monopoly of Credit.* Liverpool, 1951.
Frank, Waldo. *Our America.* New York, 1919.
Frazer, Sir James George. *The Golden Bough: A Study in Magic and
  Religion.* 12 vols. New York, 1935.
G[enzmer], G[eorge] H[arvey]. "Sam Patch." In *Dictionary of Amer-
  ican Biography.* New York, 1934.
Goodwin, K. L. *The Influence of Ezra Pound.* London, 1966.

Jameson, J. *Narratives of New Netherlands, 1609–1664*. New York, 1909.

Josephson, Matthew. *Edison*. New York, 1959.

Kenyon, James B. *Industrial Localization and Metropolitan Growth: The Paterson-Passaic District*. University of Chicago Department of Geography Research Paper no. 67. Chicago, Sept. 1960.

Keyserling, Count Hermann. *America Set Free*. New York, 1929.

Kitson, Arthur. *The Bankers' Conspiracy! Which Started the World Crisis*. London, 1933.

McDowell, Bart. "Mexico's Window on the Past," *National Geographic*, CXXIV (Oct. 1968), 493–521.

McLoughlin, William Gerald. *Billy Sunday Was His Real Name*. Chicago, 1955.

Mullins, Eustace [Clarence]. *The Federal Reserve Conspiracy*. Union, N.J., 1954.

Mumford, Lewis. *The Culture of Cities*. New York, 1938.

O'Callaghan, B. E. *History of New Netherland: Or New York under the Dutch*. 2 vols. New York, 1855.

Parker, Jennie Marsh. *Rochester*. Rochester, 1884

"Paterson." In *Encyclopedia Americana*. New York, 1962. Vol. XXI, 391–392.

Pearce, Roy Harvey. *The Continuity of American Poetry*. Princeton, 1961.

Pound, Ezra. *Guide to Kulchur*. Norfolk, Conn., 1952. Originally published in 1938.

———. *The Letters of Ezra Pound*. Ed. D. D. Paige. New York, 1950.

———. *Social Credit: An Impact*. London, 1935.

Rosenfeld, Paul. *Port of New York*. Introduction by Sherman Paul. Urbana, 1961. Originally published in 1924.

Seldes, Gilbert. *Mainland*. New York, 1936.

Sinclair, Upton. *The Profits of Religion*. Pasadena, 1918.

Tolson, M[elvin] B[eaunorus]. *Libretto for the Republic of Liberia*. Preface by Allen Tate. New York, 1953.

Trelease, Allen W. *Indian Affairs in Colonial New York: The Seventeenth Century*. New York, 1960.

Wildes, Henry Emerson. *Twin Rivers: The Raritan and the Passaic*. New York, 1943.

DATE DUE